D0067873

CultureShock!
A Survival Guide to Customs and Etiquette

Paris

Frances Gendlin

Marshall Cavendish
Editions

This 3rd edition published in 2011 by:
Marshall Cavendish Corporation
99 White Plains Road
Tarrytown, NY 10591-9001
www.marshallcavendish.us

First published in 1998 by Times Editions Private Limited, reprinted in 1999, 2000, 2001; 2nd edition published by Marshall Cavendish Corporation in 2007, reprinted 2008.
Text Copyright © Frances Gendlin
Design Copyright © Marshall Cavendish International (Asia) Private Limited
All rights reserved

No part of this publication may be reproduced, stored in a retrieval system or transmitted, in any form or by any means, electronic, mechanical, photocopying, recording or otherwise, without the prior permission of the copyright owner. Request for permission should be addressed to the Publisher, Marshall Cavendish International (Asia) Private Limited, 1 New Industrial Road, Singapore 536196. Tel: (65) 6213 9300, fax: (65) 6285 4871. E-mail: genref@sg.marshallcavendish.com

The publisher makes no representation or warranties with respect to the contents of this book, and specifically disclaims any implied warranties or merchantability or fitness for any particular purpose, and shall in no events be liable for any loss of profit or any other commercial damage, including but not limited to special, incidental, consequential, or other damages.

Other Marshall Cavendish Offices:
Marshall Cavendish International (Asia) Private Limited. 1 New Industrial Road, Singapore 536196 ■ Marshall Cavendish International. PO Box 65829, London EC1P 1NY, UK ■ Marshall Cavendish International (Thailand) Co Ltd. 253 Asoke, 12th Flr, Sukhumvit 21 Road, Klongtoey Nua, Wattana, Bangkok 10110, Thailand ■ Marshall Cavendish (Malaysia) Sdn Bhd, Times Subang, Lot 46, Subang Hi-Tech Industrial Park, Batu Tiga, 40000 Shah Alam, Selangor Darul Ehsan, Malaysia

Marshall Cavendish is a trademark of Times Publishing Limited

ISBN: 978-0-7614-5875-3

Please contact the publisher for the Library of Congress catalogue number

Printed in Singapore by Times Printers Pte Ltd

Photo Credits:
Black and white photos from Zeny Cieslikowski: pages xii, 7, 22, 32, 98, 158, 202, 212, 221, 224, 228, 244, 275; Photolibrary: pages xiii, 60, 71, 112, 134, 170, 175, 260, 269, 289, 305. Colour photos from Photolibrary. ■ Cover photo: Photolibrary

All illustrations by TRIGG, except pages 20,23 (John Zaugg).

ABOUT THE SERIES

Culture shock is a state of disorientation that can come over anyone who has been thrust into unknown surroundings, away from one's comfort zone. *CultureShock!* is a series of trusted and reputed guides which has, for decades, been helping expatriates and long-term visitors to cushion the impact of culture shock whenever they move to a new country.

Written by people who have lived in the country and experienced culture shock themselves, the authors share all the information necessary for anyone to cope with these feelings of disorientation more effectively. The guides are written in a style that is easy to read and covers a range of topics that will arm readers with enough advice, hints and tips to make their lives as normal as possible again.

Each book is structured in the same manner. It begins with the first impressions that visitors will have of that city or country. To understand a culture, one must first understand the people—where they came from, who they are, the values and traditions they live by, as well as their customs and etiquette. This is covered in the first half of the book.

Then on with the practical aspects—how to settle in with the greatest of ease. Authors walk readers through topics such as how to find accommodation, get the utilities and telecommunications up and running, enrol the children in school and keep in the pink of health. But that's not all. Once the essentials are out of the way, venture out and try the food, enjoy more of the culture and travel to other areas. Then be immersed in the language of the country before discovering more about the business side of things.

To round off, snippets of basic information are offered before readers are 'tested' on customs and etiquette of the country. Useful words and phrases, a comprehensive resource guide and list of books for further research are also included for easy reference.

CONTENTS

FOREWORD

'Fluctuat nec mergitur—It tosses on the
waves but does not sink.'
—Paris motto

This book is designed for anyone who loves Paris. Loving Paris is not hard, as even cold statistics attest, for each year it is rated as the most visited city in the world. It's true that many world capitals have ardent admirers, but there seems to be something unique, something almost palpable about Paris that inspires love. It's not about you or me, this love, nor about anyone else; it is about the city itself and how being here makes us feel about our own lives. But why Paris? Certainly its charms are not unique. Rome is as historic and Venice as beautiful, Hong Kong is as bold and Marrakech as exotic. But somehow Paris has it all, including an ability to insinuate itself into our souls, demanding so much of us—and giving so much in return. Yet the spirit of this magnetic city is hard to convey: its impressions are so personal and its offerings so varied that each person who arrives for the first time ultimately seems to discover it anew. Perhaps it's best that way.

A tourist who comes to Paris for a week or two is fortunate, to be sure. There is so much atmosphere to soak up in the city's streets and there are historical monuments to stop and admire, outstanding works of art to appreciate and parks landscaped so beautifully that they take one's breath away. And what about the food and the wine? There are too many opportunities and not enough time. Yes, such visits are necessarily short, so before departure, before anything can be forgotten, people often jot down in the back of their guidebooks the museums to include for the next visit, a few restaurants to recommend to friends and which neighbourhoods remain to be explored. Unfortunately, these must be left until the next time.

So imagine, as many tourists do, actually living in Paris—having the Louvre nearby every day of the year and the world's temples of gastronomy to satisfy any culinary whim... how wonderful that must be! Fortunately, life here is as good as one imagines, even if few residents go to museums every day or—if they are at all concerned about their budgets—frequent restaurants on a daily basis. Yet

Paris truly is a city in which it is ultimately better to live than visit—for the reasons above to be sure, but also for deeper, more lasting reasons that are understood little by little, as life in *La Ville Lumière* (the City of Light) unfolds. Immersion into any new culture takes some effort, but this is Paris after all, the most entrancing—and yes, romantic—city in the world and worth whatever effort it takes.

Think of the thousands who have come before who thought the same. Pablo Picasso painted his masterpiece *Guernica* while living on rue des Grands-Augustins, around the corner from rue Christine, where the American writer Gertrude Stein lived for a time. Farther north, at Square d'Orléans, the Polish composer Frédéric Chopin settled near his lover, writer George Sand. Artist Amadeo Modigliani, the 'king of Montparnasse', died young and broke in Paris, but composer Virgil Thompson (who claimed that if he had to starve to death, he would prefer to do it where the food was so good) found fame in time. Ultimately it was Ernest Hemingway who summed it up: "There is never any ending to Paris and the memory of each person who has lived in it differs from that of any other... Paris was always worth it and you received return for whatever you brought to it."

Actually, much about being in Paris is easy. It is easy to get around and to find out what is going on, no matter how deplorable your spoken French. The city has one of the most efficient public transportation systems in the world, reaching into every hidden nook you would want to explore. Everything you need or want is available somewhere within the city's confines. Both the Tourist Office and City Hall provide more information about the city than you would think possible—from brochures you can pick up to information on the Internet that is updated daily. In addition to museums, tours, monuments and interesting current events, you can find every sports facility and municipal pool, get advice on how to raise and educate healthy children, and even an explanation of why the city's water is so good. Descriptions of public gardens, suggested walks through historic neighbourhoods and schedules for cultural and entertaining events are available to visitors and residents alike. Shops sell guides, history books and restaurant critiques, and you can find directions to intriguing shops and compendiums of helpful advice from what is open on Sunday to what can be delivered to your door. There are also several locally produced English-language publications to keep you updated on the area's events. Actually Paris may well be the most comprehensively covered city in the world.

So, what is it that takes an effort? It's moving. Moving to any new city, settling in, getting used to manoeuvering and finding the things you need when you descend upon a city not yet your own. Don't underestimate the time required to get your bearings, or to begin with, to cram the furniture you had shipped into a space that turns out to be too small. Or to deal with the fact that there is no hot water tap to hook up to the washing machine you brought from home. Or that the documents you were told to bring were not the right ones after all. Or that you cannot get a bank account without proof of domicile, but without a bank account you cannot get an apartment... These difficulties are wearying to be sure, but they can be overcome with dispatch—we hope—by using the information in this book.

USING THIS GUIDE

The first guidebook to Paris was published in 1685 and hundreds have been published since. Today, guidebooks for tourists recount the city's history and describe in their own ways its remarkable sights and sensations. In varying detail, they review restaurants and suggest hotels of all categories. Each tries to present the material in a more eye-catching manner than the others, and each has its own approach to capturing the glory of *la Ville Lumière*. All, however, have one thing in common: they are designed for people visiting for a short while, tourists who think that what they see in a week is what they would get every day of the year.

This book, although encompassing information for the short-term visitor, is different in approach. Its main purpose is to offer specific advice and assistance about daily life in Paris for those who are planning to stay longer, for people who have the time for byways rather than straight paths, for sojourners who want to get into the deeper Parisian life that is often hidden from the tourist's eye. Whether your stay is for a month or a year, the type of information you need for a successful stay is different—deeper and more detailed than that found in standard tourist guides: where and how to look for appropriate housing, how to manage finances, how to stay healthy and where to get fit, how to access the Internet and where to buy a computer, where to get a fun meal for your kids, etc. are just a few examples of basic information that should help you move with minimum discomfort into the Parisian scene.

Of course, there is a difference between learning how a city works and adapting yourself to its cultural rules. In Paris, this is what takes the real effort, requiring more adjustment than you might suspect. How much you want to adapt is up to you, for Paris is flexible above all. You can spend all your time with English speakers— some 100,000 live in the Greater Paris area—and learn just enough French to ask a grocer if the melons are ripe. Yet, if this is the route you choose, you'll never really feel at home. If you don't understand why your colleagues or new friends act as they do, you'll always be an outsider to them. This book will come in handy in this regard, with cultural tips, some do's and don'ts—and there are many of them—and even a quiz to see how many of the 'Paris Rules' you've absorbed.

Your success at this will depend for the most part on your expectations. Preconceived ideas about an unfamiliar society may not always prove true, and it's best not to assume that life in Paris will more or less be like life at home, except for the language—it isn't. Start from scratch and take Paris as it is, appreciate its remarkable beauty, explore its delicious novelty, enjoy its agreeable differences, cope with its difficulties and try to laugh (if only to yourself) when your own cultural assumptions collide head on with the differing assumptions of the French.

LIVING WELL

Parisians have long felt that they have mastered *l'art de vivre*—the art of living well. Tourists who stroll the length of the beautiful Champs-Elysées may get a whiff of the French traditions of elegance, culture and poise, but it is the total absorption of *l'art de vivre* that truly enriches the soul. It is the habits of everyday life—walking down the city's beautifully designed historic streets on your way to work, passing graceful apartment buildings and landscaped squares, shopping in the bustling markets, or lingering in the spring sunshine at a sidewalk café—that continually remind you of how gracious Parisian life can be. Watching a film under the summer stars at La Villette, hearing organ music soar to the high reaches of the Cathedral of Notre-Dame, or gathering with new Parisian friends at a neighbourhood bistro where you have become known as an *habitué* (regular customer)—these will remind you of the fullness of life in Paris as well. Make no mistake: appreciation of experience is what Paris is about, whether you are here for a day or a year. And this never stops as long as you are here.

Eventually you'll find your way—everyone does after a while. As your Parisian life unfolds, you'll come to discover which neighbourhood *fromagerie* (cheese store) is your favourite and which teller at the bank goes a little out of the way for you, and so you will be dealing less with strangers and more with people you know. You will walk down the streets and suddenly realise that those byways and hidden nooks are familiar, that they're become your own. The essence of your life will seem more vibrant, your conversation more animated, your days fuller. Now you will be developing your own *art de vivre*, keeping the best of your own culture and traditions while adding on those of the French. This is the beginning of *la belle vie*, the good life you could only imagine at first, but now coming true in ways you had not expected. And when these things happen, you'll understand—almost without thinking about it—that you're at home.

Be patient, for it will happen, with openness to new ideas, observation of life around you and even a little assistance. In this regard, we hope this book will help guide you and perhaps even keep you on course. *Bienvenue à Paris*. Welcome home.

This book was originally researched in 1996 and I had a lot of encouragement when I was still so new to Paris. Colette and Claude Samama read every word of the manuscript and saw me through the project from beginning to end. My stalwart friend Jean Coyner offered invaluable advice, her humour often sorely needed. The late Jean and Warren Trabant (who loved Paris every day for their fifty years here), Sally Leabhart, Judith Oringer, Jaem Heath-O'Ryan, Fenn Troller and John Zaugg (who also created the elegant maps in Chapter Two) all read drafts of the manuscript. Your help was invaluable, and I thank you once again. *Je vous en suis très reconnaissante.*

In addition, in Paris, Doctor Francis Bolgert, Mary Briaud, Mme Henriette Chaibriant (l'Assistance Publique), Rabbi Tom Cohen, Véronique Gaboriau, Georges Gross, Drew Harré, Juan Sanchez and Mme Michèle Simonin (Chambre de Commerce et d'Industrie de Paris) all read parts of the manuscript and made suggestions. Legal and cultural consultant Jean Taquet commented extensively on sections concerning residence permits. In the United States, I had comments from Bill Benoit, Robert Cole, Ann Overton, James Keough and Linda Sparrowe. I still thank you all for your kindness and support, and as I assured you in 1996, if there were any mistakes herein, readers would understand that they were mine lone and not yours.

And now 14 years later we are doing a new edition—updated, modernised and expanded. Although I have been living in Paris for some years now, I still needed some feedback on the new material created. So, to the above list I add with pleasure and gratitude: Virginia Crosby, Lois Grjebine, Joy Eckel, and Iris Grossman. *Je vous remercie beaucoup.* And again, to Jean Taquet, whose expertise cannot be measured. I thank you all.

A FEW NOTES ON FOREIGN WORDS

Throughout the book, foreign words are shown in italics, even those that have been assimilated into the English language and appear in the Oxford English Dictionary. This includes the word 'anglophone', which is how the French refer to native English-speakers, and which is used here occasionally in the appropriate context. When listing services or shops (e.g., bakeries) in the vicinity, they are listed by *arrondissement*; where the services might be needed regardless of their location (e.g., churches), they are listed alphabetically. Where full addresses are given in the text, including the entire number of the *arrondissement* (e.g. 75012), the word Paris has been omitted; if writing to these addresses, be sure to include the city name.

DISCLAIMER

Readers should understand that information about regulations, addresses and Internet websites were current as of December 2009, to the best of our knowledge. Also, please note that the sites and services listed are informational only. The author and publisher bear no responsibility for any changes in immigration laws (which are currently under review), the sometimes unhelpful service, discrepancies in rates or prices, quality of products or accommodations, the disappearance of a shop, the occasional bad meal (yes, even in Paris), or any other misunderstanding or inconvenience that might arise. As the French say, *"C'est la vie"*—that's life.

La Palette is a well-known café in Paris. Parisians flock to outdoor cafés as soon as the spring weather permits.

Paris as far as the eye can see—
a city awaits your exploration.

MAP OF FRANCE

ENGLAND

NETHERLANDS

ENGLISH CHANNEL

BELGIUM

GERMANY

LUXEMBOURG

● **PARIS**

ATLANTIC
OCEAN

FRANCE

SWITZERLAND

BAY OF
BISCAY

ITALY

CORSICA

SPAIN

ANDORRA

MEDITERRANEAN SEA

IMPRESSIONS

CHAPTER 1

'If every soul left it one day and grass grew in the
pavements, it would still be Paris to me,
I'd want to live there.'
—Katherine Ann Porter

Do first impressions endure? Is love at first sight a reliable indicator for the future? Perhaps not, but then we wouldn't be talking about Paris. If Paris is the most visited city in the world, it is because those who pass through, again and again, whenever they can, understand something that reaches their hearts as soon as their feet touch the first cobblestone or their eyes soar to the spire of a medieval church. Paris has something special, and what makes it so is plain to see.

Paris is, in fact, a city of impressions. When you first arrive, you can't help but take in the beauty right away, even if you can't quite define it—the open squares with charming cafés, the landscaped parks and verdant esplanades, the ancient palaces turned into museums, the gracious stone buildings vibrantly alive with pots of red geraniums on so many windowsills. And the colour of the sky—why does no one call it 'Paris blue'?

Then, as you look around, you notice that except for the Montparnasse Tower that looms large and rather out of sync, the city is of a human scale. It's just the right size for walkers. The boulevards are broad enough for several lanes of cars to zoom along, but the residential streets are narrower and welcoming to those who stroll, curving in unexpected directions and lined with small shops and outdoor tables that beckon you to stop for a moment to take it all in. The buildings are low—few extend beyond five stories—windows are tall and doorways are wide. Occasionally there's a door ajar, allowing you to peek in. You see a courtyard, perhaps. Or a bicycle propped against the wall. Sometimes there's a stone cherub looking down on you as you pass. Or an antique streetlight, curved and ornate, waiting for dusk. And just around the corner there's a church with a fountain, where a dog is splashing itself and everyone else along with it. Paris is constantly a surprise.

And suddenly you notice the noise, or at least, the quality of it. Paris is a city with some dignity, is it not? Certainly there are automobiles rushing about, but they rarely honk their horns, and some *métro* trains have only whooshing rubber wheels. There's no music intruding on your dinner in restaurants or in elevators, no one interrupting or shouting in stores. There's just a bustle and hum as the city works. And without thinking, you relax and take it down a notch yourself, hearing each sound for what it is.

Hungry, you stop at a fruit stand and browse through the artistically displayed produce: fresh, colourful and abundant fruit in season. Or you decide to drop in at a bistro and you choose one of the specials of the day written on a chalkboard propped up next to your table, the selections also in season and carefully prepared. Or perhaps you rest your feet at a café, where the waiter dressed in black allows you to sit with your coffee and postcards until you're ready to take on the city once again.

And then you walk some more and finally back to your hotel. The concierge greets you quietly, but he asks you nothing about your day. He does not want to intrude on your privacy, on those thoughts that are swirling around in your head. You nod back and say "Good evening" in French, if you can. You understand though, that he is letting you know that he is there, ready to help if need be. But you are fine, if a little overwhelmed. A few minutes later, you have your shoes off, ready to run a bath and replay those hours that even now seem too short.

"Yes," you think, at the end of this first day awash with your first impressions, "Yes, I could live here, and quite well." And this is an impression that turns out to be true.

OVERVIEW

CHAPTER 2

'It is the only city in the world which
understands the world and itself.'
–Henry Adams

PAST AND PRESENT ENTWINED

Paris is, without a doubt, the most beautiful capital of the world, and it should well be. For more than a millennium, kings, emperors and presidents have devoted their patriotic, religious and imaginative energies to creating their capital. The result is Paris, a city of splendour unmatched on the world's stage. Yet it is a city designed to be lived in as well as admired, and it is the almost seamless weaving of the city's intricate history into everyday life that makes the Paris experience so rich.

It is hard not to think about Paris' history wherever you go. Every street name is a voice from the past, from rue Vercingétorix, which recalls the Celtic warrior who fought against the conquering Romans in 52 bc, to boulevard Haussmann, named after the man who, 150 years ago, designed much of the structure of Paris today. If you are stuck in traffic on the 36-km beltline highway, the *périphérique*, remember that your slow path traces the city's final fortress walls of almost 200 years ago. And as you stroll, plaques on buildings will remind you of historical events and the people who shaped them. Wherever you are, the saga of Paris is in plain view.

The Beginnings

It's hard to say when the city was 'founded'. A small band of Gauls called the Parisii lived in the hills of the Paris Basin as long ago as the 7th century BC and on what is now the Île-de-la-Cité from about 250 BC. From this island in the middle of the river Seine and surrounded by the rivers Oise, Aisne, Ourcq and the Marne, the Parisii plied a lucrative river trade by commanding a strategic stop for all travellers.

No wonder the Romans wanted it, taking it in 52 BC and staying some 400 years. They first established themselves on the island of the Parisii, then slowly expanded their city across the water to the south, into what is still called the Quartier Latin (named after the Latin-speaking students of the university quarter during the Middle Ages). North of the river was a marsh—a *marais*—and the trendy 21st century neighbourhood there still goes by that name, Le Marais.

Some 9,000 people lived in what was then called Lutetia, but by 212 AD, it was officially named Paris, after the displaced Parisii. Some ancient ruins from that time have survived, for example, those in the crypt in front of the Cathedral of Notre Dame and ruins in the Quartier Latin.

By the 3rd century AD, however, Christianity was spreading and the Pope sent his bishop Denis to Paris to convert the Gauls. To the displeasure of the Romans, he succeeded, so he and two fellow Christians were beheaded near the top of the region's highest hill, now called Montmartre or 'hill of martyrs'. Saint Denis became the patron saint of France.

The patron saint of Paris itself is Geneviève, a devout girl of the 5th century who convinced the Parisians to trust in the Christian God and saved the city from an onslaught of Attila the Hun in 451 AD. By then, the Romans had already lost control of the area and were replaced for 300 years by the Franks from Germania—a dynasty that fought among themselves but which managed to establish Francia as Christian once and for all, though not always peacefully, to say the least.

By the 9th century, Charlemagne (whose father Pépin III was the first of the Carolingians) was using harsh military conquest to expand the domain and to impose Christianity on the realm. He preferred the Germanic city of Aachen (Aix-la-Chapelle) to Paris, so Paris declined over the decades, suffering from neglect and invasions by Norse Vikings.

Notre Dame sits along the Seine, which curves leisurely through Paris.

Charlemagne's descendants fought amongst themselves as well, so just before the turn of the first Christian millennium the time was ripe in Paris for a new king to emerge. Thus came Hugues Capet who founded the Capetian Dynasty that lasted in direct male lineage for more than 300 years.

It's important to remember that the territory of Francia then does not correspond to the map of France today. At the time of Hugues Capet, it encompassed Paris and more or less what is now the region of Île de France. In fact, Gaul was a feudal society marked by regions, each with its own dialect, culture and governance. But as the centuries rolled on, and as the Capetians expanded their domains into these regions, Paris, with a population numbering about 20,000, grew in importance.

It was around 1163, at the time of the Capetians, that the construction of the Cathedral of Notre Dame began. It took about 150 years to be completed and still stands, as does the

Conciergerie, as part of the Palais Royal. (The Conciegerie became a prison during the French Revolution, but is now a national monument.) It was under the Capetians that the magnificent gothic Basilique Saint-Denis and the exquisite Sainte-Chapelle were built, and the Sorbonne founded in 1253. It was also under the Capetians—King Philippe-Auguste—that the fortress of the Louvre was built and the larger streets paved with stone. The city marketplace of Les Halles was also constructed under the Capetian reign. It remained on the same spot for some 800 years, but was razed in 1969 to make way for an enormous shopping and entertainment mall called, of course, Forum Les Halles.

Medieval Paris

But what was daily life like in this beautiful city we revere today? By the beginning of the 14th century, its population had reached more than 250,000, cramped in an area perhaps one-quarter of the city's size today. It may have had an awe-inspiring cathedral and other impressive churches and palaces, and it may have become a renowned centre of learning, but crowded and dank as most cities were at that time, Paris stank. The rich, of course, lived well regardless of the conditions, but with no indoor plumbing or underground sewers; with horses traversing the streets; rubbish piling up and trenches for excrement running open in the middle of many streets—life in the city was not easy for the masses. Houses were heated by fireplaces that smoked and built up soot inside and out; food spoiled quickly; and insects and bugs thrived in bedlinens, clothes and on the people themselves, who went mostly unwashed. In addition, disease was rampant. The Black Death (bubonic plague) that hit Europe in the mid-14th century took more than 25 million people, including some 70,000 in Paris, decimating its population and its economy.

And so came civil unrest and war. As the Capetians' direct male line died out, the English king figured he was next in line for the French throne—after all, it was the Normans (from Normandy in northern France) who, long before their 1066 conquest of England, had owned and ruled northern France.

Having lost much of their holdings, these 'Anglo-Normans' wanted them—and France—back. The French barons said *"non"* and put a Valois (a non-linear descendant of Hugues Capet) on the throne in Paris, beginning a dynasty that lasted about 250 years. Think of their rule however, and what comes to mind initially is the disastrous plague and a 116-year war against England.

It's hard now to imagine a war that could last so long, but the Hundred Years' War (1337–1453) saw decades of victories and defeats on both sides in brief skirmishes and major battles, intrigues and fluctuating allegiances. It saw Joan of Arc initially victorious at Orléans, then burnt at the stake by the English as a witch. It also saw Paris being occupied by the English for some 15 years, allowing Henry VI to be crowned king at Notre Dame. And finally, in 1437 it saw Paris retaken by the Valois king Charles VII, who ultimately regained the rest. And so, through the nascent nationalism that united the disparate regional forces to defeat the English, France started to become a nation with Paris as its major cultural and administrative force.

The Early Modern Age

The Valois dynasty lasted until 1589, reigning through the Reformation and the flowering of the Renaissance. In the century after the end of the war, Paris' population grew to about 400,000 and magnificent churches and mansions were built, including the Hôtel de Cluny, now the popular Museum of the Middle Ages. The Louvre began to be transformed into the magnificent palace of today, and French officially replaced Latin as the language for administrative and legal acts throughout the realm. The first printing press appeared and more people could read and write. Under François I—a poet and patron of the arts—Leonardo da Vinci came to France bringing with him the Mona Lisa, which visitors to the Louvre now flock to see. In fact, the bulk of the art in the Louvre today is from the collection of the Valois. François also established the Collège de France, the first humanist (non-religious) university, which is still going strong. Paris was a city of culture and learning under the last Valois kings.

By now, Parisians were solidly identifying themselves with the side of the river on which they resided. From the Middle Ages, the Right Bank (*rive droite*) became the mercantile focus of the city, because boats could moor easily, servicing the aristocrats who had settled near the palace of the Louvre. The Left Bank (*rive gauche*), home to the Sorbonne and other institutions of learning, was inhabited by artists and intellectuals. Till today, the modern city continues to divide itself thus, with headquarters of banks, the largest department stores and much of the city's major commerce clustered on the Right Bank, while the Left Bank holds the universities and artists' galleries in a vibrant atmosphere of creativity and ideas. And so the Paris of today is still somewhat reminiscent of the city under the Valois.

But it was also a city of persecutions and strife. In response to the harshness of Catholicism, the Huguenots (followers of the French reformer John Calvin), who spoke out against the Pope in Rome, began converting part of the French population, including Parisians. After fluctuating degrees of tolerance, Parisians witnessed the massacre of about 3,000 Protestant 'heretics' in Paris on Saint Bartholomew's Day in 1572. (All told, some 70,000 Huguenots were later slain.) Eventually—after intrigues and the assassination of King Henri III—Henri IV of Navarre was crowned king. Henri IV set out to build a more efficient town. In 1605, he began the construction of what is now called La Place des Vosges, near Place de la Bastille, which some say is the most beloved square in all of France. He also built the exclusive Place Dauphine and, to better connect the two banks, finished the Pont Neuf, which 400 years later, is still called the New Bridge.

Henri IV began the Bourbon dynasty, and the Catholic Bourbons—periodic uprisings and unrest aside—ruled for the next 200 years, until they were overthrown by the French Revolution. Wars were waged to extend the monarchy's realm, while the arts flourished in Paris, literacy increased for both men

"Paris is well worth a mass."

These were the famous words of the Huguenot Henri IV of Navarre who was crowned king only upon his conversion to Catholicism.

and women, literature and publishing expanded and the Luxembourg Palace (now the Sénat) was built.

We've all heard of Louis XIV, the 'Sun King' who abandoned crowded and filthy Paris in 1682 for his newly built opulent palace at Versailles, one of the most visited palaces in the world today. Paris had some 600,000 residents at that time, and although the streets were paved with stone and somewhat lit at night, and in spite of its expansion to the north and south, it was still a city of overcrowded slums. Despite such beautiful oases as the Place Vendôme and the Place des Victoires, and despite the flourishing of the arts and such amenities as the first true café, Procope (which still stands at the same spot today), the city hadn't changed much overall. Disease and crime were rampant, and so for the rich and powerful, it was best to be at Versailles.

The Revolution

And thus we come to poor ill-fated Louis XVI and his Austrian wife, the pampered and hated Marie Antoinette. Actually, by the end of the 17th century, the ideas of the liberal, anticlerical Enlightenment were taking hold, and Paris had assumed its place as the cultural centre of the Age of Reason. Learning and the arts were esteemed, and life was lovely— for individuals who could afford it. But in 1788, the French treasury was almost bankrupt, owing to costly wars (including the support of the American Revolution), the lavish lifestyle of the French royalty and a disastrous harvest. People were starving all across France. Unfortunately, Louis XVI, rather a simple, well-meaning man, only indecisive and conservative, yet ultimately willing to accept some reforms, did not react. And so, the Parisians decided that they had had enough: the Bastille—a prison near the present-day ultra modern Opéra National Paris Bastille—was taken. The active revolution had begun. Paris— and France—would never be the same.

"Let them eat cake."

It was during a bread shortage in Paris that Marie Antoinette is reputed to have uttered those famous words, "Let them eat cake". It's not clear if she really did so, but the populace blamed the Austrian-born queen for France's troubles, no matter that Louis himself might have been a scapegoat for the tyrannies and excesses of his predecessors.

All the regions of France came together in a meeting in Paris to pledge their allegience to a single, common nation. The Declaration of the Rights of Man and the Citizen was adopted. The country was divided into *départements* and in 1792, the First Republic declared the birth of La France. It wasn't an easy birth. Over the next five years, there were civil war and clashes with other European states. After a period of moderation and constitutional monarchy came the Reign of Terror led by the infamous Robespierre, during which some 17,000 'enemies of liberty' (including Louis and Marie-Antoinette) were beheaded by the guillotine. The major site of the executions was Place de la Révolution, now the beautiful and much more serene Place de la Concorde.

Napoléon

Despite the ensuing 75 years of instability and the revolutions of 1830 and 1840, which caused governments to swing from republic to empire to monarchy, and then to republic, the legacy of the French Revolution was the power given to the citizens, who became—and remain—the country's dominant political force.

Napoleon, who seized power and had himself proclaimed Emperor, made lasting changes to France that are still felt today. In Paris, his legacy is seen everywhere. His successful military battles are honoured by street names—Iéna, Friedland, Wagram—and he has left his mark on the Madeleine Church, the Arc de Triomphe and the arcaded rue de Rivoli. He built the Pont des Arts and what is now the lovely Canal Saint-Martin. He also systematised the city's districts by designating 12 *arrondissements* (they number 20 today) and even creating a uniform system for the numbering of buildings. He established the *lycée* educational system and most importantly, he devised a new civic legal code that was almost revolutionary in codifying the rule of law throughout the land. Military defeats brought all this to an end: the Russians entered Paris and Napoleon abdicated into exile on Elba. He returned to Paris for 100 days but was defeated once and for all by Wellington at the Battle of Waterloo.

A City of Unrest

With Napoleon's exile to the island of Sainte-Hélène, a series of unpopular governments ruled for the next 60 years, culminating finally in the 1871 establishment of a republic, once and for all. But it was a tumultuous period in teeming and seething Paris, whose population had now reached 900,000. First the Bourbons—two brothers of Louis XVI— took power one after the other, but they and Charles X, who was too reliant on the Church and too authoritarian, didn't last long. After a riot in which some 5,000 workers were killed ended the short-lived republic, Louis-Philippe ruled as the 'bourgeois monarch' from 1830-1848. However, intolerable conditions brought the city to bursting point, and explode it did.

By about 1848, the Industrial Revolution and the rise of science and reason were taking hold in Europe. Railroads were being built and ports expanded. French workers were flocking into the small city and its growing suburbs. Paris now held more than a million people, and it was still dark and dense, with warrens of narrow alleyways running with rats and filled with filth and disease. Fresh water was still rare and a crowded tenement stood directly in front of the Louvre. The streets were open sewers as in medieval times, the Seine was part of the sewer system and in 1848 alone, some 19,000 people died of cholera. Factories overworked their employees and there was a high rate of unemployment. Paris may have been the world capital of culture, but the air was polluted with smoke and soot, and crime was uncontrollable.

First came what was meant to be a peaceful demonstration near the Madeleine. But troops on the boulevard des Capucines (in the 8^e *arrondissement*) started a riot by firing into the crowd. Revolution became the order of the day. Barricades shot up in the streets, the king abdicated and fled, and finally some 50,000 poverty-stricken citizens marched in protest in June. This was too much for the new conservative government, and in putting down the rebellion, some 1,500 Parisians were killed and another 5,000 deported.

As his name was known thoughout France, Louis Napoléon Bonaparte, Napoléon's nephew, was elected president in 1848. In 1852, he changed his mind and named himself Emperor

Napoléon III. It is true that Napoléon III's reign only lasted for 18 years—until war and another revolution terminated monarchy in France for good—but it was important, for much of the Paris that we see today was created during this period.

Imagine Paris then: workers from the countryside were streaming into the city and living conditions were untenable—the city simply couldn't be sustained. The Emperor knew something had to be done and asked his prefect, Baron Georges Haussmann to remake Paris into a 'new Rome'. Baron Haussmann went to work, demolishing the slums by relegating the poor to the eastern edges of the city and replacing the dark little alleyways with straight streets and broad avenues (so police could control any future uprisings of the masses). Gracious apartment buildings that adhered to safety standards were constructed, as well as modern glass-and-iron public edifices. Open squares were created and landscaped, streets were paved with asphalt, and he brought Parisians into the sun with 5,000 acres of parks including the Bois de Boulogne and the Bois de Vincennes. He built hospitals and schools, dug an efficient 600-km underground sewer system and also constructed aqueducts and reservoirs that brought fresh water to all. Gas mains fuelled 15,000 street lamps, making the city safer after dark, thus transforming Paris into *La Ville Lumière*—the city of light.

But if Paris was beautiful and if sophistication and fashion ruled, the poor people had made few gains. There were also the wars. France had enough military successes under Napoléon III to erase the humiliation of Waterloo, but in 1870, a disastrous war was declared against Prussia, and that was the end of the Emperor, who abdicated into exile. Prussians were besieging the city, the people were hungry, cutting down trees on the Champs-Elysées for firewood just to keep warm. In the midst of this bombardment of Paris, revolution once again took hold, perhaps the bloodiest the Paris streets had ever seen.

The Paris Commune
The Paris workers had had enough. After the elected government had capitulated to the Prussians, they angrily

forced the leaders to evacuate to Versailles, electing their own extremist council, named the Commune, to run the city. Immediately it tried to impose reforms, including the abolition of the guillotine, the conversion of abandoned businesses into workers' cooperatives and a separation of church and state. But the Versailles government was not to be thwarted. After a few weeks, it retook Paris, street by street, neighbourhood by neighbourhood. (Owing to those open boulevards constructed by Haussmann just a few years before, it was hard to erect the barricades necessary to keep the 'Versaillais' at bay.) Atrocities and murders were committed on both sides, but the 'Versaillais' prevailed, slaughtering thousands of Communards. By the time it was all over, some 40,000 people had been arrested, 13,000 imprisoned or deported to Devil's Island and 20,000 left dead. Even after peace had been restored and the elected government returned to power, hard feelings and unrest lasted for decades, and the Commune is remembered till today.

The Belle Epoque

In spite of the upheavals and reshuffles under the Third Republic, Paris, with a population of some 2.8 million, seemed to glow. The torched Hôtel de Ville (City Hall) was rebuilt and old buildings began to be conserved and restored. The *métro* system was built, as was the beautiful basilica atop Montmartre—Sacre-Cœur. More open boulevards were constructed according to Haussmannian standards and theatres and gracious apartment buildings shot up. The staging of Expositions Universelles gave rise to the Trocadéro, the Grand Palais and the Petit Palais (now museums) and, of course, the Eiffel Tower. Impressionist painters, whose work can now be viewed at the Musée d'Orsay (which was then a railway station), emerged.The first department store, Au Bon Marché, opened in 1876, followed by Au Printemps. Literature thrived, theatres were packed and popular composers such as Camille Saint-Saëns, Claude Debussy and Maurice Ravel epitomised the cultural ethos of the time.

The Great War

However, World War I, known as the Great War, changed the face of Paris once again. Paris may have faced sporadic bombardment, but it was the aftermath of the war that had the greatest impact on the city. More than 1.5 million Frenchmen between the ages of 25–45 were killed and another million maimed during the long war. It was said that 'a generation was lost'. The birth rate plummeted, and women went to work in Paris. They also smoked in public, wore short skirts and were open about their love affairs (although they didn't get to vote until after World War II). Skilled workers were desperately needed to rebuild and modernise the city, but had disappeared. If previous influxes of workers into the city were from the French provinces, now Paris opened its doors to foreign immigrants, and they came by the thousands. Some new arrivals integrated themselves, but others formed their own ethnic enclaves within the city confines and beyond. The 'crazy years' of the 1920s also saw foreign writers and artists flocking to Montparnasse, the new artistic *quartier*, and the entire Left Bank was populated by such lights as Ernest Hemingway, Pablo Picasso, James Joyce and Gertrude Stein. World War I may have ended with the Great Depression for the Americans, but the arts and high living in Paris still thrived—until Hitler made the city his own.

World War II

On 16 June 1940, Paris capitulated to Germany and the city was occupied by the Nazis. In May 1940, the population of Greater Paris stood at 3.5 million, but a month later it had diminished by more than half, those with resources to do so having fled. What was left in Paris, as one can imagine, were the workers and the poor. A puppet government was set up in Vichy under the World War I hero Marshall Henri Philippe Pétain. General Charles de Gaulle left for London, where he announced a government in exile, calling upon all 'Free French' to resist.

World War II is recent enough that the atrocities committed, the concentration camps and the deprivations need not be elaborated upon here. In Paris, life on the surface may have looked 'normal' with restaurants, nightclubs and theatres functioning (mostly for the occupiers), children playing in the parks and Parisians still going to church, but the newspapers were closed down and censorship and curfews established. Forbidden to own cars, Parisians crowded the *métro*, except on weekends when it was closed to them. Clocks were set to German time. Signs and restaurant menus appeared in German, and while the Germans lived well, Parisians were cold and hungry. But in the face of brutal repression and privations, executions for infractions of Nazi rules and a roundup and deportation of thousands of Jews by the Vichy government itself, there was nothing to do but endure, and clandestinely, to resist.

After D-Day on 6 June 1944 and the breakthrough of the German lines by the Allies, Paris rose up. Look around as you walk around Paris today and see the plaques remembering the brave French individuals who fought in the city's streets and died for La France. Stop on the corner of rue de Rivoli and rue Saint-Florentin, as you come out of the métro, where there are ten such plaques in a row, often covered by wreaths, and thank those heroes for having defied the Nazis' tanks right on that busy street. Finally, on 25 August 1944, after heavy fighting in the streets of Paris, General de Gaulle marched triumphant into the city, ready to take on the rebuilding of France.

From Then Until Now

It would be nice to say that all has been peaceful in Paris since then, but that wouldn't be true. For the next 12 years, the Fourth Republic (1946–1958) focused on rebuilding a country whose infrastructure had been destroyed by war. Hardship finally gave way to recovery, riding on the American-led Marshall Plan, combined with a French economic plan, and Paris seemed on its way to modernity. But the country's North African colonies, especially Algeria, wanted their independence, and a grizzly war (1954-1962) complete with massacres, torture and finally exodus, brought more than 500,000 colonists into France, especially Paris, where many were settled into faceless residential suburbs. Fifty years later, these suburbs are openly seething with unrest.

Nonetheless, city life after the war began to shine. Intellectuals once again rose to the forefront—Jean-Paul Sartre, Simone de Beauvoir and Albert Camus frequented the cafés on the Left Bank, foreign writers again found Paris as their muse and the film industry gained prominence worldwide. Haute cuisine and haute couture rose to their greatest heights and Paris became a tourist Mecca once again. Not even the explosive student unrest of 1968 could dent the reputation of Paris; today Paris is the most visited city in the world.

Indeed, over the next several decades of the Fifth Republic (1958–), under presidents from both the Right and the Left, Paris continued to build, restore and modernise. Some streets were widened and the *péripherique* was built to alleviate the clogging of the roads brought on by the proliferation of cars. Historic buildings were restored and cleaned under a 1962 law. The poor neighbourhood of Beaubourg was replaced by the ultramodern art museum, the Centre Pompidou. The Tour Montparnasse that arose in the city centre reminded Paris that it didn't want such eyesores, and thus throughout the 1970s, the enormous, modern business-residential city of La Defense was built on the city's western edge. Its dominating Grande Arche was later constructed as part of President François Mitterrand's *Grands Projets* that envisioned urban revival and architectural modernity for a city whose cultural and economic position would be cemented in the European Union and beyond.

Mitterrand cleaned up those eastern slums to which the poor had retreated during the Haussmannian improvements. He also constructed a new science museum, park complex La Villette on the site of the city's former slaughterhouse, as well as the huge Opéra Bastille. The Bibliothèque Nationale arose in the wasteland of the 13th *arrondissement*, an area that is becoming populated once again. More parks were landscaped and an ultramodern Finance Ministry building brightly commands the riverfront of the 12th *arrondissement*. Even the Louvre, that ancient oasis of elegance, was restored to its former glory and modernised with a spectacular glass pyramid to welcome the millions of visitors who pass through every year.

Into a New Millennium

And now we are at the beginning of a new millennium, and despite political upheavals, the advent of the European Union single market, wars abroad and the threat of terrorism around the world, Paris continues on its glorious road. Of course, its longtime residents grumble about the state of their urban environment, with 2.3 million people in the city and another 10 million in the suburban surrounds. Talk about the traffic and the smog! And what should be done about the crowded, angry suburbs, seething with immigrants from former French colonies in North Africa, people who have French nationality, but who have been assimilated neither into society nor the workforce as 'true French'? In a formerly Catholic country with a separation of church and state, how does one deal with the fact that some eight per cent of the population is Muslim and that some 13 per cent of the Paris population is made up of immigrants? How many more should the country admit? How many of the limited number of jobs will they take from the French, and how can they be integrated into French life? Of course, other European capitals are dealing with problems of the same sort and answers are slow in forthcoming. But France, in particular, with a culture that believes in rational solutions to most problems, is at a loss when they do not appear. Protest marches call for solutions while cars are burnt in the northern suburbs, and Parisians—who love to talk about politics—have differing views on what should and can be done.

So this is a time of some confusion as Paris strives to maintain its traditions while adapting to the modern world. Yet the marvel of Paris is that the city, for the most part, is managing to hold on to its appreciated traditions while meeting the future, as it must. As for Parisians, despite all the uncertainties and changes, they are proud of how the history of their city melds into their comfortable modern surroundings and they know how fortunate they are.

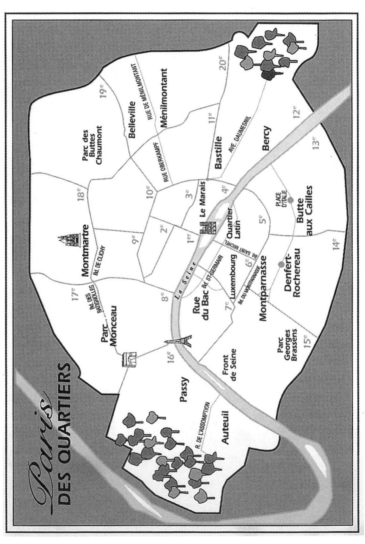

The *quartiers* and some landmarks of Paris.

PARIS NOW: THE CITY AS IT IS
Paris Overall

Still a small city as world capitals go, Paris encompasses no more than 80 sq km and is only about 12 km across. Although officially Paris is *intra-muros* (within the old city walls), Greater Paris today includes the outlying towns that border the *périphérique*. About two million people live intra-muros. 10 million more live in the suburbs, giving the metropolis a population of more than 12 million.

If Paris is the sum of its history, as any city is, it is also creating a new history as the days go by, changing and evolving into what this new millennium requires. Too much traffic in the city? Construct bicycle and bus lanes to encourage a reduced use of cars, or develop a tram line that circles the city edges, and provide 20,000 rental bikes for public use, docked in every neighborhood. Not enough open space for the increasing population? Create a 3-km-long summer sandy "beach" along the riverfront, and offer recreational activities late into the night. These are already accomplished and, except for the car drivers who are slightly inconvenienced, few people complain.

And more is in the Paris wind. That enormous warren of shops at Les Halles is to be upgraded and additional residences for students are being planned. There is also a need for more affordable housing throughout the city. Although more than 5,000 apartments have been built in the past decade, future building might require changing zoning laws and reaching higher into the Paris sky. In this beautiful city, this is not popular at all.

Yet, for now Paris still retains a very human scale. Buildings are low, few neighbourhood streets run straight, and there is always something unexpected, often charming, to catch the eye. Thanks to Baron Haussmann 150 years ago, Paris is an open city, characterised by ornate, spectacular squares and wide boulevards that converge at open junctions where residents do their shopping or sit at sidewalk cafés. Formally planned gardens and parks and casual, leafy squares dot the landscape; 100,000 trees line both narrow streets and wide boulevards; and two beautiful wooded parks, the Bois de

Boulogne to the west and the Bois de Vincennes to the east, provide respite at Paris' flanks. The Seine flows through the city, joined from the northeast by the Canal Saint-Martin, itself crossed at intervals by little metallic bridges and partially by pleasant rows of trees.

Although the climate is fairly mild overall and Paris often shines gloriously in the sun, the city's uneven weather can bring problems in any season. In winter, the temperature may hover below freezing for weeks, with the wind howling down those wide boulevards and nipping at narrow corners. Rains make the river rise, sometimes closing the banks to traffic; occasionally there is snow. Spring, even well into the supposedly romantic April, is often unpleasantly grey and wet, but there are also splendid, almost warm, sunny days. True spring begins in May—the first signs are newly planted flower boxes on windowsills and the tables that begin to reappear outside cafés. By the time summer is in full swing late in July and August, the sometimes sweltering temperatures and high pollution drive Parisians out of town until the beginning of September, when they return in a burst of energy. This is an event in itself, known as *la rentrée*. September and October can be the best months, pleasantly sunny and warm.

Tulips appearing at the florists usually mean Spring is round the corner.

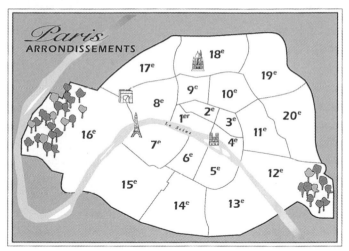

The 20 *arrondissements* of Paris.

The Layout

Since the time of Napoléon in the early 19th century, Paris has been divided into administrative zones called *arrondissements*. Originally there were 12, but in 1860 Napoléon III annexed outlying villages, doubling the population and creating more *arrondissements*, finally reaching the current 20. Each *arrondissement* has its *mairie* (town hall), its mayor and its *conseil d'administration d'arrondissement* (district council), which elects the mayor of Paris. Most of the bureaucratic business for residents is done at their local *mairie* and it is the best source for information about all public functions in the city.

The *arrondissements* begin at the core of Paris, the Île-de-la-Cité and move in an outward spiral, enlarging toward the periphery. City maps are arranged and numbered by *arrondissement*, from the 1er *(le premier)* to the 20e *(le vingtième)*. Historically, the eastern parts of Paris were the factories and the workers' neighbourhoods, shabby and dense. The western parts—upwind from the unsanitary conditions and stench of industry—were the most aristocratic. Thus it was to the west that the nobles removed themselves after the 1789 revolution, and the west remains the most luxurious today. Nonetheless, the ambitious *Grands Projets* of the 1980s have upgraded the eastern *arrondissements* with modern public buildings, walkways and parks. Old buildings have also been refurbished, such that neighbourhoods are now trendy rather than squat. Within the *arrondissements* are the *quartiers* (neighbourhoods) with their individual characteristics and tradition.

You Are Where You Live

Although in times past Parisians could be categorised by their *arrondissement*, this is less true today as rising housing costs are forcing them to make their homes wherever prices are still reasonable. Many older neighbourhoods are being gentrified, sometimes to the dismay of long-time residents who bemoan the loss of their area's traditional character in the process of its becoming a more agreeable place to live.

Thinking about Place

Parisians live in every habitable square metre of space in their city, in spacious apartments overlooking leafy boulevards or tiny walk-up flats above neighbourhood stores. The *quartiers* can be airy and open, crowded and dense, or a succession of commercial streets that seem not to be a neighbourhood at all. Apartment buildings range from the graceful and traditional to the modern and faceless, down to the dilapidated and cheap. Some tranquil side streets have charming little houses and many large buildings look inward onto quiet courts; some must have windows with *double vitrage* (double glazing) to keep out the noise from the street. Parisians live in them all.

If an area seems strictly for business, just look up and you will see a flowerpot on a ledge and a curtain waving in the breeze of an open window. If an area seems so noisy you cannot possibly imagine anyone living there, just wait until you see someone coming home from work with a briefcase in one hand and the evening's *baguette* in the other. And if an area seems absolutely perfect, be prepared to pay handsomely for that rare perfection.

The neighbourhood you choose for yourself will, of course, depend on your circumstances and your purse. Much will depend on the length of your stay, or if you have family in tow. A residential neighbourhood may not be important if you are single and your stay is only a few months, but a home near your workplace may be less important if your children need a park and proximity to a bilingual school. Much will also depend on your personal preferences: will you prefer living in the *banlieue* (suburbs) even if it requires the use of an automobile? Or would you prefer a lively area in the *centre ville* (city centre), where you can walk to work? Perhaps living in a dense *quartier* is acceptable if it is close to restaurants and exciting cultural activities? Remember that not all areas look residential, but Parisians and newcomers alike live in them.

After deciding on your priorities, given the ever-present need for compromise, look carefully at each *quartier* you are considering. Are there open spaces in which to stroll, sidewalk cafés in which to relax, the kinds of shops you use, a park for children? Is there a *métro* stop nearby, and even better, a *correspondance*, meaning a junction of two different lines? Is there a major street artery nearby, but not too near? If you look at an apartment on a weekend, come back during the rush hour to get a realistic gauge of the traffic and noise. Look at the mix of people walking on the street, do some window-shopping... do everything you can to understand if this is the best place for you.

The River Islands

The Île-de-la-Cité, the oldest part of Paris, remains the sentimental heart of the city. *Kilomètre zéro*, the point from which French distances are measured, is a dial embedded in the square in front of the Cathedral of Notre-Dame. From its beginnings 2,000 years ago as home to the Celtic Parisii, the island has been an area of constant activity. Today, tourists congregate at Notre-Dame and Sainte-Chapelle, the Conciergerie and a memorial to the deported French of World War II. Parisians come to the Préfecture de Police, the Hôpital Hôtel Dieu and the Palais de Justice, built on the site where Roman governors and later the kings of France, once resided. Hardly a residential neighbourhood, there are nonetheless pockets of elegant apartments, especially north of Notre-Dame, along the quais and around the intimate Place Dauphine, an enchanting, tranquil triangle of brick and white stone dating from 1607.

Both the grandeur of the island and its apparent lack of neighbourhood character can be traced to the redevelopment of Baron Haussmann, who demolished a warren of slums and who brought order to the island while dispossessing its 20,000 residents. It is this centrality that makes the Île-de-la-Cité convenient, especially for a short stay. Bridges go directly into the 5e and 6e on the Left Bank and into the 1er and the 4e on the Right Bank. Even the *métro* stop on the island opens onto Place Lépine, the popular market for flowers and birds.

Just to the east is the Île Saint-Louis. Despite tourists who stroll down its main street, rue Saint-Louis-en-l'Île, the island remains peaceful and gracious. Although bridges connect it to both river banks and to the Île-de-la-Cité, the feeling of remove from modern life reminds one of how Paris must have looked 300 years ago.

Poplar trees shade the streets and the views of Paris from the quais are exceptional. Since development began only in the 17th century under Louis XIII, there is an architectural unity to the island, its harmonious, gracious buildings being of about the same width and height. The old *hôtels particuliers* (townhouses) and the large restored apartments still house affluent Parisians, and some foreigners have bought apartments to rent them to tourists for a well-deserved, often hefty price. Unfortunately, few long-term apartments are available, and when they are, their prices are steep, but the residents clearly think the Île Saint-Louis worth the price.

First Arrondissement (1er)

Encompassing many tourist attractions such as the Louvre, the Tuileries gardens and the long rue de Rivoli, along with some of the city's most fashionable hotels, the 1st *arrondissement* is populated day and night, but not particularly by residents. From its beginnings, this has been among the most commercial area of the city; today, just a few streets away from the tourist attractions, financial and administrative offices continue to rule.

The atmosphere of the 1er is, in a sense, determined by the Louvre. To its east are the busy traffic junction of Châtelet, the former site of a dreaded prison, now home to several popular theatres and Les Halles, the ancient marketplace transformed into an enormous shopping complex, Forum des Halles. Les Halles has extensive gardens, a cultural pavilion and a popular play facility for children, but its periphery is a hangout for young tourists and street entertainers.

Yet, typical of Paris, tucked just a few streets away is one of the most peaceful oases of the city—the quiet and romantic Jardins du Palais-Royal. Spacious old apartments nestle amidst discreet offices, and residents can still enjoy the sensation of being buffered from modernity while situated right in the heart of the city. An interesting neighbour is the lovely, circular Place des Victoires, home to fashion designers who occupy the harmonious 17th-century buildings. This may not be what one considers a real neighbourhood, but it has its attractions, including a variety of restaurants.

The royal heritage extends west of the Louvre. Kings lived at the Tuileries in a palace destroyed toward the end of the last century during the protests of the Paris Commune. What remains are the Jardins des Tuileries, one of Paris' most popular parks. Across the rue de Rivoli are both tourist shops and high-class enterprises of the type that once catered to the aristocrats who lived in the shadow of the king. Bordered on the west by the imposing Place de la Concorde, the size of a small town in itself, the area culminates nearby in the spectacular granite Place Vendôme, a royal square begun by Louis XIV in 1686, now home to exclusive banking establishments, jewellers, offices, a few plush apartments and the Hotel Ritz.

This remains the upscale end of the *arrondissement* and the apartments in the side streets and above the shops along rue du Rivoli can be comfortable and gracious; much depends on the shops below and where the tour buses stop. The parallel street, rue Saint-Honoré, is lined with shops and restaurants, and the charming modern Marché de Saint-Honoré has enlivened the place Saint-Honoré. Although little of this area is truly residential, it might be fun for a short stay.

Second Arrondissement (2e)

Extending the commercial centre of Paris, the tiny 2nd *arrondissement* contains La Bourse (Stock Exchange), financial offices of every type and nationality, airline offices, travel agencies and insurance companies. Cafés, cinemas and theatres keep the western edge alive well into the night. This is an area that is becoming more residential, as formerly rundown areas are being revitalised by a younger set of Parisians, and the area is becoming increasingly fashionable.

Toward the east are hundreds of factories and warehouses at the heart of Paris' clothing industry, culminating at cart- and traffic-jammed Sentier and Place du Caire. Except for streets near the fashion designer enclave of rue Etienne-Marcel and Place des Victoires and a few streets toward the east, there are only a few areas one would consider for a residence. Away from Place de l'Opéra, much of the area is deserted at night and on weekends, except for the broad avenues and the eastern boundary of boulevard Sébastopol. There is little open space and this is the least green area of the city.

The 2e, however, is the site of some *passages*—covered shopping arcades dating from the end of the 19th century. Several have been beautifully restored for upmarket shopping and dining, while others remain full of jumbled stores. Here too is one of Paris' important market streets, the pedestrian-only rue Montorgueil, an attractive combination of food emporiums, *traiteurs* (take-out delicatessens) and terraced cafés. People used to come here only to do their shopping, but since refurbishment has spruced up the area and prices are still fairly reasonable, people are increasingly calling this area home.

The Marais (3e and 4e)

The 3rd and 4th *arrondissements* are collectively known as the Marais, that ancient swampland that was once part of the river basin of the Seine. As noted, it is the one of the oldest parts of the city, encompassing half of the Île-de-la-Cité; this was also the first part of the Right Bank that was inhabited—around the present rues des Blancs-Manteaux and Vieille-du-Temple—more than 1,000 years ago. Although not all parts of the Marais conform to the trendy image the name now evokes, this is certainly one of the most chic parts of town.

The Marais became popular with royalty and aristocrats about 400 years ago. Henri IV built the Place des Vosges, the first royal square, which has been authentically restored to look much as it did in 1612: a square of almost identical, warm brick-and-stone townhouses with steep, pitched roofs, surrounding an exquisitely sculptured, symmetrical garden. From the 16th century, the southern part of the Marais had seen the building of *hôtels particuliers* for nobles and aristocrats, but in the 18th century, the area was abandoned when the court moved west toward Versailles. Sadly, with the vicissitudes of time and politics, the Marais declined.

How it has changed! Now one of the city's most colourful districts, the Marais benefitted from the 1962 Loi Malraux, which mandated the preservation of historic districts. Decrepit medieval streets and once-stately *hôtels particuliers* were refurbished without succumbing to the faceless modernisation suffered by other parts of the city at the time. Now this area is an unexpected delight of ever narrow, angled streets, low-rise buildings,and just one *métro* station, Saint-Paul. Art galleries, fashion shops, nightspots and restaurants enliven this good-natured district that is more and more in demand every day.

Although a Jewish community lived here until its expulsion from France in 1394, it is only since the last century that the influx of Eastern European Jews has given the quarter much of its character. Clustered around the 13th-century rue des Rosiers and rue des Ecouffes are kosher restaurants, bakeries, delicatessens and groceries. That they draw crowds on Sunday, when the rest of the city is closed, has encouraged neighbouring boutiques and galleries to stay open as well, making this a lively area every day.

The Marais has also become a major focus of Parisian gay

life. Starting near Châtelet and moving east, gay nightspots and restaurants contribute to the area's eclectic 24-hour atmosphere. The bookshop, Les Mots à la Bouche, in rue Sainte-Croix-de-la-Bretonnerie is a central information point for this increasingly open and accepted community.

All in all, the part of the Marais that stretches west from Place de la Bastille to rue des Archives is a fun and somewhat affordable area in which to live. Comfortable apartments can be found in a range of prices, but parking in the crowded streets is scarce. Another residential area is the small *quartier* below rue Saint-Antoine. Buildings of homogeneous architecture line its sides, most of which are well maintained. There are just a few museums, some antique shops and the remnants of the medieval city wall that draw visitors. Convenient shopping for both areas stretches along the rue de Rivoli, where it takes over from rue Saint-Antoine.

The 3^e *arrondissement* begins above the fashionable rue des Francs-Bourgeois, once the northern perimeter of the city walls, although here it is indistinguishable from the 4e. On lovely rue Payenne, the Museum of the History of Paris was, in the 17th century, the *hôtel particulier* of the literary Marquise de Sévigné. This area declined when the nobles moved on, melding in dilapidated spirit with the *quartier* farther north, toward what is now the rather gritty Place de la République.

This northeastern corner (known as Temple) is where the Knights Templar in the 12th century settled after their return from the Crusades. Their Enclos du Temple was a powerful, fortified city containing a palace, a church and commerce, and it provided safety for workers and artisans within its walls. It is all long gone, even the tower in which Louis XVI was kept prisoner until his execution in 1793. When it was finally torn down by Napoléon, all that remained were the workers and tradesmen, and the area took on a rather shabby character, which it still has today.

It was precisely the inexpensive aspects of this sector that drew its present population. The post-World War I influx of Asians into the 3e constituted the first Chinese community in Paris, and there is still an Asian presence around rues des Gravilliers and rue au Maire. At rue de Nazareth there is an important Jewish synagogue, as this was the Jewish community's centre before it moved south toward rue des Rosiers.

Much of this northern border remains dull, with old housing in drab streets, although this means that rents are not high. The rag trade extends here: a cheap clothing market is always on the verge of being shut down and some factories employ the immigrants who continue to come. Nonetheless, gentrification is slowly moving north, up rue Charlot and around the pretty little Square du Temple. As the ambiance of the Marais expands and housing becomes scarce, this area is sure to benefit.

The Latin Quarter and Saint-Germain (5ᵉ and 6ᵉ)

Encompassing the 5th *arrondissement* and by extension some of the 6th, the Quartier Latin is where many romantic images of Paris come true. This can be one of Paris' most exciting areas in which to live. Judging from the number of people—French and foreign alike—who, day and night, stroll the boulevards, explore the medieval streets, browse in the bookshops or frequent the cafés or cinemas, this ancient part of Paris is a most intriguing place to be.

The 5ᵉ is named for the medieval scholars who were required to speak to each other in Latin, but the part of the 6ᵉ that borders on the crowded boulevard Saint-Michel was also part of the Quartier Latin until Baron Haussmann widened the ancient Roman road and distanced an integral part of the quarter to the west.

Famous initially for the Sorbonne, founded in 1253 by Robert de Sorbon, the Latin Quarter is today an area of diverse intellectual endeavours. (Even the Sorbonne is just one part of the seventeen-school University of Paris system, much of which is spread throughout the city.) This *arrondissement* contains educational institutions such as the Collège de France founded in the 16th century, several of the prestigious Grandes Écoles, the famous lycées Louis-Le-Grand and Henri-IV and the Institut du Monde Arabe; various institutions; a government ministry; museums; the impressive Islamic mosque, the Val-de-Grâce

The famous café, Les Deux Magots, at place Saint-Germain-des-Prés, once frequented by such literary lights as Hemingway, Sartre and Simone de Beauvoir, among others.

hospital; a botanical garden with a zoo; the oceanographic institute and an aquarium. Here too are important historical churches and, rising imposingly above the area's village-like streets, the famous Panthéon.

Fortunately for those who live in the area, the Latin Quarter remains agreeably residential. Its low buildings nestle securely amid the massive institutions that dominate its core. Along the narrow, medieval streets on both sides of the bisecting boulevard Saint-Germain, apartments of all types can be found—large and small, for long-term and short-term rentals—for this is an area that caters to faculty and students, a population that comes and goes.

Rents may be high, especially for the larger apartments in the narrow streets north of Saint-Germain, heading toward the quais. South of the boulevard, going up into the winding hilly streets, the residential area is slightly more affordable. Of course there are tourists here, particularly on the charming rue Mouffetard and at Place de la Contrescarpe, but somehow they do not intrude. The area that borders the 13ᵉ is fairly inexpensive, and lively and popular as a result. Just about any street will do nicely here, but do not look for apartments in October, when the students return and are looking as well.

What draws tourists as well as locals are the international book stores and music shops, offbeat boutiques, world-renowned jazz clubs and cabarets, theatres, an inviting mix of restaurants and cafés and a large selection of cinemas that show foreign and art films. Tourists congregate around Place Saint-Michel, where shops are downmarket and restaurants overpriced. Nonetheless, this all contributes to the exuberant, youthful atmosphere that pervades the Quartier Latin.

The intellectual and artistic focus of the 5e becomes more sophisticated as one moves west toward Place Saint-Germain-des-Prés. Located here, where the Romans dedicated a temple to the goddess Isis, is the heart of the 6e—the 1,500-year-old site of Paris' first Christian church, now the Eglise Saint-Germain-des-Prés. This square is one of the most visited in Paris, and the crowds who come here every day of the year, whether to visit the ancient church or to sip a coffee across the street, experience all of Paris, then and now.

For centuries this area was just an extension of the Latin Quarter but is now more known for its place in the post-World War II scene. Existentialism and a liberated, intellectual life unfolded at this area—at the famous cafés, the Deux Magots and the Café de Flore, at the Brasserie Lipp and at the bookshop, La Hune—where Simone de Beauvoir and Jean-Paul Sartre held court. Jazz had long been hot nearby on rue Saint-Benoît. Today the cafés are the province of tourists, of the chic set coming to see and be seen, and of a few writers trying to soak up the atmosphere of the past.

This part of the *arrondissement* has it all. From Place de l'Odéon, past Mabillon, the well-trodden streets off the boulevard have antique shops, art galleries, cinemas, theatres, restaurants, cafés galore, upmarket boutiques and markets at rue de Buci and near rue Mabillon. Toward the Seine, in the *quartier* Beaux-Arts, named for its prestigious arts school, the narrow, angled streets have low-rise 17th-and 18th-century buildings with apartments rented by both Parisians and foreigners—currently the most expensive residential niche.

This is certainly one of the most agreeable *quartiers* in the city. Between the relaxed 5^e on the east and the reserved 7^e on the west, housing here shares the character of its neighbours. It starts at a reasonable price along the east and gradually becomes extremely expensive the farther west one goes, particularly between boulevard Saint-Germain and the Seine. The atmosphere is unique, and it is one Parisians are fighting to preserve, although the battle seems lost. Local shops have moved out as rents have risen and impersonal giants such as Armani, Louis Vuitton and Cartier have taken their place.

Although the atmosphere may change from street to street, it doesn't change for the worse. Around Place Saint-Sulpice, with its fountained square and fashionable surrounds, and along such streets as the classy rue de Tournon, rue de l'Odéon, the wide boulevard Raspail and rue Notre-Dame-des-Champs, the apartments are large, airy, and expensive. This holds true especially for buildings overlooking the spectacular Jardin du Luxembourg, one of the nation's most beloved public gardens and once the exquisite palace grounds of Marie de Médicis. This residential part of the *quartier* may be more quiet in spots, but it picks up once again as the busy rue de Rennes reaches Montparnasse, where the atmosphere of quiet sophistication begins to disappear.

Seventh Arrondissement (7e)

Despite the tourists that stream constantly to the Eiffel Tower, Les Invalides and the Musée de Quai Branly, the 7th *arrondissement* is one of the most tranquil areas of the city. The broad, leafy streets provide a haven for residents, for the government ministries and embassies that have moved into the 18th-century mansions of the aristocracy and for some erstwhile nobles who still live in their ancestral homes. This is 'old money' Paris. The presence of the Assemblée Nationale, UNESCO and the area's most famous official resident—the French prime minister—at the Hôtel Matignon, makes this the safest *arrondissement* in the city.

Living here is extremely agreeable, with some parts seeming like a suburb in the city centre. In general, this is an open and airy *arrondissement*, with its widest border along the Seine and several long green stretches that bolster the feeling of luxury. The Champ-de-Mars, the longest grassy promenade in Paris, is a charming park stretching from the École Militaire to the Eiffel Tower, and the Esplanade des Invalides has a welcome green strip down to the river. A popular area for families with children, there are several small playgrounds and a sweetly hidden park at Square Récamier. Apartments tend to be large, gracious and well-maintained.

Commerce clusters toward the edges of the 7e—to the east near rue du Bac and rue de Sèvres, and toward the west along rue Saint-Dominique and rue de Grenelle. Some of the city's best options for dining are in this *arrondissement*; otherwise there is little evening activity. Antique shops and galleries thrive in the compact area known as Le Carré Rive Gauche. Especially popular with foreigners are the chic rue du Bac area and other small streets throughout the *arrondissement*. Many provide commercial services, and on rue de Sèvres is the famous department store and food hall, Le Bon Marché. The charming market street, rue Cler, is conveniently near the old townhouses and modern apartments of rue Bosquet and rue de Grenelle.

Eighth Arrondissement (8e)

The spectacular avenue des Champs-Elysées and the tourists who have taken it over dominate much of the 8th *arrondissement*. Although a major overhaul of this 17th-century aristocratic promenade brought back a touch of its distinction after years of decline, its high rents are now affordable primarily for international chains such as Virgin Megastore and the hotels and restaurants that cater to the ubiquitous tourists. Despite the persistence of such traditional institutions as Fouquet's restaurant and the Lido Cabaret, this is one of the least Parisian parts of Paris.

This was not always the case. When the Tuileries Palace was burned down during the uprising of the Paris Commune in 1871 and the 1er dropped from aristocratic favour, this adjacent area took its place. Preferred by the upper classes since the area was laid out by the famous Le Nôtre during the time of Louis XIV, the rue du Faubourg Saint-Honoré was then a street of 18th-century townhouses belonging to wealthy Parisians, with gardens overlooking the still bucolic Champs-Elysées. But not today! The old mansions are now occupied by embassies and offices, and the Palais de l'Elysée is the official residence of the president of France. Few of the old gems of apartments still exist, so when the corporate types go home for the evening, the side streets are left empty and dull. Contributing both to the commercialisation and elegance of this eastern edge is the Golden Triangle of the haute couture salons of famous French and international designers, high-class shops of other sorts and some of Paris' finest purveyors of haute cuisine.

Nonetheless, people live here and live very well. Around Place François-1er, tucked quietly toward the Seine and farther west at avenue George-V, graceful buildings house a privileged few—primarily older, wealthy Parisians. The apartments are large and comfortable, but rarely available. These areas are fairly quiet, with high-class *traiteurs* and a few services catering to the rather sedate population.

Fortunately, the 8^e offers much more. The lovely and formal Parc Monceau at its western edge, dating from the late 18th century, is one of the more desirable districts of Paris and popular with both Parisians and newcomers. Here are wide streets, including avenue Hoche, rue de Monceau and the residential end of the long boulevard Malesherbes, plus small, charming side streets abutting the park. Apartments are plush and airy, with high ceilings, floor-to-ceiling windows, and upmarket prices. In general, the elegant atmosphere of the Parc Monceau area and its proximity to the markets and services of the 17e can make it a lovely place to live.

Ninth Arrondissement (9e)

The dense, southwestern edge of the 9th *arrondissement* is home to the famous Opéra Garnier, department stores, shops, cinemas, theatres, banks and the American Express office. It is always crowded and always on the go. Restaurants of all levels line the boulevards, the broad streets that 'aerate' one of the few areas of the city that has limited residential desirability and few green, open spaces to provide relief from the stress of urban life.

To the east and just out of the tourists' line of sight, the *arrondissement* continues with a fitful character. A Jewish community lives around rue Richer, its Sephardic kosher restaurants and Middle Eastern shops incongruously situated near the famous Folies Bergères. Rue Cadet is the area's market street, and the only bit of green in this otherwise colourless commercial area is the small Square Montholon.

Farther north, however, the atmosphere becomes more agreeable, although it can change in character from street to street. Winding up toward the Place Saint-Georges is a long-time artists' quarter that once linked sophisticated Paris to the village of Montmartre in the north. Here too is a section built around 1820, known as the Nouvelle Athènes, which became fashionable after the construction of the church of Notre-Dame-de-Lorette. Today one still finds pleasant streets amid the uninspired, and although many of the old buildings have been taken over by offices, others offer agreeable apartments. Place Gustave-Toudouze and a triangular space on rue Henri-Monnier are little oases lined with small shops and cafés, and the Square Alex Biscarre is a hidden touch of green. At the northwest is Place Adolphe-Max, a charming square surrounding a small park and playground, but just beyond is boulevard de Clichy, which can be rather seedy.

In the 9e are some of the most reasonable rents and purchase prices in the city. If you are attracted by the prices, the interesting nightlife toward the northern edges, or even by the international mix of population that is trickling down from Montmartre, choose carefully, as almost every street has its own atmosphere.

Tenth Arrondissement (10^e)

Much of the 10th *arrondissement* is truly drab. Unfortunately close together and dominating most of the area, the Gare du Nord and the Gare de l'Est exist in the atmosphere that train stations generate, and their railroad yards cut through the entire northern part of the district. Much of the housing is working-class and uninspired. People come for the low prices, to visit several important hospitals, to frequent some theatres, museums and the rue de Paradis (known for its china shops), but they do not come for the neighbourhood. This holds true all the way to Place de la République.

Toward the busy rue du Faubourg Poissonnière, however, is an area that was once home to prosperous Parisians who wanted to live north of the city in homes with gardens and fresh air. Now some of the old buildings are being restored and some interesting possibilities can be found. Close to rue d'Enghien there are still areas to avoid at night, but this should gradually change.

Toward the east, however, is where the *arrondissement* deserves increasing respect. The Canal Saint-Martin opens up the area and refurbishment is making the quai de Valmy area one to consider for housing—if anything is available. The cobblestone strip is shaded by plane trees, arched footbridges cross at intervals and the quais are lined with graceful, 19th-century apartment buildings, trendy cafés and shops. Nearby, the eastern surrounds of the lovely Jardin Villemin are agreeable, despite their proximity to Gare de l'Est. This area is sought out by young Parisians who are attracted to its vibrant atmosphere, openness and reasonable prices.

Bastille to Nation (11ᵉ and 12ᵉ)

One of the most up-and-coming areas of eastern Paris, the southern strip of the 11th *arrondissement* and the adjacent northern area of the 12th are much in demand. Starting at Place de la Bastille and stretching to the enormous Place de la Nation, this former furniture craftsmen's suburb of Faubourg Saint-Antoine is being completely revitalised. Prices are still moderate in areas, though on the rise, as formerly shabby neighbourhoods are spruced up. Only pockets of the old proletarian atmosphere can still be found, distressing those who fear that the area is becoming too homogeneous and losing its village feel. Most people seem to agree, however, that the youthful, electric atmosphere is bringing a new energy to eastern Paris.

It begins at Place de la Bastille, which, from 14 July 1789 (Bastille Day) to the mid-20th century (site of the student uprising of 1968), was known for protest and resistance. Now, however, it is an engaging, open area that is dominated on the east by the Opéra Bastille, one of Mitterrand's *Grands Projets*. In the south reappears the Canal Saint-Martin, which goes underground at rue du Faubourg du Temple, flowing below the broad, green boulevard Richard Lenoir. In summer, sunbathers—old and young, gay and straight—sit on the canal's landscaped and cobblestone banks and watch boats slowly pass through the lock to the Seine. The rest of the square is taken by chic terraced cafés—a taste of what is to come.

Actually the area is mixed in spirit, partly by habit, partly by design. Some established artisans and furniture makers still inhabit the *cours* (courtyards) and *passages* on the sides of the picturesque, vibrant rue du Faubourg Saint-Antoine, but others are slowly disappearing as redevelopment raises rents and forces them out. Replacing them are bistros, cafés and shops that draw the crowds, as well as new businesses, galleries and the consulting and high-tech firms that are drawing young professionals. The major streets of rue de Charonne and rue de la Roquette are connected by the popular cobblestone rue de Lappe (once known for prostitutes and pimps), rue des Taillandiers and rue Keller, a centre for the gay community.

Old warehouses converted into lofts, restored buildings and new apartment blocks make for an eclectic mix. There is an interesting market and a park-like setting on the wide boulevard Richard Lenoir. As in the Marais, gentrification is expanding northwards as older buildings are restored and retail activities expanded. Although the recently trendy rue Oberkampf is upgrading its character, the renewed atmosphere does not yet extend to Place de la République or to the northeastern border with Belleville in the 20e.

To the south of rue du Faubourg Saint-Antoine, in the 12e, the life of the *cours* and *passages* continues. Just a few streets away however, the bustling crowds and exotic aromas of Place d'Aligre take hold. The covered Marché Beauvau gives over to an inexpensive, international extravaganza that spills out into rue d'Aligre and down to rue de Charenton.

Owing to its proximity to Gare de Lyon, which opened Paris to southern Europe and then to Africa, this has long been a varied area, changing once again with the influx of young, professional Parisians. Although housing blocks intrude on the otherwise low-rise residential *quartier*, the neighbourhood spirit persists.

Almost a secret in the eastern area of the *arrondissement* is the Allée Vivaldi, a hidden greensward surrounded by modern offices and residences. Across an arched footbridge, the open Jardin de Reuilly has gardens, playgrounds filled with children and a grassy expanse; it too is surrounded by pleasant, unobtrusive, modern housing. To the northwest of the garden, connected by a footbridge, is the charming Promenade Plantée, a landscaped, 4.5-km path on a former elevated railroad bed. How welcome is this bucolic promenade that originates at the Bastille and how interesting the arched vaults below, now called the Viaduc des Arts! Its galleries and artisans' ateliers draw visitors into what is becoming a lively, upmarket area, despite its proximity to the Gare de Lyon.

The *quartiers* of Picpus, Bel-Air and Daumesnil at avenue de Saint-Mandé and below have long been a solid, unpretentious, residential district. Increasingly as this area is revitalised with new shops, offices and housing, it will be even more in demand.

To the south, the former wine warehouse district of Bercy was once isolated from the rest of Paris by the train yards of the Gare de Lyon. No longer! Bercy, one of the dynamic *Grands Projets*, is now one of the liveliest areas of the city, reached easily by the high-speed *métro*, Météor. At one end of the exquisite Parc de Bercy is Bercy Village, an attractive complex that includes a long promenade of upmarket boutiques and stylish restaurants, culminating in a huge cinema complex. At the other end of the park, which incorporates ruins and old plane trees into its varied modern landscaping landmarks, is the Stade de Bercy, which is the venue for major sporting and musical events. To the sides are commercial areas, both old and modern apartments (many with balconies overlooking the park), artists' studios and some hotels. This is one of the trendiest areas of town, influenced by the thousands of people who work in the area—just across the river is the Biblithèque Nationale François Mitterrand. This area is quickly developing a vibrant personality of its own.

Thirteenth Arrondissement (13e)

Three bridges—including the lovely Simone de Beauvoir footbridge—connect the lively area of Bercy to the 13th *arrondissement*, which is finally feeling the effects of the revival spurred by the construction of the Bibliothèque Nationale François Mitterrand.This area modernises itself almost every day, especially in the area around the library, with new commerce and entertainment possibilities springing up, yet the large 13e, situated along the city's southern edge, is already one of the more interesting districts of Paris, known primarily as home to some 30,000 of the city's Asian population.

It's hard to imagine how this area must have looked centuries ago—an area of sweet pastures and vineyards, the little hamlets of Saint-Marcel and Gentilly and the river Bièvre—all now long gone. First came the butchers, then the tanners of hides and finally the factories for textiles that disposed of their wastes into the Bièvre. Along its banks were workers' housing, cheap shops, squalid nightspots... and crime. If Parisians today complain about the area's homogeneous atmosphere and its impersonal apartment blocks, they have forgotten the cholera epidemics of the mid-1800s and the open sewer that the Bièvre had become, finally covered over only around 1910.

The *arrondissement*'s eastern edge flows along the Seine, across from Bercy. Here, several imposing edifices mark a rather colourless area. There is the ultra modern four-building library complex, the Hôpital Pitié-Salpêtrière and the busy Gare d'Austerlitz. With new housing being built and planned, this is becoming a new *quartier*, the Seine-Rive-Gauche, and galleries are already starting to move in. Currently, however, as one heads into the *arrondissement*, it is the broad avenue des Gobelins that has the lively atmosphere and residential popularity of the 5e, its neighbour to the north.

Along with the seemingly ubiquitous apartment towers built in the 1970s are hidden enclaves of the old, charming Paris. Unassuming private homes sit next to faceless apartment projects and longtime Parisians live side-by-side with Asian immigrants—immigrants who descended on Paris in the 1970s and who did not mind the apartment blocks that had been built to replace old slums.

To the south of the enormous commercial Place d'Italie is what makes the 13^e so famous: its Asian population, which lives in an area known as the Triangle de Choisy. Between the avenue d'Ivry and avenue de Choisy, a dense international community has sunk its roots, renovating older buildings and enlivening the new blocks. Here are several large Asian supermarkets, many small groceries and shops and dozens of Asian restaurants, creating an atmosphere unlike any other in Paris. Yet, even in this Asian stronghold, more traditional surprises can be found: just a few streets west, by the placid, unassuming Place de l'Abbé Henocque, are little streets of private houses and gardens. And the Cité Floréale, to the south, is a triangular, flowery nook just off Place de Rungis.

To the northwest is one of Paris' few remaining true villages—la Butte aux Cailles—an intricate set of hilly streets with old-world charm and small town flavour. Low, five-storey houses, small shops and narrow streets characterise the area. The small steep park, almost hidden on its northern edge, is used by locals, as is the large market on boulevard Auguste-Blanqui.

Montparnasse and Beyond (14^e)

Legendary for the bohemian Montparnasse, the 14th *arrondissement* actually includes so much more that its residents often consider it to be the best kept secret in Paris. In fact, aside from busy Montparnasse, the hospital complexes that dot the area and the broad avenues that cut the *arrondissement* into a pie, the 14^e has as many residential attractions as any other area in the city.

Montparnasse sits at the northwest corner of the *arrondissement* and encompasses small edges of the 15^e and 6^e. It stretches east to the Observatoire built under Louis XIV and south to the pleasant junction of Denfert-Rochereau. But Montparnasse is known not so much for its geography but for its intriguing atmosphere. It was a hangout in the 18th century for students venturing away from the Latin Quarter; later it became famous for its bohemian and intellectual life.

Imagine the intensity of this area less than a century ago, when cheap rents for studios and cheap booze drew poverty-stricken artists to this worker's district from the increasingly expensive Montmartre. Now world-renowned Amadeo Modigliani, Marc Chagall and Pablo Picasso were a few of these unknown artists who descended upon Paris. Eastern European Jews without a franc to their names also came to escape pogroms and Russian thinkers such as Lenin and Trotsky contemplated revolution during their stays here. In the 1920s, after World War I, came the Americans: writers, artists and their patrons. Paris was a playground for those with American dollars, and unlike in the United States, the alcohol flowed until all hours in cafés we frequent even now—Le Dôme, La Coupole and La Closerie des Lilas. Unfortunately in 1929,

Modigliani arrived in Paris in 1906 and first stayed at Montmartre before moving to Montparnasse. Tubercular and drug-addicted, he was even known as the 'king of Montparnasse'. Two films have been made about Modigliani's life: Jacques Becker's *Les Amants de Montparnasse* and Mick Davis' *Modigliani*, starring Andy Garcia and French actress Elsa Zylberstein.

the stock markets crashed, pockets were emptied and the Americans went home. But not, of course, the French. It was about this time that a new breed of intellectuals such as Sartre and Beauvoir congregated at the area around Carrefour Vavin, but when World War II came and the Germans took over the cafés of Montparnasse and closed the nearest *métro* station, the crowd moved up to Saint-Germain.

Legends die hard: the commercial area and cinemas are always crowded and the cafés and nightspots hum into the wee hours of the morning. The sterile Gare Montparnasse, the Tour Montparnasse, its shopping mall and several concrete apartment blocks do nothing, however, to remind us of what once was.

The residential secret begins around the expansive Place Denfert-Rochereau. Although the *quartier* has changed and high-rise development has tried to encroach, much of the area remains reminiscent of a Paris that has elsewhere disappeared. Broad streets close to the square, such as rue Froidevaux and boulevard Saint-Jacques, have stately buildings and an open atmosphere. The massive, concrete Place de Catalogne, part residential, part offices, dominates toward the west, but it gives way to the long rue Vercingétorix, whose top portion is now a neighbourhood promenade and park. Renovated studios and apartments with quiet courtyards nestle in some of the short streets (the *impasses*, *cités* and *villas*) and artists' ateliers still dot the entire area. Off the busy avenue du Général Leclerc and just a few steps from the market street, rue Daguerre, is the astoundingly beautiful Villa Adrienne, a community of gracious apartments overlooking a lovely little park.

The area from Plaisance to Alésia is lively, with both commercial and residential buildings and interesting little streets mixed in, some of which will, no doubt, soon be renewed. Rue d'Alésia is known for its discount clothing shops, but it is also the commercial artery in this agreeable part of the *arrondissement*.

But it is the southern area that has it all. Parc Montsouris has beautiful gardens, a charming, terraced restaurant featuring band performances, a puppet theatre for the children and a sizeable lake that is home to graceful aquatic birds. Overlooking this wonder are the apartments on rue Nansouty. Adjacent—and dotting this *quartier* throughout—are exceptional private villas. Just across boulevard Jourdan, lying admist another green expanse, is the Cité Universitaire, a cluster of 40 international student residences of eclectic styles dating from the 1920s. This greensward stretches west to the Porte de Vanves, the scene of one of Paris' most popular weekend flea markets.

Getting around these southern reaches has been made easier recently, with the opening of the new modern tramway that runs from Porte d'Ivry to the Pont de Garigliano.

Fifteenth Arrondissement (15e)

The largest *arrondissement* with the highest population in Paris, the 15th *arrondissement* is a comfortable middle-class community. Located southwest, it stretches north to the subdued 7e, east to Montparnasse and south to the *périphérique*. Until recently the province of chemical factories, metallurgies and gasworks, the 15e has few tourist attractions, save perhaps for some offbeat museums and the lovely, futuristic Parc André Citroën. It is the locals who dominate: young Parisian families, middle-level professionals and retired persons, many of whom come for the reasonable rents and the family atmosphere. Prices here are moderate in comparison to other areas on the Left Bank or in the 16e, just across the Seine.

Apartment blocks built in the 1960s and 1970s dominate in an area along the river called Front de Seine, with an elevated, landscaped walkway connecting the buildings. Here children play in the evenings while their parents chat on benches close by. On rue Linois is the multi-level Centre Beaugrenelle, a shopping mall, but just a few streets away, at Place Saint-Charles, modernity gives way to graceful Belle Epoque buildings and various services catering to a middle-class French population.

Further down the river, the 14-hectare Parc André Citroën, a beautifully designed green space built with much imagination on the site of a former automobile plant, adds to the revitalisation of the area. Citroën-Cévennes is a residential *quartier* surrounding the revamped rue Balard, with both modern housing and refurbished old apartments. This revitalisation will only increase now that the large, ultramodern Hôpital Européen Georges Pompidou is open after years of construction.

Elsewhere, little communities hold their own. The commercial rue du Commerce, with its shuttered houses, barely looks any different from how it might have been 50 years ago, especially around Place Etienne-Pernet. Here are inexpensive restaurants, neighbourhood shops and the Place du Commerce, a pleasant, leafy square. Past rue Lecourbe, the streets around rue de Vaugirard and rue de la Convention are popular for their comfortable, middle-class ambiance.

Another park surrounded by a residential area is the southeastern Parc Georges-Brassens, built on the site of a former slaughterhouse. With grassy areas, a small lake and a carousel for children, this bucolic park breaks the monotony created by the modern apartment blocks that tower over older buildings. Nearby, however, in Passage de Dantzig is La Ruche, the famous beehive building of artists' studios used by Chagall, Modigliani, Soutine and Léger, among others of Montparnasse fame; studios are still available today.

Montparnasse, whose northeastern corner abuts on the 14e, is perhaps the 15e at its most interesting. Despite the district's commercial nature and the domination by the Tour Montparnasse, the streets off rue de Vaugirard and rue Pasteur are residential, with proximity to a market, supermarkets and the Maine-Montparnasse shopping complex. Hidden above the railroad station is the Jardin Atlantique, a landscaped roof garden with fountains, play areas and tennis courts. Close by are the large Hôpital Necker and the famous Institut Pasteur, around which are agreeable little residential nuggets, which benefit from their proximity to the elegant 7^e, with its oases such as Place de Breteuil and the elegant market at avenue de Saxe.

Sixteenth Arrondissement (16^e)

The most aristocratic of Paris' *arrondissements*, this large area at the western edge of the city was among the last to be incorporated into the city system. Its two main *quartiers*, Auteuil and Passy, were formerly small villages set amidst farmland and a forest stretching west, which were the hunting grounds of the French kings. Underground mineral springs turned the area into an aristocratic spa in the 17th century, and it was to this area of rural elegance that the nobility retreated during the Revolution.

Today the 16th *arrondissement* still enjoys a small town atmosphere. Just past the western edge is the Bois de Boulogne—what is left of the royal woods. Some Parisians claim the 16e is boring, for there is little nightlife, and in the summer, many of its residents close their homes and depart, returning only at *la rentrée* (return to work and school after the summer holidays, an event in itself). Whether this is a disadvantage is debatable, for the *arrondissement* is also appreciated for its tranquility, its graceful mid-rise buildings with spacious, costly apartments and its little villas and *hameaux*—leafy lanes with a country feel. Indeed, this is one area that is extremely suitable for families with children.

Starting from what was once the hill of Chaillot and is now Place Charles-de-Gaulle, the streets around the spectacular avenue Foch are residential. Avenue Foch itself, the broadest in Paris, has long been home to Parisian wealth. Close by, avenue Victor-Hugo is also chic and expensive, as one would expect from these avenues that radiate out from l'Etoile.

Toward the Porte de la Muette is the Organisation for Economic Cooperation and Development (OECD), its surrounding streets home to many of its diplomats and to old Parisian wealth. Starting at the Place du Trocadéro and cutting across the *arrondissement* to the Porte de la Muette, the wide avenue Georges-Mandel continues as avenue Henri-Martin. Buildings are set back from the double boulevard, whose trees provide shade and cushioning from noise. Somewhat south is the Villa Beauséjour, with some surprising old Russian-style cottages. Families like this area close to the charming Jardins du Ranelagh and to the Bois de Boulogne.

Past the Trocadéro gardens, Passy takes hold. Here one enters the village: a residential neighbourhood, a church square, several commercial streets, including rue Bois-le-Vent and the main street, rue de Passy, with its high-quality shops and services. The prized residential district lies mainly between avenue Mozart on the north and the long rue Raynouard, although areas around Square Charles-Dickens and rue des Eaux are well worth exploring.

South of Passy, the village and vineyards of Auteuil were among the last areas to be urbanised, and Auteuil remains a small town with a church square. Rue d'Auteuil, the main street, formed part of this picturesque village, along with still charming streets such as rue Boileau and rue La Fontaine, the extension of Passy's rue Raynouard.

Even in this staid area, there are surprises: the gated community of Villa Montmorency holds 80 private houses in curved, leafy streets in an almost rural setting. Just north, closer to the Jardins du Ranelagh, the buildings in the short Place du Docteur-Blanche are strikingly Art Nouveau. Housing anywhere in this area is expensive and it is a popular area for foreign residents.

Seventeenth Arrondissement (17ᵉ)

Encompassing the old farming areas of Monceau and Ternes on the west, and the workers' villages of Batignolles and Epinettes on the east, the 17th *arrondissement* of today is largely residential, but the area has several 'moods'. Cut neatly in two by railroad tracks heading out from Gare Saint-Lazare, the western area is open and upmarket, while the east is distinctly working-class and crowded.

On its southern and eastern edges and above the stately Parc de Monceau, the 17ᵉ has the feel of its affluent neighbours near l'Etoile. What was once the Plaine de Monceau has been replaced by broad avenues and gracious apartments that were, 100 years ago, the most modern in the city. The avenue de Wagram leads from l'Etoile into the heart of the district, opening up at Place des Ternes with its charming flower market. Off boulevard de Courcelles and rue de Prony is a residential district only somewhat less aristocratic than the 16ᵉ—extremely genteel residential pockets can be found particularly toward l'Etoile .

The area is conveniently near the markets of rue de Lévis and rue Poncelet, both holding fast to an atmosphere that is disappearing all too quickly. Radiating to its west on streets such as rue Lebon, rue Bayen and rue Guersant, is a solid *quartier* leading to the boulevard Pereire, flanking a grassy esplanade that covers the railroad tracks. Just beyond is Villa des Ternes, leafy and comfortable.

The area northeast of the railroad yards has long been a solid workers' quarter, with only a few pleasant residential streets amid others of little distinction. Two parallel streets typify this dichotomy: the working-class rue des Moines, with drab five-storey buildings, markets and cafés, in contrast with the nearby Cité des Fleurs, a quiet pedestrian zone of houses with gardens. Yet, the Square des Batignolles with its rolling lawns and little lake is pleasantly shared by all, and the city is taking steps to refurbish the entire area, constructing modern apartments, offices, public facilities and a new park.

Eighteenth Arrondissement (18ᵉ)

Known for the tourists who swarm the *butte* (hill) every day to visit the Basilique du Sacré-Coeur, or for others who hang out at seedy nightspots on the southern edge, Montmartre nonetheless manages to retain some of its old-time character in places and can be an extremely agreeable place to live. Ranging from lovely to shabby, from enclaves of old-time Parisians to those of recent immigrants, the 18th *arrondissement* ascends winding picturesque streets from the boulevard de Clichy and boulevard de Rochechouart, peaks at the Butte Montmartre and flows out to the *périphérique*. It is probably one of the most unpretentious areas of the city, with few historic monuments and little modern development. Some areas are well worth considering and some are definitely not recommended.

An area of fields, vineyards and gypsum mines until the early 20th century, Montmartre became a place of pilgrimage after the decapitation of the Christian bishop, Saint Denis in ancient times. It was more recently that Montmartre acquired its present reputation when, attracted by the fact that the hilly area laid outside the city's toll walls, the low rents and cheap nightlife, workers descended here from the countryside during the Industrial Revolution, as did artisans, struggling artists, political protesters and anarchists during the Paris uprisings. Today, however, the southern edge teems with tourists who savour the artificial bohemian atmosphere created by shopkeepers.

Nonetheless, at the western side of Butte Montmartre, between Sacré-Cœur and the Montmartre cemetery, there are some wonderful residential nooks, charming squares and winding narrow streets with both older and newer homes, some with gardens. Real estate prices here can be high—though still lower than in more trendy areas—and the views and atmosphere may be worth the price. Look above rue des Abbesses, which intersects rue Lépic, the famous market street; or west, near rue Damrémont. Farther up the hill, rue Caulaincourt is interesting and avenue Junot has been nicely restored. Although tourists may wander here, the touristic atmosphere is kept at a distance. The small, green Place Casadesus is frequented by locals and Villa Léandre, one of a few charming alleys of small houses, feels like a quiet country lane, as does the nearby Hameau des Artistes.

Unfortunately, claiming the southeastern edge of the *arrondissement* are Pigalle and Barbès, home to both dubious nightlife and crowded clubs. This unsettling ambiance stretches to rue de la Goutte-d'Or, just off boulevard Barbès, long a poor, cramped workers' *quartier* and now an area of immigrants. The crowded, bargain department store Tati can be fun, as can the exotic shops and inexpensive markets and restaurants, but this area has the worst crime rate in the city and may not be one to frequent at night.

On the back slope of Sacré-Cœur is the rest of the 18e, deeply cut into by railroad yards coming up from the rue du Poteau of the 10e. North of the *butte* is a good market street and there are some oases around Square de Clignancourt. Nonetheless, along its top, the *arrondissement* is fairly charmless and drab, despite the presence of Paris' most famous flea market, jammed every weekend with bargain hunters.

Belleville and Ménilmontant (19e and 20e)

The 19th *arrondissement* is the 1860 addition into the city system, comprising the slaughterhouse town of La Villette and part of Belleville, then an industrial, working-class town. The rest of Belleville sits to the south, entwined with its neighbour Ménilmontant and belongs to the 20th *arrondissement*. Once a slum of radical politics and protest, Belleville was split apart in the final expansion of the *arrondissements*—an attempt by the government to quell the zone's rebellious spirit. But these areas, along with the former villages of Bagnolet and Charonne, remain inextricably linked and retain an atmosphere of their own.

At the northeastern tip, above avenue Jean-Jaurès, is the ultra-modern La Villette, a 55-hectare green expanse, science museum and entertainment complex. It begins alongside Canal Saint-Denis and straddles the Canal de l'Ourcq that cuts across the top of the area and ends at the impressive Bassin de la Villette. In the day, families come for the museum, children's programmes, themed gardens, promenades and bicycle rides along the path. In the evening, entertainment takes over and all of Paris comes. As interesting as this all is, it is currently not much of a residential district, although it's on its way as old warehouses are being converted into studios and apartments. Morever, when Baron Haussmann's refurbishing of Paris' central slums sent many lower-class Parisians migrating to Belleville, cottages went up willy-nilly on small, hastily carved roads. These are the spruced-up, charming culs-de-sac, *impasses*, and villas of today—a large district that remains mixed in population, atmosphere and price.

The *quartier* is most agreeable from Buttes Chaumont to Place de Rhin-et-Danube, benefitting from its proximity to the beautiful hilly Parc des Buttes Chaumont. How amazing that in forcing the poor to these already overcrowded areas, Baron Haussmann created one of the city's loveliest vantage points! Around the park's perimeter are the broad residential rue Manin and rue Botzaris. Off rue Mouzaïa and rue du Général Brunet remain the villas of private houses, coveted places to live in, as are some parts of rue de Belleville, still like the high street of a small town. But these and other nooks strewn across the southern part of the *arrondissement* are interspersed with others of dilapidated housing and faceless high-rises designed to replace them, especially around Place des Fêtes, once the village square.

It should be no surprise that this area drew a population looking for work and cheap housing. Immigrants came, some legal, some not: Eastern European Jews came seeking refuge, first from pogroms, then from the Nazis. Then came Greeks, Armenians and Turks, and most recently Asians, Arabs and Africans—again, some with legal papers, others without—bringing a tangible instability and some anger (sometimes explosive) to the area, as the French endlessly debate how to handle the large immigrant influx and its high rate of unemployment. Today this population congregates to the sides of the boulevard de Belleville at the Arab and Asian shops, Muslim and Jewish establishments and the crowded, inexpensive market. Much of this western side where the 20^e and the 11^e abut is rundown, but some parts bear the mixed results of urban renewal.

In the 1960s, the 20^e began to experience the same faceless development as parts of the 13^e and 15e, but the outcry of the residents, les Bellevillois, caused at least some areas to be preserved. Thus, this hilly northern part of the district contains apartment blocks, charming cottages and dismal slums. The area immediately above the steep Parc de Belleville is up-and-coming, with new cafés and bars enlivening the area; downhill, it approaches boulevard de Belleville and the unsettled area described above. The commercial rue de Ménilmontant cuts across the multiracial area, separating it from the neighbourhoods below.

West of the cemetery Père-Lachaise—the largest garden in Paris—and toward Porte de Bagnolet, lie the old hamlets of Charonne and Bagnolet. In this generally residential area around Place Chanute and Square Séverine are small cottages on hilly, flowery side streets such as rue Paul Strauss. There are also interesting niches off rue Saint-Blaise. Of course, these are all nestled amidst apartment blocks or adjacent to areas that are still waiting to be refurbished. It just depends on where you look.

La Défense and the Western Suburbs

Although the suburbs are beyond the province of this book, some should certainly be considered, for many are extremely popular with the international community. Many foreign residents, especially those with families, commute into the city or to La Défense from the *banlieue* (suburbs), which offer a tranquil lifestyle, spacious gardened homes and proximity to some of the international schools. The suburbs are categorised by those that are near (*la proche banlieue*) and linked by the *métro* to Paris, and those farther out (*les banlieues plus éloignées*), reachable by RER (commuter railway). *La banlieue ouest* (western suburbs) are most in demand, especially by new arrivals to Paris. The standard of living is high and housing is more spacious for property of comparable prices in the city centre. Having a car is essential, however, as not all services or shopping needs can be found in every small town.

Look at elegant Neuilly-sur-Seine and its neighbour, Levallois-Perret, at the western edges of the city. Try Boulogne-Billancourt and its neighbour across the Seine, the charming, affluent hill town of Saint-Cloud. Suresnes and Puteaux are also home to many Anglophones, as is Courbevoie, beyond La Defénse.

Just beyond Paris' western suburb of Neuilly-sur-Seine rise 2,000 acres of modern skyscrapers—high-rise residential blocks, France's largest shopping mall and miles of landscaped, connecting walkways. This is La Défense, a multi-use business/residential complex planned in the 1930s, realised in the 1960s and 1970s and topped off in 1989 with the construction of La Grande Arche, a 400-m high arch of two hollow towers, connected at the top and larger than the Cathedral of Notre-Dame.

Some 100,000 people work at La Défense, in the offices of 800 of the world's most important corporations. Thirty thousand people live here, in a pleasant, homogeneous area close to some of the international schools. Housing is modern and affordable, agreeably built around landscaped squares and elevated walkways that hide the public transportation systems below. The Quatre-Temps shopping centre holds hundreds of shops and restaurants and the hypermarché Auchan. In fact, all conveniences are here, including a variety of cultural attractions, and central Paris is no farther than a *métro* or RER ride away. If La Défense does not have the traditional charms of the city centre, it has its advantages worth considering.

If the south interests you, look at Issy-les Moulineaux— a town of winding streets, its own town square and an atmosphere more casual than some of its neighbours. Just beyond, look too at Meudon, accessible by RER, prized both by commuters into Paris and those who work in the industries that border the Paris side of the Seine.

Of the outer reaches, Saint-Germain-en-Laye is probably the most well-known. A charming, affluent country town, it has provided upmarket services to Anglophone residents since the 17th century, when the English James II and his retinue lived in exile here. All conveniences that residents could possibly want are here, which also benefit its less famous neighbour Le Vésinet. The tranquil lifestyle of these areas make them extremely popular for the Anglophone community—do check them out.

Be careful, however, when thinking of the northern or northeastern *banlieu*, which are currently more problematic. Dense housing blocks and industrial compounds characterise these areas, for this is where many immigrants were settled during the various influxes into the Paris region. Overcrowded and monotonous, these northern inner suburbs have recently been in the news for unrest and protests by young, underemployed people with few prospects. France has long grappled with the assimilation of these immigrants—many of whom are French but of North African descent—into society and the job market. After the incidents of car burnings of late 2005, the government finally realized that it had to make a more concerted effort toward improving living and economic conditions for immigrants throughout France. This was much easier said than done, given the resistance to change by the French, even when the citizenry knows conditions must change. So in terms of housing, at present, it's best to stick to the west or south when thinking of a suburban place to live.

MEETING THE PARISIANS

CHAPTER 3

'How can foreigners say they like France, but not
the French? It's the French who made the France
they like—and keep it that way.'
—Getrude Stein

WHEN YOU FIRST COME TO PARIS, you'll wonder, "What are the Parisians like?" In fact, Parisians are a constant topic of conversation among newcomers, at least until they think (they think!) they have finally understood the essence of the French. But the truth is that the answers—for there are many, and they may not always be consistent—come slowly, or as the French say, *petit à petit*. This is only partly because fathoming the intricacies of any culture takes time. The French are also traditionally private and reserved and do not readily open themselves to people they have just met or accept anything new. The main reason, however, is that the populace of Paris is changing and if it was once easily categorised, this is no longer the case.

The younger generations of Parisians—even those whose roots have long been in this city—live in a world and have attitudes their grandparents could never have imagined. Their Paris is one of plenty, without the scars of privation and hardship due to wars or depression. Their sphere is that of instant news on television and of chatting on the Internet, of universal education, Facebook and Twitter, and inexpensive international travel. Even without leaving Paris, they can explore the world. And they like it that way—keeping, in their opinion, the best of French refinement and culture while partaking of the international scene. It has moved them to an openness and tolerance even their parents couldn't have foreseen: of gays who openly make up about five per cent of the French population, of Parisians of different races and religions, of newcomers to their city and to the ideas of the new millennium that will affect their lives.

But they also live in a time when half of the marriages in France end in divorce and where their friends often don't choose the option of marriage at all. Abortion is legal. Real estate prices are high and jobs are scarce. They know that the political and economic realities of the uncertain 21st century influence their futures. Competition is fierce, so they must pay attention and learn. Some of these people are ambitious young professionals who may well, eventually, bring about change to the hierarchical, top-down structure of French society. And others, even young shopkeepers and clerks, will perhaps start businesses of their own that cater to the needs of future generations, broadening the definition of what it is to be both modern and French.

As for their parents, they perpetuate the stereotype that, while knowing it is necesary, the French don't like change. They worry that foreign cultures—pervasive American commercialism and even the different cultures of their confrères in the European Union—are infiltrating their own. They see their children as being too influenced by external ideas that don't reflect the traditions they revere. There's also too much uncertainty all around. Knowing that globalisation is inevitable, and even understanding that, in many ways, they are benefitting from greater opportunities, they still don't like all this newness one bit. If you talk to these older Parisians—even on a beautiful sunny day on the terrace of a charming café—they'll tell you that everything in their city is going from bad to worse.

And they too wonder who Parisians are these days. As described in Chapter Two, Paris is no longer a city of only 'Parisians'. Some 13 per cent of 'Parisians' are foreigners, i.e., about 300,000 out of 2.3 million, including a large North African influx from the former colonies of France. Others include citizens of EU countries who may now live in any EU country they choose. It's also estimated that some 100,000 English speakers live in the Paris area, some of whom are employees of international corporations or embassies, here for a short term, then moving on and ceding their place to yet more newcomers. Parisians now hear Arabic in the streets and in the *métro*, and English everywhere as well—mostly what the French call 'American', a linguistic distinction Americans don't make.

ANSWERS STILL EXIST

Yet, if Paris is no longer that of Louis XIV and the Marquis de La Fayette, it is clear to foreigners—if not to the French themselves—that cultural legacies do linger on. Paris remains a city of Parisians, a city that is charming as well as efficient, beautiful and welcoming, and this is due to the Parisians. So, one still needs to ask the question: "What are Parisians like?" or more precisely "What can I expect from my new neighbours?" The French continue to embody their history and deeply ingrained traditions. As such, despite the variations in individual experiences that can occur, there are codes for manners and behaviour, clues a newcomer can discern, which will help in you to fit in, whether here for a week or a year. Use the 'The Paris Rules' and you will feel welcome and increasingly see why life here can be so good. In the end, it's up to you to pay attention to each situation and to react accordingly, using the knowledge and 'people skills' that you have learnt.

GETTING STARTED

First it should be said that Paris is an extremely agreeable city to live in—graceful, well maintained, efficient, with something interesting going on all the time—and this is the way the French like it.

So just who are they? Basically the French are people who are formal and respectful with others, cordial and polite, direct in their speech, and quite witty and affectionate when they get to know you. Life revolves around their families and friends. They are busy with their work, but they treasure their leisure time, enjoying *la belle vie* or the good life—concerts, cinema, their favourite bistros and cafés. Since they have created these outlets for themselves, they are at your disposition too! Of course, as anywhere else, you'll find shopkeepers you like and restaurants that please you more than others; people you want as friends and others that you don't. With those Parisians who welcome you slowly but surely into their midst, you'll create your own *belle vie* as time goes on, and what will make all this happen is less the Parisians or what they're like, but you and how much effort you make to fit in.

Legendary Rudeness Dismissed

Tourists in the past may have complained so much about the rudeness of Parisians that it has become legendary, but people who come today are surprised to find it just isn't true. In fact, manners, as well as respect, formality and privacy, are extremely important to the French. It's always a mistake to assume in a new country that because the citizens look like you, dress like you and perhaps, even seem to lead the kind of life that you do, they are like you. They're probably not. They're themselves, an amalgam of their particular traditions, as well as political and cultural history. So, bringing your own cultural assumptions and being offended when these are not met is certainly a big mistake.

Take, for example, the welcoming smile. The French had heretofore smiled only when they had a reason to, for example, when meeting a friend. In fact, although this is changing among the modern generations, the French used to be known to have a *mine d'enterrement*—a funereal look. So, if you come from a gregarious culture where people automatically smile when saying hello—even to a waiter in a restaurant or someone sitting down next to you on the bus, you may be taken aback in Paris when your smile is not returned and think it rude, although it is not.

Yet, as with most legends, this one may have once contained a glimmer of truth. Tourists who came to Paris just some 40 years ago would have dealt with Parisians who grew up during and just after World War II in a climate of hardship and loss and who subsequently faced the Algerian War and student rebellions in their youth. As such, they were often grim and perhaps even suspicious of the droves of cheerful, superficial, high-spending foreigners who were all

It's common to *faire la bise* when greeting your French friends—but even this follows codes.

around. But this generation is thinning out, and the Parisians of today are two generations hence. History has moved on and so have they.

Of course, there are people who are rude anywhere, in any city of the world. It's unavoidable. There are bureaucrats who get tired of answering the same question again and again. There are also Parisians who react negatively to something outside of their own cultural assumptions. And even French who have lived in Paris all their lives have occasional woes of how they were mistreated by someone, sometime. For newcomers, the stories we tell and retell are those that draw a laugh, most often at ourselves for having gotten it all wrong or at how we were, yet again, misunderstood. It takes some time to get it right. All you can do is be patient and have a sense of humour about it all.

How They Were Brought Up

The real truth is that most Parisians are polite and wouldn't dare be otherwise. It's important to French parents that their child be respectful, considerate and *bien élevé* (well brought up); calling someone *mal élevé* (badly brought up) is an insult. These expectations are passed down through the generations, and although parents these days despair of their children's manners (as parents seem to do everywhere), French children are basically *bien élevé* and grow up to be well-mannered adults. Think of how, when you go into a store, salespeople will say "*Bonjour monsieur*" or "*Bonjour madame*". They also express thanks at the end of a transaction and wish you "*Bonne journée*" (a good day) when you depart. This is, as they say, '*normal*' (perfectly normal and expected).

If you are elderly, someone will give you a seat on the bus. A person who bumps into you will sincerely apologise and ask if you're okay. And, if you have some kind of real problem, there's no one like the French to take it in hand. They're eager to

At the start of 2007, smoking was banned in most public places; eating and drinking establishments changed over in 2008. After the total ban was finally in effect, smokers—both old and young—readily adapted to the new conditions. There were few complaints, and those who predicted the demise of the convivial bar must have been pleasantly surprised.

help, to show you the way. If you start by saying "*Excusez-moi de vous déranger* (sorry to bother you), *mais j'ai un problème* (but I have a problem)," the French will be all ears. You'll certainly get some information, assistance, the use of their mobile phone, or whatever it is you need at.

But here's one of the important things to learn: this is where it ends. Most often Good Samaritans won't give you their names or invite you for a coffee after your *problème* has been solved. You will neither learn about their families or be asked why you are in Paris and what you do. Accepting a younger person's seat on the bus is not an opening to conversation about where you are going that day. Acknowledging an apology for being jostled requires nothing but a nod to say you're fine and perhaps the standard phrase "*Ce n'est pas grave* (it's not serious)". And when you are shopping, expecting the salesperson to volunteer an opinion on how the dress looks on you (once the question of the correct size has been resolved) will leave you disappointed. In short, the French do not intrude on your privacy and they expect you to respect theirs.

How They Grew Up

Hold The Accusations!

You should never accuse a French person of being wrong—especially if there's something you need. With such an emphasis on being correct, the French have difficulty in admitting they are wrong and so they practically never apologise. This generalisation may be going too far, but it has a great deal of truth to it. A bureaucrat may—only under duress—admit to an *erreur* (error), but since errors are innocently made, this means that there is no fault—and no apology will be forthcoming. A *faute* (fault) is something even worse to bring up, for it implies culpability. So, if you are a person who needs to put blame for something gone amiss, you have come to the wrong place!

It's best to take none of this personally for it's just the way the French were taught to be. As children, their upbringing was loving but strict, with expectations for proper behaviour. Their schooling was rigid and competitive. They were taught to get things exactly right, to be direct and to the point. They were taught the value of reason and that they should always find the rational solution. Even their handwriting was controlled, and as adults their handwriting is still scrutinised when they apply for a job. All in all, there's a great premium placed on being correct.

The Superior French?

Another legend that dies hard is that the French think they are 'superior'. (Didn't the word 'chauvinism' come from the French?) Then again, think of how the French look at their lives. They were brought up with an intense cultural pride—a 2,000-year-old history, a continual refinement of values and an adherence to the best traditions will do that for you. They have been taught to be proud of their heritage and language, their literature, art, fashion, wine and cuisine, and even the beauty of their capital. Aren't these things worth being proud of, and isn't this one of the reasons we all love to come to Paris? It isn't that a French person feels superior to any one particular foreigner, it's just that, all things said, the French—no matter of which generation—believe and feel deeply in their souls that it is excellent to be French. And it's rather nice, is it not, to be proud of who you are and where you live?

The Paris Rules

- Learn French. The French love their language and are pleased when a foreigner makes the effort to speak it. Do the best you can, even if it is not very good at first. If you don't, you will always remain an outsider. Pronunciation is the key, even though your French accent may be more reminiscent of Dracula than of Yves Montand. With just the slightest mistake, you may be looked at as though you were from another planet. For example: *salut* (pronounced 'sa-lue') means 'hello', but *salaud* (pronounced 'sa-loh') is a word not used in polite society.

- Mind your manners. Be respectful and polite. Don't interrupt if a salesperson is busy with another client. Wait for your turn.

- Look good and act in control. Appearances and confidence count. Parisians respond to people who look well put together and who come across as poised, with dignity and spirit.

- Moderate the volume of your voice. Speak softly on your mobile phone, do not shout on the *métro*, and in restaurants be considerate of people sitting close by.

- Be cordial but not familiar. Do not tell everyone your life story, just because they've asked about the weather that day.

- Do not ask Parisians anything personal about themselves, no matter how superficial it seems to you. And never talk about money or volunteer how much something costs.

- Never blame a French person for something gone wrong. Convey that you have misunderstood and ask what should be done at this point. It doesn't matter whether you are right or wrong, or even if the other person is evading the truth. What matters is that you get what you need at that point.

- Let nothing faze you. Be firm, but don't get angry. The French, whether they like it or not, will respond to manners. If someone seems unkind, do not take it personally and don't overreact. With cordiality you at least stand a chance of an easy transaction; without it, you do not.
- Pay attention. Read some of the books mentioned in the Further Reading section and listen carefully to the stories of friends who have already been through the acclimatisation process. Pay attention to each situation for they are not all the same. When you have doubts, just ask a Parisian, who will no doubt be pleased that you are making an effort to understand how Paris works.
- Read the French newspapers as much as you can and watch the news, so you know what is current in France and in Paris. In other words, be a resident of your city, know what it going on.
- Learn *le système D*. Parisians, too, make train reservations and need help from clerks, and they too get the answer "*non*". The 'D' comes from the word *débrouiller,* meaning to manage or untangle. What it really means is finagling any way you can—within socially acceptable and legal parameters—to get what you want; whether it is a connection through a friend or by using every persuasive charm you have to convince that office clerk to bend a rule (that might not even be a rule at all) just a little. In short, *séduire* or charm someone who is brusque and unhelpful. Play on their sympathy. Rely on their expertise. Be helpless but persistent. Don't take "*non*" for an answer. Ply *le système D*!
- Do not complain about Paris or France, even if Parisians gripe that everything is going from bad to worse. Love Paris every minute and let it be known that you do.

SOCIALISING WITH THE LOCALS

CHAPTER 4

'I think every wife has a right to insist upon seeing Paris.'
—Sydney Smith

IT STANDS TO REASON that the people most likely to become your first friends are those with whom you already have some personal link: contacts from people back home, parents of other children in the bilingual schools, people you've met at your English-language church or synagogue, or even those you've found through the networking groups mentioned in Chapter 10. Everyone wants to know people from their home countries, and these people may form the core of your social life, as you share the same language and culture shock is minimised. If these people have lived here a long time, they almost qualify as 'locals', for although they may not be seen as 'Parisians' by the French, they certainly know the ropes and, in addition to including you in their Parisian lives, they can help you along. Their social customs, in fact, may well reflect aspects of both cultures, for newcomers tend to keep their own while also taking on those of the French. They may, for example, invite you into their homes for dinner sooner than the French might, but would still expect you to arrive at least 20 minutes late, which Parisians consider as being on time.

BREAKING DOWN THEIR RESERVE

But you're determined to make some French friends, and rightly so. So how do you meet Parisians? It isn't at all impossible to make French friends. It takes time, patience and effort. It takes being cool and collected, and standing some disappointments. But it's all worth it at the end. If you comport

Parisian Reserve

Art critic John Russell once commented, "It must seem that in Paris every door is marked 'private', every notice means 'keep out' (even if it doesn't actually say it) and all information is classified." But Russell's is a generalisation, one that may not apply to particular individuals that you meet.

yourself as someone the French want to know, you'll already have met them halfway, but only halfway, and it is the other half—that famous privacy and reserve—that must be slowly overcome. Some people joke that if you want to make friends quickly in animal-loving Paris, just walk a dog!

Some foreigners have never met their Parisian neighbours; others have become fast friends with the person across the courtyard. Somehow, Paris brings out who you are and responds in kind. If you are someone who is easily irritated by small problems, Paris will no doubt irritate you most of the time, but if you see little problems as challenges, you will approach them with good humour. If you are a person who makes friends easily, you will eventually break down some of the barriers of Parisian reserve, but if you too are reserved in outlook, you will wind up—as is often the case with the Parisians themselves—not knowing the person next door.

Actually, the problem is not meeting Parisians, for you'll also come across them in all the places you normally frequent. Yet, they're busy with their own work and children, and when it comes to socialising, they already have their own friends and families. It's a fact that the French are most comfortable and open with people they already know—extended families and lifelong friends. That leaves you to strike a delicate balance, indicating that you would like to know them better, but allowing them the space to go to the next step at their own pace. Frankly, there's no easy answer on how to move from cordial acquaintances to friends. It depends, as with any relationship, on the individuals.

Nonetheless, there are ways—through inter-cultural groups and networking with people who have already indicated they are open to getting to know new people—and by making sure you let it be known you are interested in making new friends. You might suggest having a coffee sometime or a film that you've both said you've wanted to see. Start slowly, listen for cues and be sensitive to how far, at each point, they are willing to go.

A PARISIAN FRIEND

It may take time to make Parisian friends, but once you have made them, they will be loyal for life, going out of their way for you, including you in group dinners at a bistro, in their walks at the Bois de Boulogne or at their evenings at the Opéra Bastille.

If you are from a culture that is immediately welcoming and effusive, but which doesn't translate into deep friendships, you will be pleasantly surprised. Parisians are true friends. But this does not mean that you will be invited into their homes right away, for that takes time. And when you are, it doesn't mean you may then drop in without being invited. It does not mean that you will use the familiar *tu* (you) to address each other. It does not mean that any of the social rules may be broken (even if you do not know what they are until you have broken them). It does not mean that they will think your joke is funny if it isn't in their culture. And it does not mean you can be overly intimate, which is worse than not being friendly enough. The Parisians you come to know may enjoy your company and begin to be comfortable with you, but they still can only act like themselves—French.

So don't stereotype people according to the one or two Parisians who might not respond to your overtures. Most Parisians will look at you as an individual, no matter what they think of the politics of your country. If they see someone who is trying to fit into society, who is genuinely open to understanding Paris and who tries to follow 'The Paris rules' (see pages 64–65), they will look at you as an individual.

With each person you come to know, you will have to judge *petit à petit* how much to tell and how much to ask. Err on the minimal side. The French are astounded when foreigners—especially the open, gregarious Americans— divulge too early in a budding relationship aspects of their lives that they tell only their oldest friends. Actually, they are just as curious as you are; they just don't show it. It is still best to wait for clues and hints from the other party, and gauge each situation to figure out what comes next. If something goes amiss, ask yourself first if there's a code you have unknowingly violated. Yes, there are always more codes to learn; the difference is that with a friend, you have an ally in helping you learn them.

THE ART OF CONVERSATION

It's important to understand that the French love to talk. They love informed, witty conversation on a variety of subjects. They love repartee and banter. One of the worst things they can say about a person is "but he has no *conversation*". If you have dinner with someone, even in a *restaurant etoilé* (a starred restaurant), the dinner will almost be as much about the conversation as the food.

And even here, there are codes. Don't talk about anything intimate: they don't want to know any details about someone who is ill (not even the name of the illness), about anything dirty, about how pleased (or displeased) you are with your salary. Do not monopolise the conversation and, above all, do not complain or criticise the French—even if your friends are doing so themselves. What with all the uncertainties in the world, everyone has an opinion on politics, but that doesn't mean you should express yours immediately—not about your home country, and especially not about France.

Do talk about things you have in common—films and books or an exhibit you've seen recently; travel; current events (if it is not against the French); an amusing anecdote about something you misjudged. Compliment the food, wine and surroundings. Have a good time. That's what it's all about.

People generally don't split the bill in a restaurant. If you've been invited as a guest, your hosts will pay for the dinner. Be gracious, thank your hosts, and indicate that you'd like to reciprocate the next time. On the other hand, if you're part of a small group that has decided to get together for a drink, then expect to split the bill or to indicate that you want to pay your share. Follow the lead of other people.

The French value ideas, conversation and debate—learn the art of conversation and you'll find making friends easier.

IN A PARISIAN HOME

The French have long believed that they are the custodians of *la belle vie*—the good life. They also believe that part of this good life is adhering to accepted standards, what they call *comme il faut*, or how things are done. So, if and when you are invited to into a Parisian's home, there are also codes to be learned, the sooner the better.

Your hosts will expect you to be on time, although their concept of this may differ from yours. People generally arrive between 20 minutes to half an hour after the time called for the rendezvous. Never arrive even two minutes early or 10 minutes after—you might be interrupting your hostess in the midst of dressing or doing something in the kitchen.

Expect some physical contact. Colleagues and acquaintances shake hands when they meet and at the end of the encounter. When you know people a little better, they may lean with their face forward, indicating that they have moved from the handshake to the *bisous*—two kisses, one on each cheek. In other areas of France, some people do three and even four kisses, but two is generally the norm in Paris. These are small, friendly greeting kisses and are often repeated at the end of the rendezvous. Women also do the *bisous* with each other, as do men who are family members or, sometimes, extremely old friends. Note that even if all the others know each other well and they *se tutoient* i.e.,speak to each other in the more familiar second person singular tense, you shouldn't follow suit until you are invited to—this may take years.

If it's not a casual occasion and you are meeting people for the first time, especially older people or those more senior than you professionally, be formal. When introduced say "*madame*" or "*monsieur*", or even the rather passé "*enchanté* (delighted)" and wait for the people to indicate how they would like to be addressed. Stand up when a woman enters the room for the first time. Be aware that if it is your boss who has invited you to dinner, it is only as a courtesy—he does not expect to be invited back and to become friends.

Don't bring flowers. Your hostess probably already has fresh flowers, and she wouldn't want to spend time arranging a bouquet that you've brought. If you want to do something with flowers, send an arrangement before or after. If you decide for some reason to bring flowers, do not bring chrysanthemums, which are generally put on graves, or carnations, which supposedly bring bad luck. It's best to ask the florist to send an appropriate bouquet.

It used to be that bringing a bottle of wine was also frowned upon, as it seemed to insinuate that the host's wine cellar was not adequate or, worse, created a confusion if the host had already carefully selected wines for the evening's meal. Now, however, with a casual dinner among friends, people often bring a bottle of wine.

When your host shows you into the living room, stay there. Don't ask to see the rest of the apartment and don't wander around on your own. Don't go into the kitchen and offer to help the hostess. Just stay where you are put. Don't help yourself to the drinks that might be sitting on the sideboard and don't play the piano, if there is one. Just wait and talk with whomever else is there, or if you're alone pick up a magazine or look at the pictures on the walls or the view out the window. Be patient, that's all.

If there's something you cannot eat, make sure your hostess knows it in advance. Don't use the dinner table to discuss your allergies or dislikes. Eat what is served to you; it's rude to leave things on your plate. Your hostess will ask if you'd like more: in general, you may take more of the main course but not the others. Don't help yourself—even if platters are on the table—unless instructed to do so. Generally, there will be two glasses, one for wine and the other for water. Your host will be generous in pouring, but it is best always to quench your thirst with water and to sip the wine for the taste. The myth of free-drinking French is just that—a myth.

If you have arrived on the *métro*, you may certainly ask to wash your hands before eating dinner; otherwise, avoid using the *toilettes* or leaving the table at all if you can help it. And

Entertaining at Home

You may or may not have codes of your own, but it is the French codes you have to learn when entertaining Parisian friends in your home. Some things you'll like; some you may never get used to. Don't fight it.

- People are not usually invited over just for 'drinks'. Lately *le cocktail* (usually from 6:30 pm to about 9:00 pm) is gaining in popularity, but in effect this is still a meal, albeit one taken mostly standing up. Also, the French don't often have a buffet, where dishes are placed on the table and people can help themselves.

- Don't serve too many 'nibbles' before dinner, just champagne or fruit juice and a few nuts. The French save their appetites for dinner.

- Since your guests will straggle in late, don't prepare a dish that needs to be eaten at a certain time or one that will require you to stay in the kitchen cooking at the last minute.

- Young children will not eat with you and your guests unless it's a family dinner or lunch. If teenagers do, they are not to monopolise the conversation.

for heaven's sake, don't announce where you're going; just indicate your question quietly to your host who will show or tell you where to go. Afterwards, sit back down at the table without referring to your absence.

Keep your free hand on the table, not in your lap. This stems from ancient times, when people carried swords and daggers. Keeping the free hand on the table meant that you meant no harm to the others.

If the dinner runs late, and the host asks whether anyone would like an orange juice or some other non-alcoholic drink, it is time to go. Don't offer to help with the dishes. Just thank your hosts, comment on something that was particularly delicious or enjoyable, then go home.

- Dress appropriately for the occasion, even if you are doing the cooking. Also make sure that your dishes are 'dressed', with parsley or sauces.
- Use cloth napkins, even for lunch.
- If you are unsure of which wines or cheeses to serve, ask the *caviste* at the wine shop or the *fromager* from the cheese shop for advice. The cheeses should be at room temperature. Take them out of the refrigerator at least an hour before you are to eat them.
- Learn to eat everything with a knife and fork, even fruit. With a fruit course, make sure your guests have the appropriate cutlery. When serving salad, lettuce leaves should be small enough to eat; otherwise you will notice that your guests fold but never cut them.
- Coffee is served after the cheese, fruit and dessert. Offer coffee, decaf or an *infusion* (herbal tea).
- You may clear the table of dishes no longer in use, but don't do the dishes until after your guests leave.

SETTLING IN

CHAPTER 5

'And each day I will see a little more of Paris,
study it, learn it as I would a book.'
—Henry James

FORMALITIES FOR RESIDENCE

Citizens from European Union (EU) countries do not need a passport when entering France from another EU country. Nonetheless, some type of officially recognised identification such as a passport or national identity card is required. Also, if an accompanying spouse is not an EU citizen, he or she will need a passport to enter the country.

All non-EU citizens need at least valid passports to enter the country. Entering France entitles the passport holder to stay in France for three months, provided the French visa requirements for that country have been met. It's best to call the French embassy or consulate nearest you for the exact requirements.

Staying More Than Three Months

EU nationals have the right to decide where in the EU they want to reside and work. Thus all citizens of the 27 member states of the EU do not need a *carte de séjour* (stay permit) to remain in France. This holds true for citizens of the European Economic Area (EEA) and Switzerland as well. It might be beneficial to have the *carte de séjour*, nonetheless, since some companies, banks, or other institutions may ask for it. The Europe Direct line gives information on many aspects of the European Union (tel: 00.800.67.89.10.11, website: http://ec.europa.eu/europedirect). Citizens from the 10 newer EU countries who want to stay more than three months in France must, however, request immigration status in accordance to their situation in France. In order to work, they must also have the *carte de séjour*.

All non-EU citizens who want to stay in France for more than three consecutive months must obtain one of the six types of *cartes de séjour* currently issued; these are determined by the status of the person and the purpose of the sojourn.

The first step is to apply for the *visa de long séjour* (long-stay visa), which must be obtained before departure for France, at the French consulate with jurisdiction over your place of residence. Addresses and information on requirements can be found on their websites (see French Embassies below). The French government requires the application to be made from your own country of citizenship unless you reside in a different country. Processing the visa may take more than two months and some documents must be translated into French by a consulate-approved translator (*traducteur assermenté*). It is rarely possible for a non-EU citizen to enter France as a tourist and then change status. (For student permits, see pages 173–174.)

Some Helpful Websites

- City of Paris
  http://paris.fr. In the English version, click on "Guide for Foreign Residents" for current, helpful information.
- Préfecture de Police
  http://www.prefecture-police-paris.interieur.gouv.fr. Keep track of regulations, news of changes in the city, etc. Some in English. For personal information, you will need to go in person to the Préfecture.
- Link between administration and residents:
  http://www.service-public.fr/langue/english. Understand some of the legalities and obligations of living in France.
- Government website with information for people coming to or investing in France.
  http://www.diplomatie.gouv.fr/en/

Documents to Bring

Bring as many of the following documents as possible for the entire family; in fact, bring anything you think might be pertinent. Documents that may need to be translated into French by an approved *traducteur assermenté* are marked with an asterisk. Make photocopies of every document and keep them separate from the originals.

When you go to the Préfecture, take as many documents with you as possible: you will not always be told which documents are required, and if your dossier is not complete, you may have to come back again. You may also need to bring a stamped, self-addressed envelope.

- *Visa de long séjour*
- Proof of domicile, most likely an electricity bill in your name.
- Work permits (as required)
- Passports for the whole family
- Photocopies of the first pages of your passports
- Extra passport photos
- Visa (as required)
- Birth certificate*
- Marriage certificate*
- Divorce certificate*
- Driver's license*

French Embassies and Consulates

Citizens of non-EU countries should check the websites of the French embassies in their country or call for information on *visas de long séjour*. In most countries, the French embassy is located in the capital city. For a comprehensive list, access the Foreign Ministry's website: http://www.diplomatie.gouv.fr.

Always carry your passport or residence permit with you, as the police have the right to ask anyone to show their identity papers. Also, inform the Préfecture of any change in your residence and show evidence of the new address: lease, rent receipt, electricity bill, etc. If your *carte de séjour* is lost or stolen, make a *déclaration de perte/ de vol* (report of loss/theft) at your local *commissariat de police* (police station). Make a copy of your *carte de séjour* as soon as you receive it.

Report lost passports at the appropriate *commissariat* and take the report and two passport photos of the exact size specified to your consulate. It is always helpful to bring extra photos with you, and this is when having a photocopy of the first pages of your passport will be most helpful.

Carte de Séjour

After arriving in France with a *visa de long séjour*, all non-EU nationals must, within the first week, register at the Hôtel de Police, Centre d'Accueil des Etrangers, according to the *arrondissement* where they will live:

- 11-14e, 19-20: 114 avenue du Maine, 75014.
- 8e-9e, 1-10e, 15-18e: 19 rue Truffaut, 75017.

To obtain the *carte de séjour*, fill out the questionnaire and make an appointment with the Préfecture de Police. This may only materialise after several months, depending on the number of pending applications.

Along with the documents mentioned earlier, these are the papers you will need (at the time of writing): a valid *visa de long séjour*, three black-and-white passport photos, proof of an address in France (paid rent receipt, electricity bill with your name, etc.), and proof of financial resources and medical insurance. Other requirements (e.g., student identification card or work contract) depend on the purpose of the stay.

There are various types of *cartes de séjour*. Each depends on the situation of the applicant. It may be a *carte de séjour* cum work permit, but if it says *mention visiteur*, the holder is not allowed to earn money in France. The duration of the *carte* also depends on the applicant's situation. Heretofore, it has been renewable yearly for a period of five years, after which the card-holder may apply for a ten-year permit. Now, however, some *cartes de séjour* are renewable every 18 months, instead of a year. Dependents accompanying a person who is working in France follow the same procedures.

When dealing with *l'administration* (the bureaucracy), adhere strictly to the rules. If a form says to bring three black-and-white photos of a certain size, do not diverge from the requirements. Never lose your temper, be sarcastic, or raise your voice, even if you believe you are right about something and the *fonctionnaire* (bureaucrat) is wrong. This won't help you in your quest.

Carte de Résident

As mentioned, EU nationals have the right to live and work in France. If you have any doubts about your own status, check with the French Embassy in your country (http://www. info-france-usa.org/spip.php?article569). .

Non EU-nationals, however, must first have the *carte de séjour* to reside in France, and after five consecutive renewals, may apply for the carte de resident. This is more complicated and lengthy than it sounds. Those who have been employed one way or another [*salarié ou vie privée*] might get the carte fairly quickly, but even then they must make more than the minimum wage (SMIC) which is currently € 11,000 per annum, and if there has been unemployment at any time during the five years, that year doesn't count.

The spouse of a French citizen has to wait three years for the carte de resident, and they must have stayed married that long before being granted complete and permanent residency.

Anglophone Embassies

Foreign embassies are most helpful to their citizens during times of crisis. They replace lost passports and help in medical or legal emergencies by making referrals to appropriate doctors, dentists or lawyers. They do not, however, help people to get out of jail. In all emergencies, embassies act as a liaison between the family at home and the person in France. It's a good idea to carry the telephone number of your embassy in your wallet.

For non-emergencies, embassies renew passports; record births, marriages and deaths; notarise documents and provide advice on matters such as absentee voting and the filing of taxes. Sometimes they offer information on local services, including lists of English-speaking doctors and attorneys, translators and international schools. Some have community liaison offices (of varying responsiveness). Embassies serving the greatest number of residents in Paris provide the most information, but basic services are the same.

Some countries allow their citizens to register their address in Paris, making it easier to replace lost passports and to be contacted in case of emergency. Inquire at your embassy. Most embassies are open for consular affairs in the mornings only; find out when your embassy is open before going and bring your passport to be allowed in. On the national holidays of both France and of your own country, the embassy will no doubt be closed. See '*Ambassades, Consulats*' in the *Yellow Pages*.

- Australia: 4 rue Jean-Rey, 75015; tel: 01.40.59.33.00; website: http://www.france.embassy.gov.au
- Canada: 35 avenue Montaigne, 75008; tel: 01.44.43.29.00; website: http://www.amb-canada.fr.

The Eiffel Tower, named after its designer Gustave Eiffel, was the highlight of the 1889 International Exhibition, commemorating the centenary of the French Revolution. Although much criticized at the time, the Tour Eiffel is now the most visited paid monument in the world.

Behind the counter of a local *boulangerie* or bakery in Paris. Pastries and bread are very popular in France, and most restaurants will serve a basket of freshly-baked baguette to accompany your meal.

La defense, situated at the western edge of Paris, is the city's major business district. Its ultra-modern skyscrapers house the headquarters of numerous multinational corporations, allowing Paris itself to retain its old-world charm

Interior of the *Musée d'Orsay*, originally built as a train station for the Universal Exhibition of 1900. A work of art in itself, this museum on the banks of the Seine specializes in masterpieces from 1848 1914.

A woman enjoying the fresh air from the *balcon* of her apartment. People live in every habitable area of Paris, even in those that seem to be strictly for business. When you see flowers in a window box you know Spring has arrived.

- Ireland: 12 avenue Foch, 75016 (embassy); 4 rue Rude, 75016 (consulate); tel: 01.44.17.67.00; fax: 01.44.17.67.50; website:http://embassyofirelandparis.fr
- New Zealand: 7 ter rue Léonard-de-Vinci, 75016; tel: 01.45.01.43.43; fax: 01.45.01.26.39; http://www.nzembassy.com/home.cfm?c = 6
- South Africa: 59 quai d'Orsay, 75007; tel: 01.53.59.23.23; fax: 01.53.59.23.68; website:http://www.afriquesud.net
- United Kingdom: 35 rue du Faubourg Saint-Honoré, 75008 (embassy); 18 bis rue d'Anjou, 75008 (consulate); tel: 01.44.51.31.00; fax: 01.44.51.31.27; website: ukinfrance.fco.gov.uk/en
- United States: 2 avenue Gabriel, 75008 (embassy); 75001; 24-hour tel: 01.43.12.22.22; website: http://france.uscmbassy.gov; State Department's emergency tel (US): (1-202) 647-5226 (say it is an emergency and ask for the duty officer.)

> The Association of American Wives of Europeans (AAWE) has published the third edition of its helpful book, *Vital Issues: How to Survive Officialdom while living in France*. Order directly from AAWE: 34 avenue de New York, 75116; tel: 01.40.70.11.80; website: http://www.aaweparis.org.

Essential Resources for Anglophones

Even if you're a confirmed Anglophone, you can still find what you need in Paris, and in English too. Several websites dedicated to Anglophones display advertisements for products, jobs, housing, various types of agencies, used furniture and appliances. Note that *FUSAC (France-USA Contacts)* is issued bi-weekly as a tabloid magazine and found in English-speaking venues around the city.

- http://www.fusac.com
- http://www.paris.craigslist.org
- http://www.franglo.com

FINDING YOUR PARISIAN NEST
Choosing a Hotel

Despite fluctuations in the numbers of visitors, most of the better hotels in Paris are full most of the time. This holds true especially during the popular seasonal events such as the exclusive fashion shows that take place twice a year. It is best to make your reservations well in advance. If, however, for some reason you arrive in Paris without a reservation, you can go to the Paris Tourist Office at 25 rue des Pyramides, 75001 (tel: 08.92.68.30.30; website: http://www.parisinfo.com) or one of its branches and they will find a hotel for you for the night, or you can book online. (The main Tourist Office is open every day of the year except on 1 May.)

The Indispensible *FUSAC*

France-USA Contacts, known by everyone as *FUSAC*, is a free English-language, bi-weekly compendium of advertisements—large and small—for anything you might need in Paris (tel: 01.56.53.54.54; http://www.fusac.com). Everyone who needs something, sometime, looks at *FUSAC*. From short- and long-term housing to job openings of all sorts, from used furniture and computer technicians to yoga studios and moving companies—*FUSAC* has it all. Real estate agents who specialise in working with international clients and have English-speaking personnel advertise their services in *FUSAC*, as do relocation agencies. With 300 distribution points in Paris—in Anglophone bookshops, stores, pubs and restaurants—it's not hard to find. To see its ads online or to find a location near you, go to its website.

There are hundreds of hotels ranging from elegant and exorbitant in price, to the basic and functional. They are rated by stars, from luxurious five-star pampering establishments down to the one-star hotel where you might have to share a bath. All tourist guides have detailed descriptions of a range of hotels, often arranged by neighourhood, which can be helpful. The hotels' own websites are also useful; check especially the Accor Hotels website (http://www.accorhotels.com), which covers its Mercure, Sofitel, Novotel, Libertel and Ibis hotels, all conveniently located around the city.

- http://www.parisinfo.com
- http://www.parishotels.com
- http://www.our-paris.com

- http://www.4u-hotels.com
- http://www.parisby.com'
- http://www.hotelclub.com
- http://www.ratestogo.com

Short-Term Home Exchange

The least expensive way to stay in Paris for a few weeks or months is to exchange your home for one here. International home exchange companies list homes available worldwide in brochures and on the Internet. Members pay to list their homes, specifying the dates available, and can search for those in the city of their choice. In your listing, you should describe your home, the surroundings and amenities. You correspond with the people who respond, provide photos of the property, check recommendations of people who have stayed before in that apartment and come to an agreement.

- Homelink International: http://www.homelink.org
- Intervac U.S.: http://www.intervac.com
- HomeExchange.com: http://www.homeexchange.com

Apartment Hotels

For stays of more than a week, especially for stays of a month or more, consider *résidences hôtelières* or apartment hotels, which combine the comforts of an apartment with the amenities of a hotel. Suites are of various sizes and include cooking facilities. If regular cleaning services and a concierge are important to you, consider an apartment hotel, although, of course, they are much more expensive than an individual apartment. An apartment hotel can be an easy way to spend a month or so, especially while searching for long-term lodgings. The companies below rent short-term, fully equipped apartments of various sizes and prices in convenient locations around the city. See also English-language advertisements for other such companies, as well as short-term apartments rented by agencies and individuals in *FUSAC* (see page 84 for a description of *FUSAC*).

- Citadines Aparthôtels ; tel: 08.25.33.33.32;
  website: http://www.citadines.com. A chain of upmarket apartment hotels

- France Appartements; 97–99 avenue des Champs-Elysées, 75008; tel: 01.56.89.31.00; fax: 01.56.89.31.01; website: http://www.rentapart.com
- Paris Appartements Services; 20 rue Bachaumont, 75002; tel: 01.40.28.01.28; fax: 01.40.28.92.01; website: http://www.paris-apts.com

Otherwise, you might rent a furnished flat from a private owner or through an agency. But be aware that laws regulating this kind of rental are starting to be enforced, for the city is concerned that foreigners are buying apartments just to rent them out short-term and that Parisians do not have enough access to affordable housing. How the enforcement will take shape will take some time to be resolved. See *FUSAC* for extensive listings or one of the agencies below. All have English speakers.

- Bridgestreet; tel: 01.42.94.13.13; fax: 01.42.94.83.01; website: http://www.bridgestreet.com
- Cattalan Johnson Agency; tel: 01.45.74.87.77; website: http://www.cattalanjohnson.com
- De Circourt Associates; tel: 01.43.12.98.00; website: http://www.homesparis.com
- Paris Lodging: tel: 01.43.36.71.69; website: http://www.parislodging.fr

Thinking about Apartments

As soon as you know your departure date and have at least a temporary place to stay, start thinking about permanent housing. If your company is sending you to Paris, discuss its relocation procedures. On your own, plan to begin making contacts well in advance of your departure. Three months in advance is not too early to begin inquiries, to place or look at ads, or to commit yourself with a deposit. If you plan to deal with real estate agencies, you will need time and patience. Call on weekdays, for many agencies are closed on weekends, and in August both landlords and agents are away on holiday. If you plan to commit to a short-term apartment before you arrive, inquire about all amenities before you sign a contract, and if possible, even ask someone you know in Paris to check it out.

It is hard these days to find a decent long-term rental apartment at a decent price. Indeed, for various reasons, including a slight decline in unemployment, there are fewer apartments on the market. If you see articles discussing 'average' housing prices, this means, of course, that apartments in the less desirable *quartiers* cost less and those in the trendiest neighourhoods cost more (if there are apartments to rent in these neighourhoods at all). Visits to view apartments are sometimes *groupées*, meaning that everyone interested visits the apartment at the same time and turns in their well-presented dossier (application, along with financial and professional references) immediately. If you wait to think it over, you won't get the apartment.

Given the dearth of available rental apartments, landlords are extremely choosy. They ask that applicants for the smaller apartments earn at least four times the rent. Most landlords will ask that at least a year's rent be blocked in the tenant's interest-earning bank account, held against any transgression, such as non-payment of rent. The landlord will no doubt also ask for a *caution*, perhaps a month's rent, which may be used when the tenant leaves, in case there is any damage or remaining bills to be paid.

As for apartments for sale, sales may have dropped, but prices have in the past few years risen by some 14 per cent. Of course, the amenities of each neighourhood, the resale value of the apartment itself and convenience to the purchaser's lifestyle must all be factored into the overall cost.

Considerations

Do not dismiss a building that seems untended on the outside: many buildings are built around inner courtyards and may be pleasant and quiet on the inside. Many apartments in older buildings have also been modernised. Be sure to open the windows to gauge the amount of noise coming from the street, no matter how high up the apartment. Some relatively quiet streets become extremely noisy between 6:30 pm and 8:30 pm; others may be noisy if there is a late-running bus line or a late-night bar. Thus, do not inspect apartments in August or on weekends, when traffic is light and all of Paris seems calm. However, if the apartment has *double vitrage* (double-glazed) windows, much of the street noise will be filtered out when windows are closed.

Most, but not all, buildings have lifts. Think twice about renting or purchasing an apartment above the third floor of a building without a lift. Although the view may be lovely and the breeze cooling, it can get tedious climbing the stairs day after day, especially when carrying groceries, and the charm will fade quickly. If you wouldn't live in such a building at home, don't do it in Paris.

Decide whether having a concierge who lives on the premises is important, as increasing numbers of buildings have replaced them with a *digicode* (key panel) or interphone system for secure entry. In this case, inquire as to how packages are received, how garbage is removed and how maintenance of the building is performed. Instead of a concierge, many buildings now have a *gardien*, who is responsible for the maintenance of the building but not for personal services.

When you see an apartment, inspect the appliances, if there are any. Since most kitchens come empty except for the sink—for rentals as well as purchase—some people negotiate the purchase of kitchen appliances and cupboards from the former resident. Otherwise, expect to purchase them for yourself, either new or used through ads in *FUSAC*.

Check the electrical wiring and whether all outlets for major appliances are grounded. Inquire about the heating system and check the hot water for temperature and pressure (especially in the shower). Ask whether the heating is *chauffage collectif*, meaning that heating is paid by the building and included in the building charges; or *chauffage individuel*, meaning that the resident pays directly for the heating. In this regard, look carefully at how well the windows close, for Paris is cold in winter and hot in summer. As most buildings have no air conditioning, see if there is more than one exposure, as cross ventilation can at least bring a welcome breeze.

Inspect the facilities in the basement, including your *cave* (storage area in basement). Newer buildings may have underground parking, but the older ones do not and street parking is difficult. If there is no parking, inquire about garage possibilities in the neighourhood. (See also page 166.) In this case, visit the garage to see how cars are parked and to determine hours when the car is retrievable.

Searching On Your Own

First, scan the ads in *FUSAC* regularly. Also, good apartments can occasionally be found by referrals from friends or in *les petites annonces* (classified ads) placed in newspapers by the owners themselves, who hope to avoid paying the landlord's share of the real estate commission. These ads often say *propriété à louer* (property for rent). Some landlords advertise privately in order to escape signing a lease, to avoid taxes, or perhaps because the apartment is not up to standard. Although the price might seem reasonable, do not accept substandard facilities or fail to be protected by a written contract. Ultimately, there are few bargains.

If an apartment appeals to you, call right away to set up an appointment. Some properties will have open houses, listed as *ce jour*, giving the time of the open house and the address. Bring your passport and proof of financial means in case you decide to take the apartment. Because the rare, desirable, reasonably priced apartments go quickly, make a commitment as soon as you can.

If you do not speak French fluently, bring someone with you who does. Sign a document only after you have understood every word.

Understanding the Ads

To decipher advertisements, start with the building itself. Its location in the *quartier* is given as the closest *métro* stop. *Standing* means it is a high-class building, as does *bel immeuble*. Apartments are advertised by *pièce* (room), excluding bathroom and kitchen; by the area in square metres; or by the number of main rooms, as indicated by F1 or F2. An apartment of *deux pièces* has two rooms, a kitchen and bathroom. A *studio* is one room and a *studette* may be as small as 18 sq m. A *chambre* may be as small as a *studette*, but without cooking facilities or a shower. *Mezzanine* means there is a loft for a bed. Pay attention to size, for an apartment of 55 sq m, despite the number of rooms, might be too small for your needs. On the other hand, most apartments—except for the old, elegant and extremely expensive—tend to be small, and kitchens and bathrooms especially may not be as large as what you are used to.

Some ads will mention *wc séparé* (separate room for the toilet) plus a *salle de bains* (a room with sink plus bathtub) or *salle de douche* (with a shower).

Unfurnished apartments may have no built-in *placards* (closets) and free-standing *armoires* must then be purchased. *La cuisine* (the kitchen), as mentioned above, may be equipped with only a sink and outlets for you to install your own appliances, unless the ad says *cuisine équipée* or *cuisine aménagée*. A *cuisine américaine* means that the kitchen opens to the living room, perhaps separated only by a bar. An apartment on the *RdeC* (*Rez-de-Chaussée*) is at street level, and an apartment on the *1er étage* means it is one level above. Ads for apartments higher up usually indicate whether or not there is an *ascenseur* (lift). *Cave* indicates a storage area

in the basement. *Parking* indicates a garage space and *box* means the garage space has a lockable door.

Agences Immobilières

To look for a long-term apartment, it is best to work with an *agent immobilier* (real estate agent) or relocation service about three months in advance. Agents prefer working on exclusive contracts and smaller agents generally specialise in their own districts—this means you may have to work with several agents in different *arrondissements*. Agents in each *arrondissement* display, in their windows, descriptions of their most desirable listings, usually pinpointed by the closest *métro* stop. All reputable agencies are licensed: their documents show their financial guarantor, insurance company and other references. Also, be aware that agents represent the interests of the landlord, not the tenant.

When contacting an agent, be as clear as you can about your requirements, although these might change as you start viewing what is available. Specifying your budget, location preferences and special needs can help an agent target apartments. Contact an agent several months in advance and follow up by telephone. Ask the agent about financial documents you will need to show in order to be accepted by a landlord.

Searching on the Internet

If you register with some of these Internet sites below and list your apartment preferences, you will receive an *alerte* when there is an apartment available that matches your criteria. Check the websites daily.

- http://www.pap.fr
- http://www.avendrealouer.fr
- http://www.seloger.com
- http://www.immostreet.com
- http://www.lesiteimmobilier.com
- http://www.pro-a-part.com
- http://www.explorimmo.com

Commissions generally run from 10–15 per cent of a year's rent but are not regulated. Most often the commission is shared by the landlord and the tenant. Inquire of agents as to their commissions and the services included, which sometimes encompasses drawing up the lease and making an inventory of the apartment. There may be a separate charge for drawing up the lease.

Relocation Services

Relocation agencies provide personalised services for the new resident in Paris. Helpful when contacted several months before arrival, their services can be crucial for people who do not have much advance notice of their move, for they can step in quickly with good results. They work first with real estate agencies to find appropriate housing and are experts in negotiating prices. Used to dealing with bureaucratic requirements and formalities, they can help navigate the complicated tangle of work and resident permits, car registration and insurance. They also provide valuable information on schools, household insurance and how to get utilities hooked up. Some offer cross-cultural meetings to help acclimatisation. Staff members speak English and are used to dealing with the concerns of newcomers.

Relocation agencies charge a flat fee for all services. They are expensive, but depending on your circumstances and the extent of your needs, well worth the price. They often work with companies that are transferring their employees. See if your company works with a particular relocation service and if they pay all fees. Here are some agencies; check *FUSAC* for more:

- 7e: A Good Start in France; 8 rue de l'Exposition; tel: 01.45.50.25.30; fax: 01.45.50.25.32; website: http://www.agoodstart.fr
- 17e: Cosmopolitan Services Unlimited; 4, rue Halèvy; tel: 01.44.90.10.10; fax: 01.44.90.10.11; website: http:// www.cosmopolitanservices.com
- Sèvres: Executive Relocations; 9 rue Thomas Edison, Gennevilliers 92230; tel: 08.21.02.90.90; email: info@

executive-relocations.com; website: http://executive-relocations.com

FURNISHED APARTMENTS

Furnished apartments rented by the week or month are more expensive than those leased for a year. Studios and one-bedroom apartments are sought after and thus proportionately more expensive than large ones. There is a great deal of turnover in short-term apartments, so with some effort, reasonably priced, furnished lodgings can be found.

Most people who come to Paris to stay for less than a year rent under short-term contracts. Short-term vacation rentals are not governed by law, but furnished apartments with a rental duration of one year are subject to almost the same laws as unfurnished ones, if the apartment is the primary residence of the tenant. The lease on these apartments (*bail à usage d'habitation en meublé*) can sometimes be negotiated. Real estate agents' commissions are paid by the tenant. Generally, the rent includes the habitation taxes, building charges and insurance. Make sure to inquire, for any apartment or house must be covered for property damage and personal liability (see pages 100–101). Minimum insurance does not cover any damage done by the tenant to the furniture, to the building, or even to a neighbour's apartment, for example, by faulty plumbing. Thus, ensure that the landlord has a comprehensive homeowner's policy, even if you are just renting for a year.

The laws for furnished apartments state only that they must be equipped with a table, chair and bed, so you should inquire specifically about the items you require, such as a desk, a microwave or toaster. Ask the landlord for a detailed inventory (*inventaire détaillé*) and make sure it matches what is actually there. Check and report in writing any irregularities in the apartment, so that you will not be charged for damage upon leaving. Do not hesitate to specify every furniture scratch and stain. When vacating the apartment, check the inventory once again.

UNFURNISHED APARTMENTS

Unfurnished long-term apartments are usually offered in three-year leases (*bail de location* or *bail de trois ans*) if the landlord is a private individual, and for six years if the landlord is a professional or a corporation. Leases are renewed automatically if no notice is issued by the tenant. When giving up the apartment, three months' notice is required (less if the tenant is being transferred abroad), and the letter sent to the landlord must be sent *en recommandée avec accusé de réception* (registered mail with notice of receipt). A tenant, however, may be given notice six months prior to the anniversary date of the lease, and reasons for terminating the lease must be specified: non-payment of rent, impending sale of the apartment, if the owner intends to occupy the apartment, or if it needs to undergo major renovation. A tenant may not be evicted between October and April for any reason.

Annual rent increases are regulated by law and calculated annually. The landlord will require the *caution* of up to a year's rent, which stays blocked for the entire length of the lease. The landlord pays interest on the entire sum on deposit. You can pay your rent by cheque or have it deducted from your bank account. Whichever way you decide to pay, request from the landlord a monthly *quittance de loyer* (receipt) to keep for your records.

All residents of a building pay *charges* (miscellaneous expenses), which cover garbage pickup, maintenance of the common areas and lift, landscaping, etc. Housing law states quite clearly which *charges* may be passed on to the tenant and in which proportion, so if your prospective landlord is an individual and not an established corporation, ask about the *charges*, what they cover and how they are assessed. These *charges*, along with the rent, are generally adjusted once a year. Also pay attention to the *taxe d'habitation* (habitation tax) paid by all residents on 1 January. This tax is assessed according to the value of the property, so the more expensive apartments and *arrondissements* have higher taxes.

Before the actual move, the tenant and the landlord conduct the *état des lieux* (inspection of the state of the

premises). This is important, for it protects the tenant upon termination of the lease, when the landlord will inspect and charge for any damages. Expect to spend about an hour discussing and noting any damage to the apartment, no matter how minute. Sometimes a *hussier* (bailiff) may be asked to conduct the *état des lieux*; if so, the fee is split between landlord and tenant, since it is a service for both. If you do need to make some repairs or adjustments, get a written *devis* (estimate of charges) from the contractor before starting any work.

Each French *département* has an office that offers information on tenants' rights. In Paris, the *mairie* has a booklet *La Protection des Locataires*, which gives appropriate contacts to call concerning tenants' rights.

PURCHASING AN APARTMENT

Apartments in Paris are generally *en copropriété* (condominiums), in which the resident owns outright the apartment and, jointly with the others in the building, the common areas. The apartment building is almost always managed by an outside *syndic* (a company specialising in building management); the running of the building depends on the *syndic*.

If you are considering buying property as a speculative investment, understand that France taxes the worldwide income of its residents. This includes the sale of a residence in the former country of residence once the French residence permit has been obtained. Don't forget too, that property transfer taxes of up to 20 per cent are paid by the seller, and this affects the price of the property—upon buying and resale. In addition, if the resale is under two years, the transaction may be deemed as speculation, with a capital gains tax of about 50 per cent. Thus, if you are considering the purchase of a property with the intention of selling it again, explore fully the tax ramifications both in France and your home country.

Upon deciding on a property, the buyer signs a *compromis de vente* (contract) and makes a down payment of about 10 per cent, which commits both buyer and seller, although the buyer has the right to back out within seven days after signing the contract. The *promesse de vente* allows the buyer three months to confirm the purchase and find a loan. Do not sign an *offre d'achat*, which commits the buyer but not the seller, unless it is written with the help of a professional. A secured *offre d'achat* must describe the premises, the amount of the offer and the duration of the validity of the offer (two weeks is the standard). Here too the buyer has the right to back out within seven days.

The seller must guarantee that the property is of the size claimed and must provide an inspection certificate for the absence of lead, asbestos and termites. For the buyer, expect closing costs to add about 8.5 per cent to the costs.

All transactions are completed by a *notaire*, a member of the legal profession who deals with real estate and family law. Acting on behalf of both parties (although sometimes each party is represented by a separate *notaire*), the *notaire* researches, prepares and signs all documents. The *notaire* can be crucial to the successful completion of a business transaction. The number of *notaires* in each district is limited and their fees are fixed by law. No matter how well you speak French, choose a bilingual notary. Ask friends who have bought property, at the bank where you are considering taking out a mortgage, or contact the Chambre des Notaires de Paris at 12 avenue Victoria, Paris 75001; tel: 01.44.82.24.00; website: http://www.paris.notaires.fr. Check *Notaires* in the *Yellow Pages*.

Borrowing Money

Many French banks have mortgage plans for foreign buyers, some lending money in whatever currency is required. Mortgages can be at fixed or variable rates and usually run from 15 to 20 years. The amount of down payment varies considerably.

UCB, a division of BNP Paribas specialises in mortgages, with an English-language service (tel: 0800.169.8470; website: http://www.ucb-french-mortgage.com/index.asp). The British Bank Barclays also offers home loans and other personal loans in France (http://www.barclays.fr).

MOVING YOUR BELONGINGS

Anyone with a legal right to live in France and who has lived outside France during the previous year may transfer personal belongings—including personal vehicles—without customs charges. EU citizens do not need to go through customs formalities but must have an inventory of the goods. The rest of this section concerns non-EU nationals.

Non-EU nationals should inquire well in advance of shipping about all requirements and then adhere to them exactly. Non-EU citizens may import household goods duty free within 12 months of taking up residence in France. There must be a complete inventory in French of the goods, including the value of each object; this, along with the certificate mentioned below, must be stamped at the

A Parisian neighbourhood in autumn.

nearest French consulate before departure for France. A sworn statement must declare that the articles have been owned and used by the importer for at least six months. Sometimes sales receipts showing ownership of the item are requested. (These are also helpful in case of burglary, as insurance companies often demand proof of value.) The items must be for personal use and may not be sold within a year.

The application form from the Office des Migrations Internationales (OMI) must be completed, translated into French by a *traducteur assermenté* and certified by the nearest French consulate. Prior to departure, non-EU citizens must also obtain at their nearest French consulate a stamped *Certificat de Changement de Domicile* (Certificate of Residence Change), which gives the date of change of residence.

In addition to checking with your French consulate, information in English can be found in Paris from the Centre de Renseignements Douaniers at 84 rue d'Hauteville 75010; tel: 08.25.30.82.63.

Large international movers such as Allied, Mayflower, United Van Lines and many other large moving companies are experts in transatlantic shipping. Inquire of a mover in your area about its international procedures and affiliates in France and how it can help with bureaucratic requirements. International carriers can ship and pack almost any item, including automobiles, and will provide free estimates. Some will split shipments between the cheaper sea carriers and the more expensive and faster air carriers. Prices and services vary, so shop around. Ensure that the service on both sides is door-to-door and ask how long it will take for an expected delivery date. Insurance should cover full value of the belongings. It may take as little as two weeks for your shipment to arrive from overseas, or depending on the ports of exit and entry, it may take up to a month.

To take household possessions out of France, residents must prove that all tax statements have been filed. Upon clearance, a *quitus fiscal* will be issued, allowing the goods to leave France. See *FUSAC* for ads of movers (most of whom generally advertise their international affiliates under *Déménagement* in the *Yellow Pages*).

SETTLING INTO YOUR HOME

Once you've found your apartment, you'll want to get settled. This entails, before all else, insuring your home, changing the electricity and gas to your name from that of the previous tenant, hooking up the telephone, Internet connections and perhaps even cable TV. Each of these actions involves different procedures and must be done immediately, perhaps even before you've actually made the move. Then you can start thinking about making the improvements to the apartment that will make living more comfortable—buying the appliances and cabinets for the kitchen, light fixtures for the ceilings (many apartments don't come with them) and even the little things such as the hooks for the backs of doors.

First, Insure Your Home

Even before you move in, inquire of your relocation agency or real estate broker about insurance agencies. This concerns not only home owners but also tenants with a lease, who are required to have property insurance. The most common policy is *assurance multirisques habitation* (multi-risk insurance), covering theft and water and fire damage, as well as third-party liability. Inquire in advance as to your insurer's requirements to ensure that the locks and shutters conform to specifications. Make sure to get a *constat à l'amiable* from your agent, so you can file a claim within the required three days after damage occurs.

Most insurance agencies also handle health insurance and insurance for children in schools. Some well-known insurance companies are AXA, AGF, MACIF and MAAF. Be sure to shop around, compare prices and services and ask among your friends about their experiences with these companies when they have claims to submit. See *Assurances* in the *Yellow Pages*. For health insurance supplemental policies, see pages 124–126.

Then, Think Electric

France uses 220 volt, 50-hertz electricity. All current in Western Europe is the same and even the plugs are similar, so people coming from these countries do not need special *adaptateurs* (adaptor plugs). British appliances using 240 volts will not need a *transformateur* (transformer), but they will need the continental two-prong plug. Otherwise, if you are thinking of bringing large appliances with you that run on 120 volts, you will no doubt need a transformer as well as the adaptor. Transformers change the voltage, but not the hertz, so both must be appropriate. Some appliances will not function and others such as clock-radios may run too slowly if the hertz are not the same.

Computers and some other electronic devices that are meant to be used internationally generally switch automatically from one current to another. Look at the 'brick' (where the power information is displayed on the cord): if it says 120-240v; 50-60hz, it will switch automatically. Small appliances such as hair dryers also come with dual voltage, often with a small switch to turn to the appropriate setting. For the rest, adaptors and transformers are available at electronic shops, hardware stores and department stores.

Electricity is expensive in France and people are used to doing more with less. This accounts for the *minuterie* in the halls of apartment buildings—the button people press for the hall lights to come on, which only stay lit for a few minutes before switching off automatically. Nor do gas stoves waste gas by keeping pilot lights on all the time; instead people usually light the burner or oven each time it is to be used. These may be inconveniences at first for North Americans, but you'll quickly get used to it.

Also, the amount of electricity that comes into your apartment may not allow you to use a clothes washer and dishwasher at the same time. When you contact EDF/GDF (see below) for the initial contract, discuss the level of electricity you require and the price for each option.

Note that lamps brought from non-European countries usually needonly an adaptor and a French light bulb. Light bulbs are of three types: the French standard circular-bottomed bulb with two prongs that is turned and locked into place, a screw type (*ampoule à vis*), and the older but still-used bayonet with two pins (*ampoule à baïonnette*). The new energy-efficient bulbs are increasingly coming into use, as older styles will ultimately be phased out.

EDF/GDF

Contact EDF/GDF (Electricité de France/Gaz de France) to inquire as to the procedure for opening your electric and gas account (tel: 01.42.23.30.10; website: http://www.edf. fr). First check the website under 'Foreign Residents', then go to the EDF/GDF office in your *arrondissement* with a copy of your lease. Also bring your chequebook and *RIB* (*relevé d'identité bancaire*), which is the official identification of your bank account. (For information on the *RIB*, see page 138.) EDF will have the meter read so that you pay only for usage after you move in.

The *factures* (bills) for electricity and gas are sent every two months. They are based on the previous year's usage; meters are read only a couple of times a year. Thus, if your current usage is less than before, an adjustment will be made on a future bill. You can pay your bill by cheque if you wish, but the most common method of paying utility bills is to have the amount deducted directly from your bank account (*prélèvement bancaire*), having provided EDF/GDF with a copy of your *RIB*. Do this at the time you open your account. You receive your bills well in advance of the deduction date, giving you time to dispute the amount if needed.

France Télécom

Although it's no longer required to have France Télécom as your telephone provider, it is still the major provider in France. Along with newer providers, it now offers high-speed Internet and television programming among its options (English-speaking tel: 08.00.36.47.75; customer service tel: 1014; tech support tel: 1013). To meet the growing competition, prices are coming down and services are going up: inquire about all services and costs before subscribing and check out some of the other providers *(see pages 145–148)*.

There is at least one commercial France Télécom office in each district that handles telephone matters for that area, including bill payment, sales and rental of equipment and subscription to new services. Telephones must be registered in the leaseholder's name. To obtain service, telephones, and telephone books, bring identification and proof of domicile. Call customer service for information and installation of telephones.

At the Télécom office you may inquire about *signal d'appel* (call waiting), *conversation à trois* (conference calling), *transfert d'appel* (call forwarding), *Top Message*, a free voice mail service, as well as *liste rouge* (unlisted number).

Telephone bills are sent bimonthly and are usually deducted automatically from your French current account *(compte courant)*. An itemised bill *(facture détaillée)* will be sent to you in advance of the date the amount is deducted from your account, giving you time to dispute the bill, if needed. Otherwise, if bills are not paid on time, it is routine for the service to be cut off and a 10 per cent fine levied for reinstatement.

Les *annuaires téléphoniques* (telephone books) are usually distributed in May. They are left in the entrance hall of apartment buildings for the tenants to take. *Les Pages Blanches* (*White Pages*) are all listing in alphabetical order, while *Les Pages Jaunes* (*Yellow Pages*) contain commercial listings and display advertising by category, and within each category, by *arrondissement*.

Internet Hookup and Cable Television

To hook up to the Internet, no matter who the provider is, you will need either a telephone or a cable connection. For a telephone connection, ask France Télécom when ordering your telephone service, or with the provider you choose. (See page 149.) For a cable connection, contact Numericable, which is also the cable television company in Paris (tel: 3990; website: http://offres.numericable.fr/home.php).

Appliances

Most kitchens come empty except for the sink, so you will have to think about appliances and cabinets. If you are thinking of bringing large appliances from your country, make sure they fit the rooms—kitchens tend to be smaller than what you might be used to. Also, if your appliances are brands not common in Europe, finding parts and service when they break down may be difficult. In general, it may be more economical to purchase appliances in Paris.

Most washing machines in France heat the water internally, using only a cold water tap, so if the washer you import depends on an external hot water tap, it may wash clothes only in cold water. In addition, some apartments are not vented for tumble dryers, but convection dryers are almost as efficient.

If you have your own washing machine (as well as a dishwasher), you must remember that the water in Paris is extremely 'hard'. This means that minerals (*calcaire*) will build up in the pipes. Products such as Calgonite can prevent this build-up in washing machines and are sold next to detergents; you should put in one pellet for each load. For dishwashers, special salts (*sel*) must be inserted into the machine, as well as a rinsing (*rinçage*) product to avoid streaks on glasses. (A light comes on to inform you when they need to be replenished.)

Major department stores such as BHV (see page 106) sell appliances, as do the big supermarkets or *hypermarchés*. Occasionally, a shop will be slightly flexible in its prices when several large, expensive items are purchased, or if you are a known customer. Ask about warranties on new products and about *service après-vente/dépannage à domicile* (after sales service/repair), for some shops require 'smaller' items—even something as large as a microwave oven—to be brought back to the store, charging extra for a home call. It is best to get warranties on products and to use licensed repairmen.

Large appliances are delivered and installed. Make sure everything works before the installer leaves; the driver will take back damaged goods. Some stores claim

no responsibility for repairs or exchange if damage is discovered after the delivery person has left, although this is slowly changing as France begins to understand the concept of 'customer service'. (In this regard, inspect, too, all delivered furniture before the driver leaves.) See *Electroménager* in the *Yellow Pages* and ads in *FUSAC* for used appliances.

Darty is a major national chain of stores selling appliances and electronics and is known for its excellent *service après-vente*. There are eight stores in Paris alone, so it's best to access its website (see below) or the telephone book for the store closest to you.

BHV has a discount appliance outlet at 119 boulevard Paul-Vaillant-Couturier, 94200 Ivry-sur-Seine; tel: 01.49.60.44. 10; website:http://www.bhv.fr. Delivers to Paris.

Plugs

- Electric plug: Round with two prongs underneath and a hole centred above, which accepts the ground wire pin (*prise de terre*) that protrudes from the wall outlet. Only a few old, uncoverted outlets don't have the pin. All your large appliances should be grounded. Adaptors can be found in hardware stores, at BHV and at Leroy Merlin.
- Telephone plug: Long and narrow, with an extended one-piece insert. Plugs into which the international RJ11 can be inserted can be obtained at France Télécom shops, FNAC, electronic shops and hardware stores.

Cabinets and Equipment

Department stores such as BHV carry all equipment for your apartment, including kitchen and bathroom fittings.

- IKEA, the extensive international chain, has six stores in the Paris surrounds, with an enormous selection of home items, including kitchen and bathroom cabinets. Website: http://www.ikea.com
- Habitat has seven stores in Paris selling furniture and kitchen and bathroom items. Website: http://www.habitat.net/.

For the Bricoleur

Drogueries or hardware stores in every neighourhood sell home improvement and hardware items, but two centrally located stores offer everything the *bricoleur* (DIY enthusiast) might ever need. Both have warrens of aisles filled with stacks of merchandise and tools, and their staff is generally helpful.

- BHV (main store); 14 rue du Temple, 75004; website: http://www.bhv.fr. The entrance is on rue de Rivoli, across from the Hôtel de Ville.
- Leroy Merlin; 52 rue Rambuteau, 75002; tel: 01.44.54.66.66; website: http://www.leroymerlin.fr

Self-Storage

If your apartment is smaller than you thought it would be and it cannot hold all your household items, consider renting a self-storage locker. Units, clean and dry, come in various sizes. The renter keeps the key and has sole access to the locker. Check to see the hours of access.

■ Une Pièce en Plus/Access Self Stockage; websbite:http://www.unepieceenplus.com. Offers some 20 self-storage locations—see the website or telephone book.

A CHILD'S WORLD

Getting your children set for a long stay in Paris should not be difficult. Anything you can find at home for your child can be found here. As in most large cities, disposable diapers, baby bottles and pureed foods are found at supermarkets. Inoculations required are similar to those in other countries and there are many English-speaking pharmacists and pediatricians. Childhood diseases in Paris are the same as anywhere else, so be prepared for the usual colds and sore throats, especially when children go to school. See *pages 121–122* for health-related issues and vaccinations.

French parents expect their children to be well behaved, and they are. The French view of childhood may not be as relaxed as in other countries, but there are countless

opportunities for scheduled activities, structured events and sports. Museums have special educational programmes for children, and puppet theatres and circuses schedule their entertainment for when children are out of school. Activities *hors scolaires* (extra-curricular) are encouraged and often arranged in both public schools and international bilingual schools. Most public libraries have children's books, records and videos; several are devoted entirely to children. Playgrounds and sporting facilities are found in every *arrondissement*. So all told, a child's experience in Paris, although highly structured, should be rewarding and pleasant.

Contacts and Resources

Message (http//www.messageparis.org) is an English-speaking group for families with young children, as well as expectant and new mothers. Message organises meetings, events, parenthood classes, baby and toddler groups and a working mother's group. Message publishes *The ABCs of Parenting in Paris*, which is an extensive guide to family living in Paris. As Message is a volunteer organisation, contacts change and it's best to access the website to find the most current information.

The *mairie* has detailed information about all aspects of schooling in Paris. Ask for *Tout Petit à Paris*, a guide to everything you need to know concerning small children in Paris and *Élève à Paris*, which details education from birth to schooling.

Day Care

The French believe in early socialisation for their children. It is widely held that children who have attended day care perform better in their early school years than children who have not, so a high percentage of babies and toddlers are sent to day care.

Some 520 public *crèches* (day-care centres) operate within Paris. *Crèches* are subsidised, with fees based on income and need. *Crèches* are extremely over-enrolled, and many expectant mothers register their child even before birth. Start thinking about this even before your baby is born. Your *mairie* should have a list of the municipal *crèches* in the *arrondissement* and advice on how to enroll a child.

Children are dropped off at the *crèche* between 8:00 am and 10:00 am and picked up between 4:00 pm and 6:00 pm. A *crèche parentale* is run on the same principle, but parents volunteer in various capacities, so the fees are slightly lower.

An *halte garderie* is flexible in its hours. If there is a place available, a parent may deposit a child for a few hours. The system is designed for mothers who need to schedule appointments or go shopping for a few hours without the child. Children are not registered in advance and a place is not guaranteed on any given day. An *halte garderie privée* is more like a *crèche* in that the child is registered and comes on a regular basis, but the hours are flexible. Unfortunately, as with the *crèches*, there are few spaces available.

French Educational System

The French public school system is demanding and rigorous. For detailed information on the educational system, access the city's website at http://www.paris.fr and click on the 'Guide for Foreign Residents' tab. (For university education, see pages 173–184.)

Non-compulsory

- Age 2: *jardins d'enfants* (pre-nursery schools)
- Ages 3-6: *écoles maternelles* (nursery schools).

Compulsory Elementary Education

From the ages 6-16: each student has a *carnet du liaison*, a permanent file with grades and teachers' comments entered year after year.

- *École primaire* (can be coeducational or not). Progresses from preparatory to elementary to intermediate levels. Usually finishes around age 10.
- *Premier cycle* is the *collège* (which should not be confused with the English 'college'). Here, education begins according to each child's aptitude and interests.

- *Deuxième cycle* is the *lycée*, which usually starts around age 15 and lasts until the student graduates at about 18 years of age.
- From ages 15–17, preparation for the *baccalauréat* (*bac*). The *bac*, equivalent to and as stringent as the British 'A' levels, is obligatory for university entrance.

Holidays and Days Off

There is a major school break (*les vacances d'été*) of more than two months each summer and there are several shorter but substantial holidays throughout the year: February, November, Christmas and Easter. Public schools are often closed on Wednesdays (which is why you see so many grandparents with children on Wednesdays). Some schools are thus open on Saturday mornings.

As such, many cultural attractions and entertainment, including museums and the much-loved puppet shows and circuses, have special Wednesday and Saturday programmes. In addition, the *mairie* operates more than 500 Centres des Loisirs—activity centres attached to the public schools, which are open on Wednesdays and during short school breaks.

Foreign Children in Schools

Selecting a child's school will, of course, be based on many factors besides a school's location or reputation. The age, character and language ability of the child should be considered, as well as the expected length of stay in Paris and planned return to a school or university at home. A few parents put their children into French schools immediately. Some parents who are based abroad for the long term prefer private, bilingual schools throughout the child's educational career. Others start their children in the bilingual schools, and after a period of adjustment and language learning, move them into the public or private French schools. Some people who transfer to several countries over the years prefer international schools, such as Marymount, where the curriculum tends to be standard and grade levels are transferable from country to country.

Foreign children are accepted into French public schools if their French is adequate to progress within the instructional programme. Children in primary schools may enter a conversion programme to learn French (*classe de CLIN*), after which they are placed in the regular system. Schools are crowded and applications should be made in the spring before the fall term; places may not be available, especially in the *maternelle*.

To enroll, bring your child's birth certificate, vaccination certificate (including smallpox, BCG and tetanus), proof of domicile and school records from previous schools. Children must also be insured when they enroll in a school, so if you are asked, show proof of insurance. (See pages 123–126 for insurance companies.) Although schools are free, there are small charges for textbooks, supplies and meals.

Bilingual Schools

There is a wide selection of international, bilingual or English-language, elementary and high schools in and around Paris. The international curriculum is stringent, for acceptance into the best European universities is highly competitive. The private schools may be expensive and tuition varies greatly. In general though, costs are pretty much in line with other international schools. Transportation to schools in the suburbs can often be arranged at extra cost, although this may depend on how far into Paris the school buses go. Some important schools are in the suburbs, such as St-Germain-en-Laye. This list is not exhaustive, so check with your embassy.

Bilingual Nursery/Lower Schools and Play Groups

- 7e: Montessori Schools
  65 quai d'Orsay; tel: 01.45.55.13.27; fax: 01.45.51.25.12; website: http://www.Montessori-paris.org. For children from three to six. For other addresses in Paris, access the website.
- 7e: Lennen Bilingual School has three locations: 65 quai d'Orsay; tel: 01.47.05.66.55; the kindergarten at 145 rue Saint-Dominique; tel: 01.53.59.90.73; and the primary

There are international schools and curricula in Paris to fit your children's needs; soon enough, they should be as at ease as these French students.

school at 168 rue de Grenelle; tel: 01.44.42.99.00; website:http://www.lennenbilingual.com. An international school that offers bilingual cirriculum for students up to 11 years old.

- 15e: First Steps; rue Emile Duclaux; tel: 01.42.19.02.14; website:http://www.firststepsParis.com. For children from two to five years of age.
- 16e: United Nations Nursery School; 40 rue Pierre-Guérin; tel: 01.45.27.20.24; fax: 01.42.88.71.46; website: http://www.unns.net. Private school with an international population of students from two to six years old.
- 17e: La Petite École Bilingue; 8 place de la Porte de Champerret; tel: 01.43.80.25.34; fax: 01.43.80.37.40; website: http://petiteecolebilingue.free.fr.
  For children from preschool to fifth grade, offers education in French/ English and French/ Russian.

Bilingual Elementary/High Schools
- 7e: Collège-Lycée International de Paris Honoré de Balzac; 118 boulevard Bessières; tel: 01.53.11.12.13; website: http://lyc-balzac.scola.ac-paris.fr/
  Public French school that offers free bilingual education, adapted to the needs of international students.
- 15e: École Active Bilingue Jeannine-Manuel; 70 rue du Théâtre; tel: 01.44. 37.00.80; website: http://www.eabjm.com. Preparations for the American SAT, French or International Baccalaureate, with most substantive courses taught in English. Preschool through high school.
- 16e: Institut de la Tour; 86 rue de la Tour; tel: 01.45.04.73.35; website:http://www.institutdela tour.com. Catholic high school with a section for English speakers. Students prepare for the bac.
- 16e: International School of Paris; 6 rue Beethoven; tel: 01.42.24.09.54; fax: 01.45.27.15.93; website:http://www.isparis.edu. From preschool through high school, US and International Baccalaureate programmes. French language instruction. Separate locations for lower, middle and upper schools, all in the 16e.

- 17ᵉ: École Active Bilingue; 117 boulevard Malesherbes; tel: 01.45.63.62.22; website:http://www.eab.fr. Bilingual education for ages three to eighteen. Helps students make the transition to the French system, leading to the bacccalaureat, the American SAT and British 'A' levels.

- American School of Paris; 41 rue Pasteur, 92210 Saint-Cloud; tel: 01.41.12.82.82; website:http://www.asparis. org. Preschool through high school. American curriculum and the baccalaureate. In operation since 1946, this school has a good mix of nationalities, of which about 60 per cent is American.

- British School of Paris: Senior school is at 38 quai de l'Ecluse, 78290 Croissy-sur-Seine; tel: 01.34.80.45.96; fax: 01.39.76. 12.69; website:http://www.britishschool.fr.
  Junior school is at Chemin du Mur-du-Parc, 78380 Bougival; tel: 01.39.69.78.21; fax: 01.30.82.47.49. British curriculum, with an emphasis on French, from preschool through high school; about 70 per cent of the students are British. Students prepare for the 'A' levels. French classes. Transportation available.

- Lycée International; rue du Fer-à-Cheval, BP 230, 78100 St-Germain-en-Laye Cedex; tel: 01.34.51.62.64; fax: 01.34.51.39.36 (British section); tel: 01.34.51.74.85; fax: 01.30.87.00.49 (American section). http://www. lycee-international.com. Public school, with fee-paying international sections. From preschool through high school; British, American and French curricula are offered. Foreign students take special classes, then a fully bilingual curriculum.

- Sections Internationales de Sèvres; rue Lecoq 92310 Sèvres; tel: 01.72.77.70.45; website: http://sis-sevres.net. French public schools, with fee-paying international sections. Bilingual education with courses in English or German; special courses for non-French speakers. Preparation for the bac.

- Marymount School; 72 boulevard de la Saussaye, 92200 Neuilly-sur-Seine; tel: 01.46.24.10.51; fax: 01.46.24.93.26; website:http://www.marymount.fr. Independent Catholic coed school from preschool through eighth grade, for children of any religion. American curriculum and a

French language programme. About 50 per cent native English speakers.

Test Preparation

For information on the Kaplan Test Preparation centre, which will help your child prepare for the SAT or other exams, *see page 180*. (website: http://www.kaptest.fr)

After-School Activities

Most of the international schools arrange some after-school activities. In addition, active English-language scouting and guides troops are open to children of all ages and nationalities. Because troop leaders change, the most reliable information is usually available at your particular embassy and the international schools. For city-sponsored after-school activities, ask at the *mairie* for *Guide des Loisirs*. *Le Guide du Sport à Paris* is a comprehensive guide to all sports activities and venues in the city. And of course, both English-language and French bookshops sell guides of activities for children when they're not in school.

ADAC (Association pour le Developpement et l'Animation Culturelle), the public organisation for continuing education organisation, offers a vast variety of courses for children at centres throughout Paris. ADAC also operates *ludothèques* (games centres), which offer play-related learning activities, and games and toys to play with and to borrow. A nature-oriented *bibliothèque* (library)/ *ludothèque* can be found in the Bois de Vincennes at the Pavillon Nature in the Parc Floral (tel: 01.43.28.47.73). For information on *ludothèques*, call the Association des Ludothèques Françaises at 7 impasse Chartière, Paris 75005; tel: 01.43.26.84.62. Or ask at your *mairie*, or access the website (http://www.paris.fr).

Three *centres d'animation* (activity centres) offer educational, sporting and cultural, activities and outings to young people from 15–25 after school on Wednesdays, Saturdays and during school vacations. See the municipal sports guide for information, or the booklet *Centres d'Animation* at the *mairie*.

Parc de la Villette

Once children have discovered the Parc de la Villette, they may not want to go anywhere else (tel: 01.40.03.75.75; website: http://www.villette.com).

Encompassing about 55 hectares at the northeastern edge of the city, this urban educational park was constructed in 1979 on the site of the city's former slaughterhouse. There are theme gardens and activity parks, a lighted promenade, playgrounds, bicycle paths, pony rides, day-care centres, restaurants, entertainment centres and a spectacular high-tech, interactive museum. Films, concerts, a planetarium, undersea exhibits, etc. are all targeted at children, from preschoolers onwards. The Paris Tourist Office should have brochures describing La Villette and its schedule of events.

The Cité des Sciences et de l'Industrie at 30, avenue Corentin-Cariou, 75019 (tel: 01.40.05.80.00; website:http://www.cite-sciences.fr) is the ultravmodern, hands-on science museum. (It is closed on Mondays, 1 May and 25 December.) The Géode is an enormous hemispheric screen showing documentaries to viewers seated in the centre (for reservations, tel: 08.92.68.45.40; website:http://www.lageode.fr).

Educational Entertainment

In addition to museum programmes, educational entertainment can be found throughout the city. *Pariscope* and *L'Officiel des Spectacles*, the weekly events magazines, have listings for children's activities, as do the major newspapers. Access the websites below, which offer up-to-date details on children's and family activities.

- http://www.jeunes.fr
- http://www.lamuse.net
- http://www.commeundimanche.com
- 3e: Musée de la Poupée
  Impasse Berthaud; tel: 01.42.72.73.11.
  http://www.museedelapoupee.com
  Doll museum exhibiting some 500 French dolls. Across the street from the Pompidou Museum, this makes an interesting outing for all members of the family. Closed on Monday.

- 4e: Musée de la Magie; 11 rue Saint-Paul; tel: 01.42.72.13.26; http://www.museedelamagie.com. Interactive magic museum, optical illusions and magic shows.
- 5e: Musée National d'Histoire Naturelle
  57 rue Cuvier; tel: 01.40.79.30.00;
  website:http://www.mnhn.fr.
  Located in the Jardin des Plantes, with a zoo, hothouses and a playground. Imaginative exhibits on nature and natural history.
- 5e: Institut Océanographique; 195 rue Saint-Jacques; tel: 01.44.32.10.70; website: http://www.oceano.org.
  An aquarium. Closed on Mondays.
- 8e: Palais de la Découverte; avenue Franklin-D-Roosevelt; tel: 01.56.43.20.20; website:http://www.palais-decouverte.fr.
  Interesting exhibitions and a plantetarium.
- 12e: Aquarium Tropical; 293 avenue Daumesnil;
  tel: 01.44.74.84.80;
  website:http://: www.aquarium-portedoree.fr.
  Exotic fish and crocodiles. Closed on Tuesdays.

Parks, Playgrounds and Zoos

Paris has more than 400 parks and gardens. Both the Bois de Boulogne to the west and Bois de Vincennes to the east have extensive areas of interest for children. Almost all the parks have varied amusements for children, including playgrounds, go-karts, pony rides or carousels. Most parks are open during daylight hours only. A few of the better-equipped and interesting parks are: Jardin du Luxembourg, Parc des Buttes-Chaumont, Parc André Citroën, Parc Montsouris and Jardin Atlantique.

Some 388 *aires de jeux* (playgrounds) can be found throughout the city; most have large sand pits where the sand is changed frequently enough to be kept clean. Some small squares have carousels. For playgrounds with special attractions, see *Le Guide de la Rentrée*.

Theatres, Marionnettes and Circuses

Guignols/marionnettes (puppet shows) are among the most popular entertainment for younger children, although the shows may be difficult to understand for non-French speakers. Circuses, which are extremely popular, come and go according to the season; several come just around Christmas, and the famous, international Cirque du Soleil is an annual visitor. Look for Cirque de Paris, Cirque d'Hiver Bouglione and Cirque Alexis Grüss, a circus family that has been entertaining children for more than 100 years. Check the weekly events guides for current listings.

- Métamorphosis: Spectacle Magie de Paris. Located on a barge anchored on the banks of the Seine. In winter it's in the 6e, across from 7 quai Malaquais; in summer it's docked at 55 quai de la Tournelle (tel: 01.43.54.08.08). Website: http://www.metamorphosis-spectacle.fr Sunday brunch and weekday dinners on deck, then an entertaining, participatory magic show below deck.

Theme Parks
Theme parks outside Paris are good for weekend excursions, and they are generally easy to reach by car or public transportation. There are a variety of themes to choose from, from the Parc Astérix (named for the beloved comic character) to La Mer de Sable, an American Wild West extravaganza. Disneyland Paris is the most famous, but there are other interesting ones, such as France Miniature, which presents a miniature bas-relief of the historical landmarks and regions of France. For the extensive swimming complex Aquaboulevard, see Chapter Seven.

- http://www.parcasterix.fr
- http://www.merdesable.fr
- http://www.disneylandparis.com
- http://www.franceminiature.com
- http://www.aquaboulevard.com
- http://www.jardindacclimatation.fr
- http://www.sealife.fr

Toys
Hypermarchés and some of the large supermarket chains sell *jouets* (toys) and *jeux* (games) at decent prices, and department stores usually have a good selection of the inter-

nationally popular ones tailored to the French market. Shop around, for similar toys can vary in price from store to store. Think of the museum shops, for they often sell interesting, educational materials for children. See *Jouets et jeux* in the *Yellow Pages*. For children's clothes, see Chapter Seven.

- FNAC Eveil et Jeux (http://www.eveiletjeux.com) has six addresses in Paris, including an outlet on the 7th floor of the department store Printemps. Toys, videos and activities are available for children under 12 years of age. Programs for kids.
- 1er: EOL, 3 rue du Louvre, 75001; tel: 01.43.54.01.43; website: http://www.eol-model.fr. Well-stocked store devoted to model-making of all sorts, including figurines, cars, airplanes and boats.
- 6e: Imaginarium; 7 rue de Brea; tel: 01.43.26.18.59; website:http://www.imaginarium.fr. Chain of lively, imaginative shops for children's toys.
- 8e: Au Nain Bleu; 5 boulevard Malesherbes; tel: 01.42.65.20.00; website: http://www.aunainbleu.com.An elegant century-old toy shop that nonetheless carries the most modern of toys.
- 12e: Apache; 84 rue du Faubourg Saint-Antoine; tel: 01.53.46.60.10; website:http://www.apache.fr. Chain of modern stores, with furniture, toys, some clothing, Internet access and videos. Programs for kids.
- 15e: 1.2.3.famille; 21 rue Desaix; tel: 01.43.06.06.20; website:http://www.123famille.com. An excellent selection of educational toys and games of all sorts for children up to 15 years of age. Also at 204 boulevard Pereire, 75017; tel: 01.44.09.78.20

Eating Out With Children

Well-behaved children are welcome in just about any eating establishment. If they're bored in restaurants of haute cuisine, please them with the varied menus at the local bistros and *brasseries*, the inexpensive Asian restaurants that are in every *arrondissement*, or the American-style restaurants that offer hamburgers, ribs and fries. (*FUSAC*, the English-language advertising supplement, generally carries advertisements for the latter.) Not all restaurants, however, have high chairs (*chaises hautes*). Museum cafés and other tourist venues are generally child-friendly, as well.

Many casual restaurants have children's menus, including the citywide chains of Chez Clément and the ever-popular Hippopotamus. Try the sandwich chains Pomme de Pain and Toastissimo, Léon de Bruxelles for mussels (to be eaten with the fingers!) and excellent fried potatoes, and La Criée for fish. Some restaurants offer crayons to keep children occupied. The pizza chains offer home delivery for neighbouring areas, and delivery and takeaway are available from restaurants, ranging from sushi to Indian cuisine. And of course, wherever you go, there's always McDonald's.

TO YOUR GOOD HEALTH!
General Conditions
Medical and sanitary facilities in France often rate among the highest in the world, and the city itself is kept remarkably clean.

Water in Paris has been safe to drink (although the taste varies) since the city spent 12 million francs on water purification systems well more than a century ago. The water, however, has a high mineral content of *calcaire* (calcium and chalk), which is not unhealthy, but many Parisians tend to drink bottled water such as Vittel, Volvic or Evian, or slightly fizzy water such as Badoit or any of the inexpensive brands found in groceries. Currently the Brita water filter is popular. The pitcher and filters are widely available, with one replacement filter designed for water rich in *calcaire*.

Before You Leave Home
While packing, be sure to include all important medications in your carry-on case, as checked luggage occasionally goes astray. If medication includes syringes or other items that might be questioned, carry with you some proof of their need. To avoid needless questions, make sure that all medicines *sur ordonnance* (by prescription) are in their

original, labelled containers. But pay attention to new and changing regulations concerning liquids and creams in your hand baggage: how much you may carry and how they must be packaged.

Bring enough medication to tide you over until you have found a doctor and pharmacy of your own, and until you can determine which medications require prescriptions and which do not. Ask your physician to give you copies of records concerning ongoing treatments and to write new prescriptions using both the trade and generic name of the medication.

Many of the pharmacies listed in this chapter can translate the prescription into the French equivalent. Bring a copy of your eyeglass prescription and an extra pair of glasses or contact lenses.

For the Children

Obtain a copy of your children's vaccination and health records and make sure all inoculations are current. For a child to enter a *crèche* or school, DPT and polio vaccinations are required, as is a tuberculosis vaccination through the BCG combination; vaccinations for *rougeole* (measles), *rubéole* (German measles), *oreillons* (mumps) and Hepatitis B are recommended but optional. See 'Vaccination Centres' on page 123.

Check with your pediatrician to determine what you should have with you before you find a pediatrician in Paris. If your child has a health emergency before you are set up with a local doctor, go to a hospital (listed on page 127 by specialty) or call SOS Pédiatrie for an urgent house call by a pediatrician (tel: 01.43.94.35.01). Lastly, if you prefer to read a thermometer in Fahrenheit rather than centigrade, you might think about bringing one with you.

Once you are enrolled in the French health plan, your child will be issued a *carnet de santé*, which records all major health information, including vaccinations. The *carnet* is issued by the *mairie* of your *arrondissement* and is a permanent record of a child's health-related events from birth to age 16.

Health Resources

Finding English-speaking doctors in Paris can begin before departure. The International Association for Medical Assistance to Travellers (IAMAT) (http://www.iamat.org), a non-profit association, provides a list of approved English-speaking doctors, who have agreed on a preset fee. Membership for IAMAT is free, but donations are encouraged. IAMAT also has up-to-date information on health conditions worldwide.

Once in Paris, you should be able to find physicians through friends and colleagues. Your embassy should also be able to provide you with a list of English-speaking doctors and dentists.

All people insured under the French system must register with a *médecin traitant* or primary physician. Your *généraliste* (general doctor) is the one who will refer you to *spécialistes* (specialists) as needed in order for the costs to be reimbursed under French insurance. For up-to-date information and health-related news, you can also access the website of the Ministry of Health (http://www.sante.gouv.fr).

Vaccination Centres

If you will be travelling to countries where vaccinations are necessary for typhoid, yellow fever, malaria, etc., you can go to the Centre de Vaccinations Internationales d'Air France, at the Air France Terminal at Invalides (tel: 08.92.68.63.64). It's closed Sunday and holidays. Be prepared to wait.

For information on the city's vaccination centres, see *Centre de Vaccinations* in the phone book. You may also access the city's website at http://www.paris.fr; click on *solidarités*, then *santé* and you should see a section listing all the vaccination centres in Paris.

Insurance

Administered by the Caisse Primaire d'Assurance Maladie (CPAM), the English public health care system is part of the Sécurité Sociale. (For information in English, access http://www.urssaf.fr.) French health care is among the best in the world: doctors are well trained (some make house calls) and procedures are the most modern. The entire working community—employers, employees and the self-employed—contributes to this state-funded insurance plan. Anyone who has a *carte de séjour*—employed or not—is eligible for coverage. For information in French, access the l'Assurance Maladie website (www.ameli.fr).

Physicians and private clinics are either *conventionnés*, whereby they abide by the prices set by the Sécurité Sociale, or *non-conventionnés*, whereby they set their own prices. In the case of the latter, only some of the costs may be covered if it is determined that the prices for the services performed were not competitive. If a service is *non agréé*, the particular treatment is not covered; *agréé* means the services are covered.

People choose their own *médecin traitant*, usually a *généraliste*, who authorises visits to *spécialistes* when needed. The patient pays for treatment and medicines and is reimbursed up to only about 70 per cent. *Spécialistes* charge more than *généralistes*, and *honoraires libres* (doctors who set their own fees) are allowed to vary their prices.

When you are enrolled in the French health system, you will be issued a *carte vitale* containing your permanent health plan number and other information. You can check your information at any CPAM office by inserting your card into the machine, usually by the door.

Supplemental Insurance Companies

Remember that French insurance pays only a portion of your medical costs. Private insurance companies sell *mutuelles*—supplemental policies that cover costs otherwise not reimbursed. Shop around, for some *mutuelles* cover more costs than others and ask about dental and eyeglass coverage. Some employers offer *mutuelles* as part of their benefit plan. See *Mutuelles d'assurances* in the *Yellow Pages*. Students might inquire about health systems as below:

- La Mutuelle des Etudiants; tel: 08.25.00.06.01; website:http://www.lmde.com
- La Societé des Etudiants de la Région Parisienne; tel: 01.56.54.36.34; website:http://www.smerep.fr

Coverage for Foreigners

All EU nationals (and some others within Europe) are entitled to receive health services throughout the EU. Obtain the European National Health Insurance Card (which replaces the old E111). For information, check the websites of the EU (http://www.europa.eu) or the French health system (http://www.sante.gouv.fr). For long stays, talk with the local French health office about registering in France. Non-hospital expenditures in Paris are reimbursed up to about 75 per cent (with documentation and receipts), so it is important to check on supplemental insurance.

If your company is sending you to Paris, the personnel department should be knowledgeable about health insurance coverage for employees abroad. Check how you will be covered and the extent of the coverage. If you will be working for a French company, you will have the documents that allow access to the French system. Once in the system, you will have a *numéro d'immatriculation*, an identification number to be used in all health care situations.

Americans on short stays should ask their insurance carriers about coverage abroad and how to file a claim from abroad. Check about coverage for long-term supplies of medications. Older Americans should be aware that Medicare does not honour claims abroad and should investigate supplemental policies that offer coverage when travelling for limited amounts of time. Canadians are covered by the national health plan only to the amount that similar services are covered at home, so most buy additional insurance. Provincial Ministry of Health Offices and travel agents have information.

Entering the French system may take time, so plan to keep your own insurance until you are registered. If that is impossible, try one of the private international insurance companies that offer policies for people living outside their home countries. They are all costly and their coverage may not offer what you need for the long term. But most offer several different insurance options, and all would be helpful for interim coverage.

Do consider the Association of Americans Resident Overseas (AARO), an important organisation in Paris that represents the rights of Americans living overseas. (tel: 01.47.20.24.15; website:http://www.aaro.org). It is open to anyone and offers several comprehensive health plans for its members. Prices are comparable to other private health plans.

- ASA, Inc.; 1300 North McClintock Drive, Tempe AZ 85226; tel: (1-840) 753-1333; website:http://www. worldhealthinsurance.net
- BUPA International; 15-19 Bloomsbury Way, London WC12BA, England; tel: (44-0) 1273-208-181; website:http:// www.bupa-intl.com
- International Medical Group: 2960 N. Meridian Street, Indianapolis IN 46208; tel: (1-317) 655-4500; website: http://www.imglobal.com).
- AXA PPP International; Phillips House, Crescent Road, Tunbridge Wells, Kent, TN12PL England; tel: (44) 207-198-1304; website:http://www.axappphealthcare.co.uk
- Wallach and Company; 107 West Federal Street, PO Box 480, Middleburg VA 22117; US tel: (1-800) 237-6615; (1-800) 540-687-3166; website:http://www.wallach.com

Hospitals

For non-life threatening emergency care, go to the hospital nearest you. After treatment, you might be referred or transferred to another hospital that specialises in the treatment you require. Two major English-speaking hospitals are headquartered in nearby suburbs and both are easily reached by public transportation or taxi.

- American Hospital of Paris; 63 boulevard Victor-Hugo, 92202 Neuilly-sur-Seine; tel: 01.46.41.25.25; website:http://www.american-hospital.org. Full-service private hospital with English-speaking personnel, accredited in the United States. Also offers dental services. Expensive but accepts Blue Cross insurance for inpatient services and provides forms for outpatient reimbursement of insurance. Credit cards accepted in the emergency ward. *Agréé* but *non-conventionné*.

- Franco-Britannique Hospital (Hertford British); 3 rue Barbès, 92300 Levallois-Perret; tel: 01.46.39.22.22; and 4, rue Kleber; tel: 01.47.59.59.59 (check website for specialties at each address: http://www.ihfb.org).

Most public hospitals have *urgences* (emergency rooms). See *Hôpitaux* in the *Yellow Pages* and *Hôpital* in the *Pages Blanches*. The ones below are centrally located, but make sure you know the hospital nearest you. Generally, your doctor will recommend the most appropriate hospital.
- 4e: Hôpital Hôtel Dieu; 1 place du Parvis-Notre-Dame; tel: 01.42.34.82.34. Important public hospital, centrally located on Ile-de-la-Cité.
- 10e: Hôpital Fernand Widal; 200 rue du Faubourg-Saint-Denis; tel: 01.40.05.45.45. Poison centre.
- 13e: Hôpital de la Pitié-Salpêtrière; 47 boulevard de l'Hôpital, 75013; tel: 01.42.16.00.00. Large, comprehensive hospital complex.
- 14e: Hôpital Broussais; 96 rue Didot; tel: 10.43.95.95.95. Major cardiac centre.

- 15ᵉ: Hôpital Européen Georges Pompidou; 20 rue Leblanc; tel: 01.56.09.20.00. The newest and thus most modern of the hospital complexes in Paris.
- 15ᵉ: Hôpital Necker; 149 rue de Sèvres; tel: 01.44.49.40.00. Children's services and burn centre. Ear, nose and throat services.
- 17ᵉ: Hôpital Marmottan; 10 rue Armaillé; tel: 01.45.74. 00.04. Drug crisis centre.

Emergencies

In a dire health emergency, call SAMU (tel: 15) or the *pompiers* (fire department) (tel: 18), rather than going on your own to a hospital. The caller's number is automatically registered, and response is swift and effective. Ambulances are routed to the correct hospital by trained personnel. The *pompiers* have the equipment to enter an apartment when the occupant is unable to open the door. For other emergency numbers—including 24-hour doctors who make house calls—see the Resource Guide, Chapter 10.

Clinics

Private *cliniques* (clinics) often specialise in particular fields. Generally their accommodations are more pleasant and personal than in a public hospital, but their prices are somewhat higher. When you need a particular service, talk to your doctor about the advantages of a hospital or clinic that might be recommended.

Dentistry

Although Paris has excellent dental services with the most modern equipment and trained practitioners, it would be wise to have as much dental work as possible done by your regular dentist before you leave home, giving you adequate time to find another in your new home. If you have ongoing dental problems, bring a set of x-rays with you.

As with doctors, both your friends and your embassy should be able to provide you with recommendations of English-speaking dentists; this should not be hard, for many

French dentists have trained in North America or in the United Kingdom. In France, there are no dental hygienists, so it is the dentist who does the routine tasks such as tooth cleaning, giving the dentist a complete understanding of the patient's mouth and dental condition.

Hôpital Hôtel Dieu provides 24-hour emergency *stomatologie* services (dental and mouth care), as does the American Hospital. For emergencies you can also contact SOS Urgences Stomotolagie et Dentaire at 87 boulevard Port-Royal, 75013 (24-hour tel: 01.43.36.36.00).

The Centre de Santé Dentaire George Eastman is a dental institute at 11 rue George Eastman, 75013 (tel: 01.44.97.88.88). It is closed on Sundays.

Pregnancy

French maternity care is excellent. In a public hospital, just about all costs are covered under Sécurité Sociale. Women in the French health care system must declare their pregnancy and undergo a minimum of four examinations and one *échographie (*ultrasound). A *carnet de maternité* (maternity notebook) will be provided.

Inquire about your obstetrician's hospital or clinic. The services at both public hospitals and private clinics can be equally good, but while clinics may be more comfortable, hospitals may have more extensive equipment and facilities. Except for complicated deliveries, many babies in France are delivered by a *sage-femme* (midwife).

The three hospitals below are well respected for maternity care, especially for high-risk pregnancies. Your doctor will guide you as to the best resources for your pregnancy, but you should also be aware of Message, the important English-speaking support group for new and expectant mothers.

- 14e: Hôpital Saint-Vincent de Paul; 84 avenue Denfert-Rochereau; tel: 01.58.41.41.41
- 14e: Hôpital Cochin; 27 rue du Faubourg-Saint-Jacques; tel: 01.58.41.41.41
- 12e: Hôpital des Diaconesses; 18 rue du Sergent-Bauchat; tel: 01.44.74.10.10

Birth and parenting classes for expectant parents are held independently by *sages-femmes* and also at many hospitals. Hôpital Notre-Dame de Bon Secours at 66 rue des Plantes, Paris 75014 conducts a *sophrologie* programme of relaxation, including Yoga and Lamaze techniques (tel: 01.40.52.41.48). The English-speaking hospitals provide prenatal and childbirth care as well.

All births must be registered within three days at your *mairie*. The hospital provides the forms and information. New parents should ask for a copy of *La Naissance à Paris*. All births should also be registered immediately at your own embassy.

Pharmacies

Pharmacies display a green neon cross outside; the cross is lit when the shop is open. Pharmacies carry only health products such as prescription and over-the-counter homeopathic remedies, skin preparations, suntan lotions, tooth brushes and healthy cosmetics; beauty and skin products are widely available at department stores and supermarkets, often at better prices.

To fill a prescription under French health insurance, hand the *ordonnance* (prescription) that your physician has given you to the pharmacist.

Pharmacists are highly trained and extremely knowledgeable about medication, of which there are many, since French physicians tend to medicate heavily. Generic equivalents are used and the pharmacist may ask whether you will accept a generic equivalent, which is less expensive and most often equally effective. If you have doubts about a particular product, ask your doctor. Without any prescription though, you can discuss your symptoms (cold, flu, headache, etc.) with the pharmacist, who may recommend non-prescription remedies.

The pharmacy in each neighourhood should display a poster (*placard*) indicating the nearest night and Sunday pharmacy (*pharmacie de garde*). The local *commissariat* will also indicate doctors on call and open pharmacies. The pharmacies listed below have English-speaking personnel and several carry English or American products. For 24-hour pharmacies, see Resource Guide in Chapter 10. See *Pharmacies* in the *Yellow Pages*.

- 1er: Anglo-American (Swann Rocher) Pharmacy; 6 rue de Castiglione; tel: 01.42.60.72.96. Closed on Sundays.
- 6e: Pharmacie Saint-Germain des Prés: 45 rue Bonaparte; tel: 01.43.26.52.92. Open daily until midnight; Sundays and holidays until 11:00 pm.
- 8e: Drugstore Champs-Elysées (Publicis): 133 avenue des Champs-Elysées; tel: 01.47.20.39.25. Open until 2:00 am.
- 8e: Pharmacie Anglaise des Champs-Elysées; 62 avenue des Champs-Elysées; tel: 01.43.59.22.52. Open daily until midnight.
- 8e: Pharmacie Les Champs Dhéry; 84 avenue des Champs-Elysées; tel: 01.45.62.02.41. Open 24 hours.
- 9e: British-American Pharmacy; 1 rue Auber; tel: 01.42.65.88.29. Open until 8:00 pm; closed on Sundays.
- 14e: Pharmacie des Arts; 106 boulevard du Montparnasse; tel: 01.43.35.44.88. Open until midnight; Sundays until 10:00 pm.

Parapharmacies

Parapharmacies, which are generally *libre-service* (self-service) carry cosmetics and non-prescription health care products, including vitamins, homeopathic remedies and skin preparations. Not as tightly regulated as pharmacies, *parapharmacies* are often less expensive and some offer a *carte de fidélité*, giving a discount for frequent purchases.

HIV/AIDS/STD

City-sponsored health centres do free and confidential AIDS testing and several hospitals offer extensive care. Ask at the *mairie* for *SIDA et IST*, a comprehensive information booklet about sexually transmitted diseases and AIDS care in Paris.

- Médecins du Monde has a private centre
  62bis avenue Parmentier, 75011
  Tel: 01.43.14.81.50
  Website:http//www.medicinsdumonde.org

- SIDA Information Service
  24-hour hotline tel: 08.00.84.08.00
  Website: http://www.sida-info-service.org
- Act Up Paris
  Tel: 01.48.06.13.89
  Website:http://www.actupparis.org.
  International activist association with weekly meetings.

Deaths

Deaths must be certified by a physician and reported to the *mairie* within 24 hours. The certifying doctor will explain the procedures. Only after such official registration may a funeral or repatriation take place. Notify your embassy officially and it will provide assistance with the paperwork. For information when someone dies, contact the municipal Urgences Funéraires (tel: 08.00.88.00.88; website: http://www.servicesfuneraires.fr). See *Pompes Funèbres* in the *Yellow Pages*.

MANAGING YOUR MONEY
The Euro

On 1 January 2002, the euro (€) replaced the national currency of 11 countries. As of this writing, five newer members have qualified to be part of the euro zone. Thus, if you travel in any of the 16 countries here mentioned, you need not worry about exchanging currency or whether you will be left with unused foreign cash when you return. (The EU zone now consists of: Austria, Belgium, Cyprus, Finland, France, Germany, Greece, Ireland, Italy, Luxembourg, Malta, the Netherlands, Portugal, Slovakia, Slovenia, and Spain). For more on the EU, see Chapter 9.

Each country pegged the euro to its previous currency. In France, for example, one euro was deemed to be worth 6.559 francs. There was thus a permanent rate for people to convert their currency to the new one. Even now, some shops and real estate brokers still give their prices in francs as well as in euros, but this is slowly being phased out.

Although currency values themselves do not fluctuate within the eurzone, prices do. During the transition, for

WORK HARDER!

example, most merchants rounded up the fractions of their local currency to the next higher euro, but others seized the opportunity to raise prices freely. There are also other factors to consider: for example, an Italian car may cost more in Germany than in Italy, so if you want an Italian car you may well decide to go to Italy and drive it back across the open border. Therefore, you still have to shop around for the best deal on high-priced items. Such pricing differences are currently being discussed within the EU.

Currency values do fluctuate greatly outside the euro zone, even for the three EU countries that opted not to enter the monetary convention and for the 10 new members. Thus, if you know in advance when you will be travelling outside the euro zone, you still have to pay attention to currency rates and buy when it is advantageous. Rates are published in daily newspapers; unfortunately, these are bank rates and individual purchasers do not get exactly the same rates.

Unfortunately too, for Americans, the dollar is currently low against the euro and informed opinion is that it will remain that way for some time. In 2001, the price of one euro was US$ 0.87, but at the time of writing, one euro costs about US$1.26. The British pound, however, although having fallen somewhat against the euro, still remains high. Rates change almost daily, so it is worth keeping your eye on the exchange rate.

The Need for Cash

If you are arriving in France from a country that does not use the euro (including Great Britain), you will need to have at least enough cash to get into the city from the airport. Try to buy some euros before your departure, for the exchange rate at the airport *bureau de changes* (currency exchange counter) is usually not advantageous. In many airports and train stations however, there are *distributeurs* (automatic cash dispensers), and if these are linked to banks, the exchange rate will be that of the bank.

Distributeurs

For those with credit or debit cards, cash is available 24 hours a day at the *distributeur* (automatic teller machine). Most have instructions in both French and English. Pictures of the cash networks accepted (Visa, Master Card, Cirrus, Plus, etc.) are displayed, making it easy to know which machines take which cards. Make sure that your Personal Identification Number (PIN) has four numbers only, which is the European standard. If you are going to be using your credit card for cash advances, inquire in advance about the interest rate, for it is usually higher than that of normal purchases.

With your card, you may receive cash up to the daily limit that the home bank allows, linked to the exchange rate.

Obtaining Cash

If you decide to use a *bureau de change* in the city to exchange currency, it's worth checking out several, for the rates may differ even on the same street; in tourist districts they can be

Look out for signs like these to withdraw money from a *distributeur*—this one is of the Caisse d'Epargne, one of the major banks in France.

particularly unfavourable. Ask for the rates before proceeding with the transaction, even if they seem to be posted; occasionally they seem advantageous, but they may only be for large transactions. Also, do not be taken in by signs that say 'no commission', for no *bureau de change* may charge a commission—the profit is built into the rate. Occasionally the exchange seems flexible, depending on the person behind the window, but don't ever think you are getting a rate that is better than what the next cash point will offer.

Most currency exchanges are open on Sunday. This includes American Express and the city-wide chains of Thomas Cook, Global Change, Travelex and Chequepoint. See *Change* in the *Yellow Pages*.

- American Express; 11 rue Scribe, 75009; tel: 01.47.14.50.00. For the bureau de change, tel: 01.47.77.77.59; website: http://www.americanexpress.com. Open seven days a week; on Sundays from 10.00 am to 4.00 pm.

Banks offer the most favourable rates of exchange, but they charge a commission, usually one to two per cent of the monies changed. Some banks display a sign saying 'no cash', and unfortunately, banks close earlier than *bureaux de change*. And most, though not all, are closed on Saturdays.

Traveller's Cheques

Banks, currency exchanges and post offices exchange traveller's cheques. Neither American Express nor Thomas Cook charge a fee for exchanging their own cheques, but unless you want to keep large cash reserves or you can get your traveller's cheques without a commission from your bank, it's best to just get euros when you need them from a *distributeur*.

Traveller's cheques are helpful only if you would otherwise make many small withdrawals from the *distributeur*, as banks in your home country and in France may charge a fee each time. So, it's best to withdraw large amounts occasionally or to have traveller's cheques, which your own bank may issue you without charge.

For Lost or Stolen Items

For lost traveller's cheques, most issuers require a police report: go to the *commissariat* in the *arrondissement* in which the loss occurred. The police will issue a *récépissé de déclaration de perte ou de vol* (declaration of theft or loss). Bring the report and your passport to the issuer of the cheques. For those issuers without an office in Paris, ask at the time of purchase for a toll-free number to call in case of loss. Remember that you must note the numbers of the traveller's cheques, so be sure to keep this record separately from the cheques themselves.

Report lost or stolen credit cards immediately. Often a replacement card with a new number can be issued within 48 hours; be sure to inform any company that is making automatic deductions from your card (such as online services) that the number has changed. Should you be using a French Visa or Master Card, after you have notified the bank, it will inform you of the procedures for informing others.

- American Express; tel: 01.47.77.72.00
- Visa & Carte Bleue; tel: 08.00.90.11.79
- MasterCard; tel: 08.00.90.13.87
- Diner's Club; tel: 08.10.31.41.59

Sometimes lost articles—even credit cards and traveller's cheques—are turned in to the police. See Resource Guide in Chapter 10 for the address of the city's Lost and Found Departments. For lost bank cheques, call 08.92.68.32.08. For items lost or stolen on SNCF trains, call 01.55.31.58.40.

French Banking

There are many banks to choose from in Paris and these generally offer savings and current accounts, investment opportunities and money market funds. Take your time in choosing. Bring to each bank you are considering a list of questions concerning your particular banking needs. Ask too, if necessary, about the commission charged for processing an international cheque or electronic transfer of funds—these can be high and vary from bank to bank.

Ask how long it takes to have access to transferred funds. (If your home bank is affiliated with one in France, transfers of funds from one to the other may be somewhat more efficient, although this isn't always the case.) All banks these days have Internet access for viewing accounts on line. Inquire, too, about the conditions for their *carte bleue*, the Visa debit card. If you are considering investing through the bank, ask about their pricing policies. There should be written information on the bank's services.

Convenience of location and opening days and hours might factor into your decision. Banks are generally open from 9:00 am to 5:00 pm, weekends and holidays excepted. Some banks are open on Saturday mornings. If a national holiday falls on a Tuesday or Thursday, banks may *faire le pont* to bridge the long weekend, closing on the previous Monday or following Friday, to give the employees a four-day weekend. Small neighourhood branches may offer more personal service after the staff gets to know you. Otherwise, banking in Paris can be extremely impersonal. Do not ever expect special treatment.

Current accounts may pay interest, and some banks may automatically sweep funds above a certain level into interest-bearing accounts. Interest earned is taxable, so make sure you take into account in which country your taxes will be paid.

Each bank has its own specific guidelines and documentation needed to open a *compte courant* (current account), although there are some general guidelines: when you go to open your account, bring your passport, your *carte de séjour* (either affixed in the passport or a plastic card) and proof of your domicile, such as your lease or a gas/electric bill in your name. This may not be easy, for without a bank account it's sometimes hard to obtain a lease, and without a lease it's hard to get a bank account. Proof of employment generally suffices, but a letter of reference from a home bank may also be helpful.

Most banks open non-resident accounts. A few will require a hefty initial deposit, especially if there is no direct deposit of a salary cheque.

Opening an account is not immediate. Most often you must make an appointment just to see an account representative.

Then it takes a few days for the paperwork to be completed and even longer for a chequebook and the *carte bleue* to be issued. Don't assume that anything is provided automatically. Ask for the chequebook (they come in different sizes, so ask to see all available sizes and choose one that suits you best). There is no extra charge for cheques.

Cheques are accepted by most establishments with proof of identity and sometimes with a minimum purchase of € 10 or € 20. The penalties for returned cheques are so severe that cases of a person writing a cheque with insufficient funds are extremely rare. Some banks will arrange an overdraft limit, but if the bank's procedures for covering a bounced cheque are not followed, the account holder may be blacklisted (*interdit bancaire*). Thus it is important to ask how your bank structures the *dates de valeur*, the amount of time it takes for deposits to be credited, including money orders and bank drafts—withdrawals made on the same date as a deposit may result in an overdraft. Cheques are payable on the date presented, so post-dating a check is not advisable.

If opening a joint account, ensure that both parties may make bank transactions and sign cheques separately and that banking transactions do not require both signatures. Cheques are not endorsable to a third party and banks will not cash cheques made out to someone else; do not accept such cheques as payment of any kind.

The RIB

When you open a bank account, you will be given several copies of a RIB (*relevé d'identité bancaire*), which contains the identifying numbers of your bank and account. This is the coupon you will show your landlord, the telephone and electric companies and all the other institutions when you arrange for their payments to be automatically deducted from your account. Your chequebook may also have copies of the RIB at the back.

Carte Bleue

La carte bleue, the French Visa card, is actually a debit card. Linked to the customer's bank account, the amount of the purchase is deducted immediately (*débit immediat*) or at the end of the month (*débit différé*), depending which option you choose when setting up your bank account. In either case, there are no installment payments, no grace period and no bill sent at the end of the month.

Cards are accepted everywhere as payment because they are seen to be safe. Monthly purchases on the card may be limited to between € 1,500 and € 2,500, unless prior arrangements have been made.

Carte bleue functions with *distributeurs*, with a PIN that the bank has assigned. *Distributeurs* throughout Paris are electronically linked and bank cards may be used in any of them. There is no charge for using the machines at branches of your own bank, but some banks charge for withdrawals from other banks. Cardholders whose cards have been illegally used by others are generally liable for the amount withdrawn until the date they notify the bank of the problem; the PIN is a secret number and if someone else has used it, the bank considers that it was negligently given out by the cardholder. Some banks offer card insurance or can recommend where to obtain it. Make sure no one is looking over your shoulder when you are at the *distributeur*.

Moneo

Moneo is a 'smart card', a kind of prepaid credit card that can be used in some shops to make purchases of up to € 30. It's anonymous, so there's no risk of identity theft. You can refill it up to € 100 so even if it's stolen, that's the most you can lose. Moneo can be bought and refilled at post offices and banks.

La Poste

Post Offices (*bureaux de poste*) are the most widespread banks in France and as they are all connected, they have more branches than any other. In terms of convenience, the local post office may be the most practical place to open a bank account, depending on the types of services you need. La Poste offers all the usual services available at any other bank. They are also *bureaux de change* and many are Western Union agents. However, they are rumoured to be the least flexible and personalised in service. If you are after the convenience, check out several Post Offices in your neighourhood.

International Banks
Some foreign banks have *succursales* (branches) in Paris. They are all full-service banks and adhere to French banking law. In some, in addition to showing proof of your income and your nationality, you need only show that you have a pernament address somewhere, even if it is not in France. Those listed below provide the same services as French banks, but with added services for foreigners. Their services and websites are in both French and English. Prices for services also vary, and they may be more expensive than French banks.

- Banque Transatlantique; 26 avenue Franklin D. Roosevelt, 75372 Paris Cedex 08; tel: 01.56.88.77.77; fax: 01.42.25.33.33; website: http://www.transat.tm.fr
- Barclays Bank; 32 avenue George V, 75008; tel: 01.53.67.82.20; website:http://www.barclays.fr. Other addresses throughout Paris.

Money from Home
Don't expect cheques or money orders sent from abroad to clear at the bank quickly enough to provide emergency funds; if you have a bank account in France, it would be better to make a bank-to-bank electronic transfer. Other faster options exist for receiving funds. In all, the sender pays the fees based on the amount sent; these are fairly expensive, so should be seen only as an emergency measure. The Travelex *bureaux de change* are MoneyGram agents (http://www.moneygram.com) and La Poste is an agent of Western Union (http://www.westernunion.com).

How Much Do Things Cost?
Forget the old stories of Europe as being inexpensive. Not only is this no longer true, Paris fitted that mould only for brief periods when the franc was low. Now Paris rates just a bit lower than Tokyo in cost-of-living surveys. This may particularly affect Americans for the dollar remains low

against the euro. But for the British, although the pound is less strong than just a few years ago, prices are still advantageous.

Estimating how much it will cost to live in Paris will depend on several factors, including whether you are paid in dollars, pounds or euros, etc., that is, how much spending power your income actually has when converted to euros. Although you'll surely start by comparing prices in Paris with those at home, it's best to start, early on, by comparing prices in euros from one shop to another. Remember that tax is included in the price quoted and that the tip is already figured into every restaurant bill.

Expensive in many regards, Paris is nonetheless agreeably liveable, as its residents can attest. Most middle-class Parisians have learned how to live satisfactorily, setting their priorities and looking for good value at each turn. They frequent the semi-annual sales, look for promotions, and hound the discount houses. They shop for seasonally plentiful produce at the outdoor markets and eat and entertain well at home—except for meals at their favourite bistros or *brasseries*, at the inexpensive Asian restaurants or, on occasion, in a fine restaurant.

Assume that domestic goods will be cheaper, imported more expensive. Fresh produce, cheeses and breads are the least expensive, and some items such as canned goods may be more expensive than what you're used to. Wines range from the drinkable and cheap, good and moderately priced, to the fabulous but astronomical—it just takes a little tasting to figure out what you like and can afford. Goods in tourist areas may cost more than in outlying neighourhoods. The cinema and theatre cost about the same as in most cosmopolitan capitals, as do sporting and theatrical events.

Gas and electricity bills may be higher than what you're used to, but telephone calling plans vary greatly and are getting cheaper, given the increasing competition in the field. Large appliances and electronic equipment that used to be more expensive in Europe than in North America are now generally competitive in price. Imported appliances may still be more expensive, owing to high import duties and taxes. Yet even the prices of these items are quickly becoming more competitive, especially with the advent of the *hypermarchés*.

French Taxes

Residents with income in France are liable for taxes on income from sources worldwide. This includes salaries and investments but not foreign real estate income. Non-residents are taxed only on earned income in France (salary and rental income) and non-resident foreigners with vacation homes in France are generally not subject to income taxes. Some countries have multilateral treaties with France by which citizens working abroad are not double-taxed. You must still file your tax return on time. Find out the deadline for people living abroad.

The French tax year coincides with the calendar year. Tax filing for salaried employees and independent contractors is due by the end of May. Taxes are based on *le revenu* (earned income) and *capitaux mobiliers* (unearned income). Taxes can reach up to 40% of gross income (but are set to go down at least somewhat), and there are also other forms of tax: capital gains tax, death duties, gift tax, wealth tax and land tax, etc.

There are some rebates, exemptions and a standard deduction for married people and those with children. French employers do not withhold any amount for tax. After the tax return (*déclaration de revenus*) is filed, the government calculates the tax due and sends a bill. After the first year in the tax system, the bill may be paid in three installments or debited monthly from a chequeing account. First-time taxpayers must declare themselves and their taxable income to the appropriate Centre des Impôts.

Taxes at Home

Everyone must determine their tax status at home and in France while living abroad.

EU countries have treaties by which there is no double taxation, but since French taxation is based on the length of annual residency, everyone should check with their employer or the tax bureau in their home country to determine its domicile requirements. EU nationals working in France on secondment are generally not liable for French taxes, but determinations should be reached in advance.

British citizens should request a non-resident ruling by the Inspector of Taxes. Inquire at Inland Revenue: General Services Unit; enquiries tel: (0845) 010-9000; website: http://www.inlandrevenue.gov.uk.

All Americans must file a federal tax return, although there is a tax exemption on income earned abroad. A *Tax Guide for U.S. Citizens and Residents Abroad* or the *Overseas Tax Package* is available from the Internal Revenue Service Forms Distribution Centre, PO Box 25866, Richmond VA 23289; US tel: (1-202) 874-1460. Check with the tax department in your home state before departure because state requirements vary widely. You might also contact the IRS office at the American Embassy in Paris (Tel: 01.43.12.25.55; website: http://france.embassy.gov/irs.html). Much of this information is available online at http://www.irs.gov.

Sécurité Sociale

Cotisations sociales are paid by companies and all workers, both salaried and self-employed. For salaried employees this generally covers health insurance, disability, retirement pensions and unemployment insurance. Companies withhold a percentage from the employee's paycheck, and the amount is recorded on the pay slip.

Some embassies have booklets that detail the rights of their citizens working abroad. Self-employed people must pay taxes to URSSAF and must subscribe to a basic health and pension plan, both of which are expensive; (website: http://www.urssaf.fr). The expected amount is about 40 per cent of your revenue. For information on 'La sécu', access their website at http://www.securite-sociale.fr.

Bilateral agreements also apply t o British salaried employees working abroad for their company under 12 months. Transferred employees will need to provide an

E101 form indicating insurance coverage under the UK plan. If employed by a French company, the worker will receive a French Social Security number and be covered by the French system.

Accounting Firms

Your country's embassy should be able to provide a list of English-speaking tax consultants in Paris. International firms are up-to-date on both French and international tax laws and procedures, as well as the treaties between countries. They offer tax preparation advice, help prepare returns, handle audits and offer business-related services. They may, however, be more expensive than French accountants for dealing with strictly domestic matters.

STAYING IN TOUCH

New methods of communication are entering modern life so quickly—even in 'ancient, traditional' France—that any chapter on how best to stay in touch with friends and family abroad will need to be updated by the time it's printed. With phones that take photographs which can be emailed directly, or hand-held devices that receive wireless email wherever you are, there's no need anymore to wonder how people back home are and to wait uneasily to find out. No doubt new technology will continue to emerge to make staying in touch even easier, faster and cheaper. If France has not been on the cutting edge of communications so far, at least it never lets itself fall behind.

La Téléphonie

Until recently, France Télécom controlled all tele-communications services. However, its privatisation, as well as new regulations from the EU, has allowed both domestic and international competitors to enter the field. This has forced France Télécom to adapt, which it has by morphing into Orange, by reducing prices and expanding its calling options, and by providing competitive services in both Internet and television programming. (See the box on the next page for contact information.)

Moreover, since it is no longer required that customers use France Télécom for their basic providers, international competitors such as Italia Telecom have entered the French market, also offering packages of services as those mentioned above. (tel: 1033; website: http://www.aliceadsl.fr).

Internet providers are also offering these services at extremely competitive prices, so you should make sure to check out all the options before subscribing to a plan:

- Free: website: http://www.free.fr
- Budget Télécom: website: http://www.sfr.fr

Other Options

There are yet other options for inexpensive calling. Just taking hold in France, for example, is Skype, which uses the technology called Voice Over Internet Protocol (VoIP).

If you have broadband cable internet service (see Numericable on page 104) or DSL, which divides the phone line into voice and data, you should investigate Skype:

> **FRANCE TELECOM**
> Remains the major telephone provider for landlines.
> Customer service tel:1014
> Toll-free English-speaking help line: 08.00.36.47.75
> English-speaking line from abroad: (33).1.55.78.60.56
> Website:http://www.orange.fr
> Inquire about all their pricing plans before subscribing and check out telephone companies that offer competitive prices for telephone, Internet, and television packages.

http://www.skype.com (in English) and http://www.skype.com/intl/fr (in French). In effect, you'd be making phone calls using your computer or—depending on how you configure it—your iPhone, iTouch or other smart phones that support VoIP software. Domestic and international calls to other Skype customers are always free, and those to other landlines and mobiles are reasonably priced. It's important to know about VoIP, for this is the current wave, and if Skype has hit France, other providers will surely follow.

Check out, too, several services that offer cheap international calling without a subscription plan:

- Minutes Direct; website:www.lesminutesdirect.com. International calls at the price of a local call. Billed through France Télécom.
- Iradium; website:http://www.iradium.fr. Calling card plan with competitive rates. Access the website to understand how the process works and to sign up.

Mobile Phones

The French are great users of their mobiles. Some people are even choosing not to have a 'landline' (*téléphone fixe*) at all, using only their mobiles. So, if you have a mobile yourself, expect people to call you on it, even if you are at home sitting next to your landline.

France uses GSM 900/1800. Most newer cell phones are now tri- or quad-band and are now compatible. With a simple bi-band phone that only accesses GSM 1900, you'll have to buy a new phone.

For long or permanent stays, you will no doubt choose a French provider for your mobile phone. Before doing so, if you are using a tri-band or quad-band mobile from another country, you'll have to switch the setting to the 'roaming' option by selecting among the French providers offered. Many of the newer phones select the French provider automatically, finding the one that has the best reception where you are at that time. Roaming is expensive though, for you are charged both by your provider and by your temporary selection, so it's best used for only a short period. Do your research before you choose a French provider, for each offers its own plans and options, though all offer SMS text messaging options.

All brands of smart phones and hand-held devices with a range of apps are available, but in euros the devices may be more expensive than those bought in the United States or online. The boutiques of the three networks below sell their phones, as does the major electronic chain La Fnac.

- Bouygues; tel: 08.10.81.06.78;
  website:http://www.bouyguestelecom.fr
- Orange; tel: 08.00.83.08.00; website:http://www.orange.fr
- SFR; tel: 08.00.10.60.00; website:http://www.sfr.fr

Telephone Numbers

Telephone numbers in France have ten digits. Those in the Paris region start with 01 and those in the rest of France with numbers from 02 to 05. All lines in France can be reached with the ten-digit number, without an additional area code prefix. For international calls, dial 00, then the country and area codes, followed by the telephone number.

All French mobile phone numbers begin with 06. Keep a record of your phone's serial number (dial: *#06# to obtain it). In case the phone gets stolen—which happens frequently—call your service provider immediately.

Numéros verts (toll-free numbers) begin with 08.00 (often shown as 0 800). Others that begin with 08 are toll-call numbers. The higher the second set of numbers, the higher the cost per minute. Thus, a number that begins 08.92 costs more than one that starts with 08.36. *Numéros azur* start with

08.01 and can also be dialled nationwide and are charged at local call rates.

North American toll-free numbers (800, 877, etc.) are not toll-free when dialed from abroad. The prefix changes:

- For 800 numbers, dial 880
- For 888 numbers, dial 881
- For 877 numbers, dial 882

Public Phones

Public telephones can be found in post offices, public buildings, restaurants and on the street. Few telephones take coins; all take the *télécarte*—a prepaid card to be inserted into the telephone. Credits are deducted according to the length of the call and the number of units remaining on the card appears on the telephone as you speak. *Télécartes* are available at supermarkets and *tabacs*. Calls to emergency numbers are free from any public telephone. For operator assistance, dial 1812.

The French Internet

Currently there are dozens of Internet *fournisseurs d'accès* (providers) in France. New providers are entering the field and prices vary widely, so it is worth checking out the price structures and conveniences of several. If you continue to use your own Internet service provider, you will still need to be able to access it, whether by telephone or cable, so you will need to know the options in France.

You will have many options to choose from, including Wi-Fi, broadband ASDL (*haut debit*) and cable, which in Paris is provided by Numericable.

Some charge a monthly fee for unlimited access (*forfait illimité*) and many have a scale of fees, depending on your usage. As mentioned above, some offer calling, and television packages as well, so take into account all the options before you decide.

All software and instructions provided will be in French, as will most technical support.

- America Online; website: http://www.aol.fr
- Free.fr; website:http://www.free.fr

- FreeSurf; website:http://www.freesurf.fr
- La Poste; website:http://www.laposte.net.
- Numericable; http://www.offers.numericable.fr/home.php
- website: http://www.sfr.fr
- Tele2.internet; website:http://www.tele2.fr
- Telecom Italia-Alice; website:http://www.aliceadsl.fr
- Orange (France Télécom) website: http://www.orange.fr.

Cybercafés

These days, Internet access (including Wi-Fi) is available almost anywhere, including at hotels, train stations and cafés. In addition to checking your email at cybercafés throughout the city, the city of Paris has installed free WiFi in many of its public spaces—libraries, town halls, and parks. The American Library (see page 181) also offers Internet access to its members; daily membership is available. And, La Poste is not only an Internet provider, several of its branches in Paris also offer a Cyberposte option—Internet access using a rechargeable card (http://www.laposte.net). For both, it's important to check opening hours. For other sites, see *Internet: espaces de consultation* in the *Yellow Pages*.

The Post Office

La Poste is one of the most important institutions in France (http://www.laposte.fr). It is the country's most wide-ranging bank, handles all post office services and, as mentioned above, has its own Internet service. Its English-language website has helpful information for people "Already Living in France' (http://www.laposte.com).

There are often several post offices in one neighourhood, with yellow fronts and blue lettering. Despite long lines, service is generally helpful and efficient. The yellow post boxes on the street have two slots specifying the mail destination: *Paris et Banlieue* (Paris and Suburbs) or *Province et Etranger* (Provinces and International).

Post offices are open from 8:00 am to 7:00 pm weekdays and until noon on Saturday. For the post office in your district, look in the *Yellow Pages* under *Poste*. The city's main post office, La Poste Centrale, is open 24 hours daily: 52 rue du Louvre, 75001; tel: 01.45.28.14.18

Lettres recommandées (registered letters) are routinely used by the French, as they are legal proof that a person has communicated with another on a certain date. There are two types: *avec accusé de réception*, which has a return receipt, or *recommandée simple*, which does not.

Packages mailed at the post office may weigh up to 30 kg. To determine the weight of a letter or a small parcel, use one of the automatic coin-operated weighing machines that issues the correct postage. There is also a machine that dispenses the appropriate stickers for a package. To avoid flimsy packaging that may be rejected, you can buy sturdy, inexpensive mailing cartons at the post office. To pick up a package or a registered letter, bring identification.

Rush Mail Options

Chronopost International, La Poste's express mail service, guarantees second-day delivery of packages and letters to North America and third-day service to Asia (customer service tel: 08.25.80.18.01; website:http://www.chronopost.com). The major international air couriers are also efficient and reliable, although somewhat more expensive.

- DHL; 59 avenue d'léna, 75016; toll-free tel: 08.20.20.25.25; website: http://www.dhl.fr
- Federal Express; 63 boulevard Haussmann, 75008; toll-free tel: 08.20.12.38.00; website: http://www.fedex.com/fr
- UPS; 107 rue Réaumur, 75002; 34 boulevard Malesherbes, 75009; toll-free tel: 08.21.23.38.77; website:http://www.ups.com; Also in Office Depot stores.

Television

There are six non-cable *chaînes* (channels) in France. With cable, dozens of international and multilingual channels are available, including the English BBC, German ZDF, Italian RAI Uno and the American CNN. France 24 English is a new 24-hour news channel. For information and hook-up, call Numericable (tel: 3990; website:http://www.noos.fr). You can also subscribe to cable at any shop that displays the sign *TV Câble—abonnez-vous ici*. You might also inquire of your Internet provider whether television service is available.

Weekly television guides are sold at news-stands. Free advertising handouts at sidewalk stands also contain TV listings. Sports and other live events may take precedence over regularly scheduled programming. News and weather reports are frequent throughout the day on most channels. A single programme is an *émission*; a schedule of émissions is a *programme*.

Imported televisions and DVD/*magnétoscopes* (DVD/videocassette recorders) must operate on PAL/SECAM, the French television broadcast format. Older video players run only on SECAM, making them incompatible with the American system (NTSC), although they are compatible with the European PAL system. Multisystem televisions and VCRs are increasingly available. In order to tape and play the *magnétoscope*, the television set and the recorder must be compatible. There is a *redevance* (yearly tax) on television sets. When a set is purchased, the store notifies the tax authority and the bill comes with the annual bill for the *taxe d'habitation*.

DVD
As with video recorders, DVD players in different world regions run on different operating systems. DVD players bought in North America, for example, can only play DVDs that are labelled either 'Zone 1' or 'All' ('All' means they are playable on any DVD player). European DVDs are Zone 2, and DVDs bought in Europe generally say 'Zone 2' or 'All'. Sometimes a shopkeeper will be willing to enter a code into a DVD player making it multi-region and thus able to play all DVDs. This may, however, void the warranty, should anything go wrong.

Radio
Paris Live Radio at 963 AM broadcasts music programmes and English-language chat shows, plus some information on living in Paris. It is currently applying to the government for

FM frequency. The BBC is on long wave, Radio 4 at 198 khz medium wave, and BBC World is on at 648 khz AM. Radio France Internationale broadcasts news in English at 3:00 pm on 738khz AM. The weekly events magazines list the numerous Paris FM stations, as do the television guides.

English-language Publications

The *International Herald Tribune* is the major English language newspaper published in Paris, available at news-stands and for home delivery. *The Times*, *The Nikkei Financial Weekly*, *The Wall Street Journal Europe*, *USA Today*, *The Financial Times*, *The Observer*, *The Guardian* and *The Independent* may be found at news-stands.

In Paris, the semi-monthly advertising supplement *FUSAC* described earlier in this chapter is free (http://www.fusac. com), as are the English-language webzines (http://www. parisvoice.com) and *Irish Eyes* (http://www.irisheyes.fr). They can all be found in shops and cafés that Anglophones frequent, as well as the American Library.

OUT AND ABOUT
From the Airports to Paris

First of all, you'll have to get into the city. Intercontinental flights most often arrive at Aéroport Charles de Gaulle in the morning. This means that after clearing customs and picking up your luggage, you will be ready to enter Paris during the morning rush hour. Transit time on the highway can be at least 45 minutes, more if there is an accident or other unforeseen incidents. If someone is meeting you at the airport, they can check the arrival of any flight by calling the airport information number. To obtain information for both Charles De Gaulle and Orly airports: tel: 3950; website: http://www.aeroportsdeparis.fr.

There are several options to get into Paris from the airport. Your choice will depend on your budget and time constraints, how much luggage you are carrying and the degree of inconvenience you are willing to bear.

Taxis, of course, are the most expensive—they charge by the meter, and with surcharges for luggage, prices may run as high as € 60 excluding tips. Yet they are the most convenient, dropping individuals off at the door; with some persuasion, the chauffeur might even be willing to help with suitcases—at least as far as the door. Signs in the airport clearly indicate where the taxi stands are to be found. See also section on 'Taxis' on pages 160–161. Here are some other options.

- Paris Airports Service; tel: 01.55.98.10.80; website:http://www.parisairportservice.com.
  Moderately priced minibus service to your door from either airport, or from your door to the airports. Currently, the price is € 25 for one person from Charles de Gaulle, but the price per person is less when there are more people in your party. Reserve in advance by phone or Internet.

- PariShuttle; tel: 01.53.39.18.18; website:http://www.parishuttle.com.
  Same type of service and similar rates as above. Reserve by phone or Internet.

- Les Cars Air France; tel: 08.92.35.08.20; website:http://www.carsairfrance.com.
  Buses, with multilingual recorded information, run from both airports into the city every 15 minutes, and between airports every 30 minutes. Depending on the bus, the terminus may be Porte Maillot, place Charles-de-Gaulle, Gare Montparnasse or the Air France city terminal at Invalides. Prices depend on where you get off but currently are under € 25 for a round trip. Buy your ticket on board the bus, at any Air France ticket office or at the airport.

- RER B. The inexpensive commuter train goes to the city and suburbs from either Terminal 1 or Terminal 2. There are several stops in Paris, including Gare du Nord, Châtelet and Saint-Michel. The RER does not depend on traffic conditions, so it takes about half an hour to get into the city. Currently the price is € 8 one-way. See 'RER' below.

- Roissybus; tel: 08.92.68.77.14. The RATP bus that runs between Charles de Gaulle and Paris. The terminus is by the American Express Office, at the corners of rue Scribe and rue Auber. The trip takes between 45-60 minutes. Currently the price is € 9.10 one-way.

■ Orlybus; tel: 08.92.68.77.14. The RATP bus that runs between Orly and Paris. The terminus is at the Air France terminal near place Denfert-Rochereau. The trip takes about half an hour. Currently the price is € 6.40 one-way.

For information on the RER B, Orlybus and Roissybus, access the RATP website: http://www/ratp.fr

Finding Your Way

Addresses in Paris are surprisingly easy to find, given that each street has a different name assigned in no particular order. As described earlier, the 20 *arrondissements* are arranged in an outward-moving spiral; the smallest in the oldest, most central sections of town, the largest toward the edge. On streets perpendicular to the Seine, address numbers start at the river and increase as they go; *pairs* (even numbers) are on the right and *impairs* (odd numbers) on the left. Buildings on streets parallel to the river are numbered downstream from east to west. As numbers were assigned according to when particular streets were developed, do not assume that numbers on facing buildings are in the same range. In any case, numbers increase slowly, as different buildings may bear the same number with *bis* or *ter* added to them. Of course, there are exceptions to the numbering system, especially around the Grands Boulevards.

City plans may be obtained at the Paris Tourist Office, bookshops, large department stores and many news-stands. Maps and street atlases come in varying sizes. The best for carrying around is a *Plan de Paris par arrondissement*, one of several pocket-sized books with alphabetical indexes, indications of where a building number can be found, bus and métro routes, emergency numbers and more. Some atlases list a street named after a person with the first name first, others list the last name first.

Walking

Walking puts you in touch with the charm of Paris at every turn. Foreigners used to driving on the left must remember to look to the left before crossing the street. Do not assume that the zebra-striped pedestrian crosswalks are automatic havens from traffic. Although Paris drivers, impatient and aggressive as they may be, do tend to stop for the *piéton* (pedestrian) at the crosswalk, some do not. On the other hand, they may look as though they are about to hit you, but are actually adept at driving under crowded conditions and manoeuvering around pedestrians while maintaining their (sometimes breakneck) speed. And they do stop promptly at red lights, which are often placed directly in front of a crosswalk rather than at the corner. The concerned government, however, has started a media campaign asking drivers to 'stay zen'. Nonetheless, the best strategy is to pay attention to traffic, cross only at crosswalks and wait for traffic lights (*les feux*) to turn green in your direction. Also, watch out for bicycles, mopeds and scooters, which weave in and out of traffic and zoom around corners. Despite all this, walking is one of the best ways to see Paris, to get around and to get some exercise.

RATP

La Régie Autonome des Transports Parisiens (RATP) is the public transit authority for *l'autobus* (buses), *le métropolitain* (the subway, known as the *métro*) and the Réseau Express Régional (the RER commuter line to the suburbs) tel: 3246; website:http://www.ratp.fr.

Maps of the transport system (both for Paris and the suburbs) are available at *métro* stations, on the backs of city maps and in street atlases. Maps of the *métro* are easy to decipher, so the Plan de Paris No. 1, the standard handout at *métro* stations, is adequate. For buses, however, ask for the Plan de Paris No 2.

The public transit system is economical, efficient, well maintained and safe. More than five million people use it daily. As in any large city, women travelling alone should be careful late in the evenings; sitting in the first car behind the driver is also recommended. Pickpockets frequent the *métro*, especially in tourist areas, and riders should avoid looking like tourists by not wearing expensive jewellery, intently studying maps or carrying a temptingly thick wallet in the back pocket of trousers.

The Fares

The transit system is divided into zones: Paris falls within Zone 1 and the inner suburbs are in Zone 2. The rest—up to Zone 9—encompass the outer zones and airports. Single fare tickets are available, but a *carnet* of ten tickets costs about a third less per ticket. A ticket is good for one ride of any length on one bus within the city limits and for any number of transfers within the *métro*, so long as you do not exit the gates. There are no single-ticket transfers from bus to bus, or bus to the *métro*. Keep your ticket while in the system, for you will have to show it if asked by an inspector. *Métro* tickets and coupons are inserted into a slot and then reclaimed, at which point the entry gate opens. On the bus, tickets must be *validé* (validated) in the *valideur magnétique* behind the driver.

Visitors should inquire about the Paris Visite travel pass, which is issued for one, two, three or five consecutive days, and is valid on all public transportation, including the SNCF trains. The passes, sold by zones, are valid throughout the Île de France, meaning visits to Versailles or to either airport. Buy them at *métro* and train stations.

The Passes

Weekly or monthly passes (*coupons*) are more economical than single-ride tickets. The *carte navigo intégrale* is an electromagnetic card that is valid throughout Île-de-France on all forms of public transport and allows users to get through the turnstiles quickly, for it is swiped along an electronic *valideur*.

You may recharge the weekly pass (*hebdomadaire*) or monthly pass (*mensuel*) at *métro* stations. The *hebdomadaire* starts from Monday to Sunday, no matter which day of the week it was bought. The monthly recharge is good for the duration of a calendar month. To acquire a *carte navigo*, ask for the application form at any *métro* station. In theory, the *carte* is for residents only, but just about everybody who uses public transport has one.

The Métropolitain

Paris has one of the best underground transportation systems in the world. The *métro* is inexpensive, generally clean and efficient. It has 16 lines and 370 well-maintained stations, conveniently located in all parts of the city. It is rare to find oneself more than a five-minute walk from a *métro*.

The *métro* starts running at 5:30 am and the last train leaves around 12:30 am. Rush hours are from 7:30–9:30 am and 5:00–8:00 pm. To calculate journey time, count the number of stops from the beginning to the destination and multiply by 1.5 minutes, adding five minutes for each transfer. Remember, however, that the *métro* runs less frequently in the evenings and on weekends.

Entrances to many *métro* stations are marked with a large 'M' in a yellow circle; some older entrances even have charming grill-work. Each *métro* line is identified by a different number and colour on the subway map, and each *quai* (platform) has well-lit signs indicating the *sortie* (exit), terminus of the train and *correspondance* (interchange point). For example, a white sign indicating 'M6 Nation' is the Number Six line heading toward the last stop of Nation; the opposite direction is labelled 'M6 Charles-de-Gaulle-Etoile'. The *correspondance* signs are orange. *Sortie* signs are blue with white lettering. When there is a choice of escalator or stairs, these are also shown in blue and white.

Large diagrams of the *métro* system are at the entrance to each station and along the *quais*. In each car there is a schematic of the stations and *correspondances* on that line. At the exit of many stations, either just inside or on the street, there is often a map of the *quartier*.

L'Autobus

With some 2,000 city buses and 1,700 *arrêts d'autobus* (bus stops), the bus system is efficient though slower than the *métro*. Riding the bus, however, allows a good view of the city—a not inconsiderable advantage. Fifty-eight lines run within Paris and more go to the suburbs. Many *abri de bus* (bus shelters) have printed information in English, especially those in tourist areas.

Many of the bus schedules are being extended later in the evening, although some still run only from about 6:30 a.m. to 9:30 p.m. *Noctilien* (http://www.noctilien.fr) is a fleet of

Métro entrances in Paris are clearly marked.

35 night-time buses that run from about 1:00–5:30 am, generally every 10 or 20 minutes. Their terminus is Place du Châtelet. Bus service is reduced and some buses do not run at all on Sundays and holidays. There is usually a schedule posted at each *arrêt*.

Buses indicate their direction by displaying the terminus. Bus routes have two digits, and those going to the suburbs have three digits. Each bus route is colour-coded and is displayed on the bus and at the bus stop, which makes it easy to figure out where the bus stops. A diagonal line through the number on a bus indicates partial service. People board in the front and exit from the back, except in double buses where any door may be used. Pushing a red button requests the driver to stop and some doors must be opened by pushing a button.

RER

The RER is a network of express trains that go to the suburbs in all directions. Stations and routes are specified on *métro* maps, drawn with thicker, different-coloured lines. The RER is faster and quieter than the *métro* and makes fewer stops. RER trains run about every 15 minutes, beginning around 5:30 am and ceasing about midnight. *Métro* tickets are valid on the RER in the two-zone Paris area; going farther requires a supplement, unless you have a pass that includes the outer zones. Lighted signs on each *quai* indicate the destination and each intermediate station for the next train. There are currently four main lines, but several fork off in different directions at some point; therefore, it is important to make sure that the train you are on goes exactly to your destination. Keep your RER ticket, as inserting it into a turnstile is usually necessary to exit the system.

French Railroads (SNCF)

Each of the six Société Nationale des Chemins de Fer Français (SNCF) train stations in Paris serves a different geographical region of France and farther destinations. Train reservations may be made at travel agents and train stations, by telephone or on the Internet. Tickets may be picked up at the train station at least one-and-a-half hours before departure (toll call info/reservations tel: 3635; website: http://www.sncf.com). Transilien is the SNCF train network that services the Ile-de-France.

Some trips are discounted, depending on the passenger's age or how much in advance the reservation is made. Considerably less expensive, discounted tickets are generally non-refundable and non-changeable. Before boarding the train, make sure to punch your ticket in one of the orange machines located at the head of the *quais*, or risk a fine. The SNCF stations and the directions they serve:

- 8ᵉ: Gare Saint-Lazare; 13 rue d'Amsterdam. Northeast.
- 10ᵉ: Gare de l'Est; place du 11 Novembre 1918. East.
- 10ᵉ: Gare du Nord; 18 rue de Dunkerque. North, including the Eurostar to London.
- 12ᵉ: Gare de Lyon; place Louis-Armand. Southeast/South.
- 13ᵉ: Gare d'Austerlitz; 7 boulevard de l'Hôpital. Southwest.
- 15ᵉ: Gare Montparnasse; 17 boulevard de Vaugirard. West/ Southwest. International trains.

The high-speed Eurostar train travels between central Paris (Gare du Nord) and central London (St. Pancras Station) in under three hours (tel: 08.92.35.35.39; website:http://www. eurostar.com).

The Thalys is a high-speed train that travels between Paris (Gare du Nord), Amsterdam, Brussels and Cologne. Reservations are made through SNCF (tel: 3635; website: http://www.thalys.com).

Taxis

There are some 15,000 taxis in Paris and almost 500 taxi stands, but this does not mean that a taxi is easy to find on a rainy day or at rush hour. The best bet is to wait at taxi stands, which are in every *arrondissement* and have blue and white signs marked 'taxis'. Taxis can be engaged directly from the stand or by telephone. See *Taxis* in either phone book; in the *Yellow Pages*, they are listed by *arrondissement*.

Having called for pickup, you will be charged from the time the cab began its trip to pick you up, not from the time you get in. It is thus best to know the location of the nearest taxi stand. A cruising taxi may not pick up a customer within 50 m of a stand unless there are no taxis or customers waiting there.

The top light on the roof of the taxi is lit when it is unoccupied. Three smaller lights indicate the type of fare in the cab (day, night or to suburban zones). Each taxi has a *compteur* (meter), the fare determined by a combination of time and distance. Rates are strictly regulated, raised once annually and consistent throughout the taxi system. There are supplements for each piece of baggage, for holidays, for pickup at the airport and when there are more than three people in a cab—although often drivers refuse (legally) to accept a fourth passenger, being unwilling to have someone ride in the front seat with them (other than their dog). Do not agree to pay a driver's return trip from the airport and be wary of cut-rate offers. The driver is usually given a 10–15 per cent tip. Some, but not all, taxis accept credit cards; to avoid misunderstandings, inform the driver when you enter the cab if you want to use a card—not when it's time to pay. Below are some major 24-hour radio cabs:

- Alpha Taxis; tel: 01.45.85.85.85
- Taxis Bleus; tel: 08.91.70.10.10
- Taxis G7; tel: 01.47.39.47.39

Taxi drivers undergo several months of training and must be certified to obtain a licence, so they are usually knowledgeable about the city. If you have a complaint, get a receipt with the number of the cab and lodge a complaint with the Service des taxis, Préfecture de Police at 36 rue des Morillons, 75015; tel: 01.55. 76.20.00.

Driving in Paris

Public transportation in Paris is so good that you should not need a car for everyday use. Rush hour traffic is extremely slow and can be much worse on rainy days. During rush hour, traffic on the *périphérique* slows to a crawl and the major *portes* (entries into Paris from the *périphérique*) and large arteries are generally congested. *Bouchons* (traffic jams) and *embouteillages* (bottlenecks) are daily occurrences. Delivery trucks often block small, narrow streets, stopping traffic until a delivery has been made. Although drivers in Paris generally obey the traffic laws, they are aggressive and impatient. Take public transportation when you can.

Driver's Licence

If you drive, always carry a valid driver's licence; visitors staying less than 90 days may use a licence from home. The International Driving Licence is advisable but not required in France (but may be necessary in other countries you visit). It is not available in France but may be obtained from your own automobile association. Students may use their home driver's licence for the duration of their studies. Those with a *carte de séjour* may use their home driver's licence—but not the International Driver's Licence—for one year from the date of issue of the *carte*. The licence must be valid, translated into French and issued before the residence permit.

After residence of one year, a French *permis de conduire* (driver's license) is required of EU residents. Expect the process to take about two months, so apply to the Préfecture before the end of the year. Bring a valid, translated driver's licence, proof of domicile, your *carte de séjour*, two passport-sized photographs and the current fee in the form of a *timbre fiscal*—a prepaid stamp purchased at a *tabac* (usually a café that also sells cigarettes and stamps). Although EU citizens theoretically do not need a French licence, in practice it is often necessary for insurance and other reasons. Go to the Préfecture and they will decide whether you need one based on your nationality. (In fact, the member states of the EU are to issue a standard driving licence, which will gradually replace expiring licences.) A French driver's licence is valid for life.

Some countries and some states within the United States have reciprocal agreements with France to waive the driving test, but all applicants must take the written exam on rules

of the road. If you must take the driving exam, enrol in a course at a certified driving school. Ask at your embassy for suggestions for *écoles de conduite* (driving schools); some schools have sections for English speakers. *Code de la Route*, a booklet detailing the rules of the road, is available in most bookshops.

- Fehrenbach Driving School; 53 boulevard Henri-Sellier 92150 Suresnes; tel: 01.45.06.31.17; fax: 01.47.28.81.89; website:http://www.frenchlicense.eu. This school conducts all classes in English.

Report a lost driver's licence to the police immediately. They will issue a *récipissé de déclaration de perte ou de vol de pièce d'identité*, an acknowledgment that identity documents have been lost or stolen. Carry this when you drive until you have received a replacement licence.

For traffic violations, France, along with other EU countries, has a system whereby one loses points on the driver's licence for each infraction: the worse the infraction, the more points one loses, and the licence is forfeited when

12 points have been lost. People with foreign licences should understand that, although their licences cannot be taken away, information is computerised and shared. If a licence has become invalid in France, the information will show up on the system of the authorities in other countries. This includes British drivers, for the French system contacts British authorities for points to be subtracted.

For non-injury traffic offences, the police may require an on-the-spot *consignation* (deposit) on the fine. The matter is decided by the Tribunal de Police (traffic court). Police occasionally stop cars to check identity papers, so make sure you are carrying a valid driver's licence, along with the *carte grise* (vehicle registration document) and the *certificat d'assurance* described below.

Parking

With some 1.3 million cars in circulation each day, parking is at a premium. Fortunately, there are parking garages at the major entrances into the city, in the city centre, at most shopping centres and at numerous underground parking garages. In total, there are some 65,000 spaces and more garages are being built. Garages and parking meters are marked with a blue sign with a large white 'P' and indicated on city maps. Most ticket machines in the garages accept credit cards. Parking spaces in these garages may be available by the month—helpful if your apartment building does not have parking facilities. See *Parkings: exploitation* in the *Yellow Pages* or *Parking* in the *White Pages*.

Many city streets have areas marked *payant* (paying). The *horodateurs* (parking meters) operate from 9:00 am to 7:00 pm every day but Sunday; in August some do not require payment. Purchase a ticket from the nearest meter for the length of time you intend to park and place it on the dashboard. The time of expiration should be clearly visible to any meter reader. You can also get a parking ticket that is good all day. Meters accept the *Paris Carte*, a prepaid card that is sold at bar/tobacco (*bar/tabac*) shops.

Residents may apply to the Service Stationnement at 15 boulevard Carnot, 75012 for a *vignette de stationnement résidentiel*, a parking permit that allows reduced-rate parking in their *arrondissement* (tel: 01.44.67.28.28). The office is open on weekdays until 4:00 pm. Application forms can be picked up at the *mairie* and mailed in.

Tickets are issued for overtime parking or for parking in an illegal spot. To pay the fine, purchase a *timbre fiscal* from a *tabac* and follow the instructions on the ticket for affixing

Obeying the Laws

Obey all laws, even if it looks as though other drivers are not.

- Wear a seat belt, whether in the front or back seat.
- Seat children under 10 in the back seat; babies must sit in buckled car seats.
- Give priority to cars entering your street from the right, no matter how small the street. If it does not apply at traffic-roundabouts, it will be indicated. The *priorité à droite* is one of the most important driving laws.
- Do not use the *klaxon* (horn) except in emergencies.
- Do not drive or park in the bus lanes or the AXE Rouge express lanes.
- Do not park where it says *parking interdit* or *stationnement interdit*. Although many people double park, park at corners or edge up onto the sidewalk, this is illegal.
- Do not dash through a traffic light just as it is turning red; many traffic lights are placed not at the corner but instead just before a crosswalk, and pedestrians begin to cross immediately upon the change of the light. Do not make U-turns or cross a solid white line. Stay to the right on multi-lane roads, unless passing a car.
- Use high beam headlights only on unlit roads. Cars behind you that flash their headlights are indicating they will not slow down.
- Obey the speed limits: 130 kph on highways, 110 kph on wet highways, 90 kph on rural roads, 50 kph in the city, 80 kph on the *périphérique*.

the stamp. Tickets paid within 30 days are given a *remise* (discount), but you pay more than double if you exceed the three months' deadline. EU citizens should note that unpaid tickets might be forwarded to your home country for payment. If your car is not where you parked it (especially if you have parked near a sign saying *stationnement gênant* (with a picture of a car being towed away), it might have been *remorquée et mise à la fourrière* (towed and impounded). Go to the nearest *commissariat* to determine at which of the six *préfourrières* (car depots) the car is being kept. After 48 hours the car goes to one of four central *fourrières* (car pounds). Fines for retrieval include towing and storage charges, plus the original parking ticket.

Bringing a Car into France

Cars entering the country by road are not usually recorded by French customs; nonetheless it is important to have the car's registration and insurance papers with you. For shipped cars, the shipping company will be issued a *déclaration d'admission* at customs, given to the owner when the car is delivered. Cars that have been owned for more than six months (and on which no previous taxes are due) are considered intended for personal use and are generally exempt from customs duties; this does not apply to trucks and utility vehicles. Bring all ownership and tax payment documentation pertaining to the car.

Generally, cars that will remain in the country for less than three months do not have to change their registration. For stays longer than three months, the car should have French *plaques d'immatriculation* (licence plates). You must convert its registration to the French *carte grise* within a year at the Préfecture or *mairie*. Bring your *carte de séjour*, proof of residence and car title.

Automobiles brought into France must conform to countrywide regulations, such as being equipped with a catalytic converter, and will be tested to ensure that they do. If your car is a make that is sold in France, you might call a dealer there to determine in advance what adjustments your model needs. Since not all parts for imported cars are available in France, it is advisable to bring a sufficient quantity of small spare parts to avoid frustration.

Purchasing an Automobile

When buying a car from a French dealer, you will receive a temporary ownership title; the dealer contacts the Préfecture for the permanent registration, after which you must present the necessary *carte de séjour* and proof of residence. To determine fair prices for particular makes and models, consult the online automobile purchaser's guide *l'Argus* (website: http://www.argusauto.com/).

When buying a used car privately, you should obtain from the seller a *certificat de vente* (bill of sale). There should also be a *certificat de non-gage* (indicating that there are no liens or taxes due), the *carte grise* and a *certificat de passage* (indicating the mechanical condition of the car). Within two weeks, you should go to the Préfecture to transfer the title and register for new *plaques d'immatriculation* (licence plates). If you have obtained French licence plates for your car, do not use them until the car insurance reflects those plate numbers.

Automobiles bought in France to be exported within six months are issued a TT (temporary licence plate) by French customs. Legally, you must show proof of domicile, but you do not need to be a resident.

Automobile Insurance

For cars driven into the country, an *assurance-frontière* (temporary insurance policy) is available at the border from French customs. There are policies to cover the period until the automobile leaves France, ranging from eight days to a month; or, in the case of a long stay, until French insurance is arranged.

All automobiles must be insured. The *carte verte/certificat d'assurance* (green insurance card) must be displayed inside the windshield, along with an annually validated *vignette* (tax sticker), which can be bought at *tabacs* in November and which must be in place by December 1. The cost of the *vignette* is based on the age, horsepower and cubic capacity of the car.

Each car must also carry the *carte grise* and a *constat amiable d'accident*, a claim form obtained from the insurance company. In non-injury accidents, the form must be filled out, signed by both parties and sent to the insurance company. A *contrôle technique* (safety certification) must be kept in the car, along with spare headlight bulbs.

Unlimited third-party coverage (*au tiers*) is the minimum automobile insurance required by law, and coverage must be by a French or EU company. *Au tiers limité* includes third-party fire and theft while *tous risques* is comprehensive insurance; there are other more extensive options. Ask your friends or colleagues to recommend an insurance company and compare the services and prices of several companies before you choose. Make sure you read the fine print to find out what the insurance companies don't cover. Do your research carefully, for cancelling an insurance policy is almost as complicated as taking one out. Generally, agents handle home and health insurance, as well as automobile coverage. Policies run for one year and are generally renewed automatically. Ask your own broker for a letter documenting your insurance record. In some cases, a discount is available after one year, which is increased slightly for each year that passes with no claims.

Bicycling

Parisians love their *vélos* (bicyles). Many people ride their bikes as their main mode of transportation, as it's an easy, cheap and even healthy way of getting around. The city is encouraging bicycle riding by creating *pistes* (lanes) that are off-limits to motorised vehicles throughout the metropolitan area. Also, the bus lanes and pedestrian streets, all protected from car traffic, are open to cyclists. More lanes are being built, so cyclists have many options for safe riding throughout the city. The *couloirs vélos* (bicycle lanes) are marked by wide, white stripes. They run north and south, east and west, and all around the circular boulevards Maréchal. Ask at the Tourist Office or your own *mairie* for the brochure *Paris à Vélo*, which tells you everything you might want to know about biking in Paris and includes a map of all the current bike lanes.

It's best to wear a *casque* (helmet) even if not all cyclists do so. Car drivers tend to be aggressive and impatient, although occasionally they show courtesy to bikers, probably being bikers themselves. Also, if a car hits a bicycle, the car driver is usually liable. Riding bikes outside the *couloirs* during rush hour can be extremely difficult. Do not ride through a red light: not only is it dangerous, the same fines imposed on automobiles also apply to bikes.

In 2007, the city of Paris launched a new successful bicycle program to decrease automobile traffic in the city. The program is called the *Vélib* (sort of a contraction of *vélo* for bicycle and *liberté*, for liberty or free). Some 20,000 bicycles for public use are docked in automatic terminals in all the *arrondissements*. You register and take out a subscription, which can be purchased for a day, week, or year. At the docking station, your credit card is read; the first half hour of use is free, and after that there is a small, escalating, fee per 30-minute period (designed to give more riders more chances at bicycles). You may pick up a bike at one station and dock it to any other terminal, where your card is read once again.

Note that the city has a plan to launch a similar program of pick-up and drop-off electric cars, to be called *Autolib*, and at this writing the estimated date for launch is toward the beginning of 2011. Just as the city has reduced traffic somewhat with the *vélib* program, *autolib* is forecast to diminish private car use and congestion, plus reducing carbon dioxide emissions by 22,000 tons per year.

People with Physical Disabilities

As of this writing, only some of the public transport system is wheelchair-accessible, but it's getting better: some 25 buses are wheelchair-accessible and the *métro* has some stations with lifts. All the stations on the line 14 Météor are wheelchair-accessible. Ask at the Tourist Office for the Infomobi map, on which all the wheelchair-friendly *métro* stations are circled and the wheelchair-friendly bus lines listed (tel: 08.10.64.64.64; website:http://www.infomobi. com or http://www.ratp.fr).

Cycling has always been a convenient way to zip around, whether going to work or doing some shopping.

The city continues to improve conditions for the disabled. Almost all sidewalks are sloped at the corners for wheelchair access, and all restaurants opened after 1994 are required to have wheelchair access.

- The Maison Départmentale des Personnes Handicapées at 69 rue de la Victoire 75009 provides information relevant to people with physical abilities in Paris (tel: 08.05.08.09.09; email: contact@mdph.paris.fr).
- The Paris Tourist Office offers a service Tourisme et Handicaps (tel: 08.92.68.30.00; http://www.parisinfo.com/ paris-guide/tourisme-handicap/)
- The website of the city of Paris also provides information. (http://www.paris.fr/portail/Solidarites/Portal.lut?page_ id = 4947)

Ask at your *mairie* or at City Hall for the booklet *Personnes Handicapées sur la Culture, les Loisirs, les Sports*, which lists the museums, libraries, and sporting and leisure venues that are accessible to the handicapped. Information for people with reduced mobility may also be found on the website *Jaccede* (http://www.jaccede.com).

A comprehensive, English-language guide is *Access in Paris* by Gordon Crouch and Ben Roberts. It should be available in bookshops; the website itself is helpful (http://www. accessinparis.org).

The Travel Resource Center of Moss Rehab Hospital,in the United States has well-organised information about all aspects of travel (US tel: (1-215) 456-9900; website: http:// www.mossrehab.com).

Although taxi drivers are obliged to take wheelchair passengers, there is no guarantee they will do so. Some companies, however, offer services customised for disabled passengers. Taxis for weekends or to the airports should be reserved in advance.

- Aihrop; tel: 01.41.29.01.29
- G7; tel: 01.47.39.00.91
- Taxi Parisiens; tel: 06.82.87.56.85

THE CALL OF NATURE

Although they are slowly being phased out, Paris still has its sidewalk *sanisettes* (public toilets), which are easy to use, sanitary and cheap. Look for the oval structures with illuminated *toilettes* signs throughout the city. Museums, the larger hotels, restaurants, cafés, shopping centres and department stores all have public toilet facilities; in a bar or café you will be expected to buy a cup of coffee. Some *toilettes* have a coin slot that takes € 0.20: this usually means they are somewhat clean. In a few bars, however, you may still find the old Turkish toilets with a hole in the floor and foot rests on either side. Signs on doors might read *Toilettes*; or they might say *Dames* or *Femmes*, or *Hommes* or *Messieurs*; or they might only have pictures of a man or a woman.

SAFETY

Central Paris is generally safe. Tourist areas—the Eiffel Tower, Pigalle and Montmartre, around the Pompidou Museum, Sacre-Coeur and Forum Les Halles—see their share of petty thefts, but violence is extremely rare. It always pays to be cautious, however, and to stay on well-travelled streets late in the evenings. Don't carry more credit cards or cash than you need on a particular day, and if you're not going to drive in Paris, there's no need to automatically carry your driver's licence as you would at home. Keep your passport safe. Note down all credit card numbers so you can report any loss or theft; don't keep the numbers with the cards or passport.

Also, except for the occasional pickpocket in crowded stations (where, too often, unsuspecting female tourists leave their handbags unguarded, and men their wallets exposed), the *métro* is generally safe, even late at night. Some stations with long corridors without visibility have mirrors at the corners so you can look down the corridors before turning. Each *quai* (platform) has *bornes d'alarme* (alarm boxes). Women who ride the *métro* late at night often sit in the first car directly behind the driver.

Women should understand that in general, French men

are personal and flirty, even in professional situations. This does not necessarily mean they are harassing you sexually. A Frenchman (usually older) who kisses your hand by brushing it lightly or even just bringing it to his lips is being gallant, nothing more. Letting a Frenchman take you to dinner and pay the bill does not necessarily mean a payoff at the end. On the other hand, young French men sometimes think they are acting cool when they openly ogle a pretty woman. If a man persists when told firmly to desist, women might call out loudly to passersby, "*Il m'aggresse*", which means that the man is being too aggressive toward her, or even call the police (tel: 17).

THE STUDENT LIFE
EU Nationals
Citizens of EU countries may study in any other EU country. In France, they must be enrolled in an accredited institution, have health insurance and enough financial wherewithal to cover their stay in France. EU citizens—including students— also have the right to work in France (see Chapter Nine). Upon registering with an institution, the student will receive an identity card that lasts for the period of study and is renewable year by year.

EU nationals might inquire about the EU's Education Programme, Socrates/Erasmus, which encourages student mobility throughout the community (and in several other countries as well.) Qualifying students at a participating institution may study at another such institution for a year. British students should access the British Council website (http://www.britishcouncil.org/erasmus).

If you need to learn the language of the country you will study in, explore the Intensive Language Preparation Courses (ILPC), a short period of intense language study that takes place in the host country just before starting the Erasmus period. For more information on the Socrates/Erasmus Programme, access the EU website (http://ec.europa.eu/ education/lifelong-learning-programme/doc80_en.htm)

Non-EU Nationals

Non-EU nationals who intend to study for a degree or certificate must apply for the *visa de long séjour mention étudiant* before your departure for France. You must already have an *attestation de pré-inscription* (letter of admission) or other forms of acceptance, for example, a *certificat d'inscription* into an accredited institution. Upon arrival in France, you should apply within 30 days for the *carte de séjour temporaire* at the Cité Universitaire International de Paris, Maison International at 17 boulevard Jourdan, 75014. Bring the same documents you used to apply for the initial visa.

Occasionally the French cultural affairs officer will ask to see academic credentials such as transcripts and diplomas. If you are coming to France to study at a language school for less than six months, you may be issued a special *visa d'étudiant pour six mois avec plusieurs entrées*, which should waive the regular student permit. Be prepared to show proof of financial means, indicating that you have enough income to maintain yourself while in France. A medical examination and proof of health insurance are mandatory.

While in France, you will be expected to abide by all French laws. Ignorance of a law will not be accepted as an excuse for having violated it.

Health Insurance

Students must have health insurance. Coverage required is extensive: hospitalisation, outpatient treatment, dental care, medicines and medical evacuation. EU nationals covered by their country's health plans must enclose a French translation of the insurance coverage along with the application. Remember that not all costs of treatment are covered fully under the French health system. For health and insurance information, see pages 123–126 .

Resource Information

For information on the French university system, you might access the official websites of the Ministère de la Jeunesse, de l'Education et de la Recherche (http://www.education.gouv.fr).

The official Campus France has extensive information

on higher education in France, especially helpful for foreign students (website: www.campusfrance.org.) For Campus France offices in your country, access the website.

The *mairie* issues a booklet, *Le Repertoire des Savoirs à Paris* that details all educational opportunities in Paris: workshops, short-term, degree or certificate courses, at the city's museums, libraries, institutions and universities. The Ville de Paris also has an informative website: http://www. etudiantdeparis.fr.

Several well-organised official associations offer advice to young people on education, housing, employment, jobs, discounts on services and events, and dealings with the administration.

- Centre d'Information et de Documentation Jeunesse (CIDJ); 101 quai Branly, 75015; tel: 01.44.49.12.00; fax: 01.40.65.02.61; website:www.cidj.com
- Centre Régional des Œuvres Universitaires et Sociales (CROUS); 39 avenue Georges-Bernanos, 75005; tel: 01.40. 51.36.00; website:http://www.crous-paris.fr
- Centre National des Œuvres Universitaires et Scolaires (CNOUS); 69 quai d'Orsay, 75007; tel: 01.44.18.53.00; website:http://www.cnous.fr

- Mission interuniversitaire de coordination des échanges franco-américains Paris-Ile de France (MICEFA); 26 rue de Faubourg Saint-Jacques, 75014; tel: 01.40.51.76.96; website:http://www.micefa.org. Facilitates the access of American students into French universities and organises academic exchange programmes.

French University Education

All *lycée* graduates who have passed the stringent baccalauréat (*le bac*) examinations are entitled to admission to a state-run university (*la fac*, short for *faculté*). Universities thus tend to be overcrowded, rigid in their curriculum and impersonal. The Institut Universitaire de Technologie (IUT) is a two-year community college system offering certificates in professional and technical specialties.

Top *lycée* students may choose to apply to a business school or an engineering school, or any other *Grande École*. These schools have limited spaces available, for their graduates ultimately become the French elite—the most powerful politicians and civil servants, and the most influential business professionals in France. Among the most sought-after graduates are those from l'École Nationale d'Administration (ENA), Ecole Polytechnique (X), Institut d'Etudes Politiques (IEP or Sciences Po) and Hautes Etudes Commerciales (HEC).

For business schools, there is a one-year course to prepare for the entrance exam.This course is so stringent that many students repeat the year in order to get a better ranking in the exam and thus to be accepted into a better school. The programme for the engineering schools is similar, except that it is a two-year course. Again, some students repeat the course in order to get into a more prestigious school.

- Université de Paris: a conglomerate of some 17 separate institutions offering degree programmes in particular specialties; each institution has its specialties. The most ancient and illustrious, the Sorbonne, founded in 1253, is now also part of the system and known as Université de Paris IV (tel: 01.40.46.22.11; fax:01.40.46.25.88; website: http://www.sorbonne.fr). For information and addresses

Technology has made research more convenient and portable for students. French undergrad surfing online at a streetside cafe in Paris.

for all universities in Paris, ask at the *mairie* for its booklet *Repertoire des Savoirs à Paris* and look in the telephone book under *Université Paris.*

- Collège de France; a prestigious school founded in 1530. A research and teaching institution whose courses are open to everyone without advance registration at 11 place Marcelin Berthelot, Paris 75005; tel: 01.44.27.12.11; 01.44.27.11.09; website:http://www.college-de-france.fr.

The academic year runs from September to June, although sometimes it can start as late as November. Application for admission must be no later than 1 February, meaning that you must request application forms several months before. Forms and informational brochures on university study should be available at the cultural section of French embassies and consulates.

Degrees
The curriculum at all universities is highly regulated. A stringent core curriculum takes up the first two years, after which the Diplôme d'Etudes Universitaires Générales (DEUG) is awarded, or at a technological university, the Diplôme Universitaire de Technologie (DUT). After a third year the *license* (degree) is awarded. Some business or vocational programmes involve a postgraduate *stage* (training internship). A *maîtrise* can be added to the *license*; it requires an added year of study and completion of a dissertation or project and is roughly the equivalent of a Master's Degree. Then the student has a choice between finishing these studies with a more practical diploma called the *Diplôme d'Etudes Supérieures Spécialisées* (*DESS*) or continuing toward a doctorat (PhD) by preparing for a diploma called the *Diplôme d'Etudes Approfondies* (*DEA*).

Qualifications
Any foreign student applying to a French university for a degree programme must meet the stringent requirements of the rigorous educational system in France. British students, for example, must have their A-levels and American students

are often required to have completed two years of college. Fluent French to the point of being able to read complicated texts is necessary and proficiency tests are given before acceptance into a programme. A few of the *Grandes Écoles* have small quotas for foreign students, but in general, non-EU students are rarely admitted.

English Language Institutions

More realistic options for university study include taking a degree from one of the many fully accredited English-language institutions with degree programs in Paris or taking a year abroad sponsored by a university at home. Some schools have better credentials than others, and some may not suit your particular needs or goals, so explore all possibilities.

- The American University of Paris (AUP): 6, rue du Colonel Combes.; tel: 01.40.62.06.00; international admissions tel: 01.40.62.07.20; U.S. tel: (1-303) 993-4326; website: http://www.aup.fr. Bachelor of Arts in a variety of fields, such as art history, comparative literature, economics and modern history; Bachelor of Science in applied economics and computers.
- American Business School (ABS): 12 rue Alexandre-Parodi, 75010; tel: 01.40.03.15.04; fax: 01.40.03.15.05; website: http://www.absparis.org. French school offering an American undergraduate programme in business administration. Students must have the equivalent of the French *bac*, British 'A' levels or an American high school diploma.
- The University of London Institute in Paris: 11 rue de Constantine, 75007; tel: 01.44.11.73.83; fax: 01.45.50.31.55; website: http://www.bip.lon.ac.uk. Programmes in basic and business French, culture, current events, translation. Bachelor of Arts in French studies, leading to a University of London degree.
- Parsons School of Design: 14 rue Letellier, 75015; tel: 01.45.77.39.66; fax: 01.45.77.10.44; website:http://www.parsons-paris.com. Both credit and non-credit programmes in illustration, fashion design, studio arts, computer

graphics, etc., with flexible schedules of day, evening and weekend courses. Bachelor of Fine Arts degree.

- Schiller International University: 7–9 rue Yvart, 75015; tel: 01.45.38.56.01; fax: 01.45.38.54.30; website:http://www.paris-schiller.com. Graduate, undergraduate and business degrees. The focus is on economics and business, government and public administration.
- Paris American Academy: 277 rue Saint-Jacques, 75005; tel: 01.44.41.99.20; fax: 01.44.41.99.29; websitet: http://www.parisamericanacademy.fr. Four-week courses in fine arts, interior design, French language & civilisation, creative writing and fashion. Programmes available in January, June, July and September.

Graduate and MBA Programs

French employers are beginning to look for advanced degrees, such as the Master's in Business Administration (MBA). Corporations are also officially required through the CIF (Congé Individuel de Formation) programme to sponsor continuing education (or training) for their employees. Several schools, including those below, offer MBA programmes in English; their curricula vary, so investigate several, including those mentioned above. Most require some years of work experience in addition to a college degree. Check *FUSAC*, which has extensive ads for educational institutions. Those listed below have English-language programmes.

- INSEAD: 15 boulevard de Constance, 77305 Fontainebleau; tel: 01.60.72.40.05; website: http://www.insead.edu. Internationally known French business school, offering a ten-month MBA, as well as doctoral programmes. On the average, students have five years of business experience.
- American Graduate School of Business, International Relations, and Diplomacy: 101 boulevard Raspail 75007; tel: 01.47.20.00.94; website:http://www.ags.edu. Accredited school for MA and PhD programmes.
- International School of Management: 148 rue de Grenelle, 75007; tel: 01.45.51.09.09; website:http://www.ism.edu. Fully accredited MBA, DBA and PhD programmes

in management, plus customised programmes for senior managers.

- Paris Graduate School of Management: 242 rue du Faubourg Saint-Antoine; tel: 01.55.25.46.28; website:http://www. pgsm-group.com. Bachelor's and Master's of Business Administration; the American MBA offers a year in an accredited American university. The European MBA offers an intensive 12-month programme.

Exam Preparation

Preparatory workshops for college and graduate school qualifying examinations may be taken at the Kaplan Center, 3 bis rue Jean Pierre-Bloch, 75015, which offers courses for the GMAT, GRE, TOEFL, SAT, ISAT, etc.; tel: 01.45.66.55.33; website:http://www.kaptest.com.

Studying French

See Chapter 8, pages 296–297.

Cooking Courses

What could be better than learning to cook in this world capital of haute cuisine? Short- and long-term cooking classes and demonstrations are both instructive and fun. Some of the language schools offer their own classes, but there are well-known cooking schools that offer both serious long-term programmes for serious chefs and short-term courses for those who just love to cook. Librairie Gourmande at 4 rue Dante, 75005 specialises in cookbooks; tel: 01.43.54.37.27.

- Ritz Escoffier School: Ritz Hotel, 38 rue Cambon (Place Vendome), 75001; tel: 01.43.16.30.50; website:http:// www.ritzparis.com. Demonstrations and courses of all levels. Also offers pastry courses, wine appreciation, flower arrangement and even cocktail preparations.
- École Le Cordon Bleu: 8 rue Léon Delhomme, 75015; tel: 01.53.68.22.50; website:http://www.cordonbleu.edu; Short-term courses and demonstrations are held in English; long-term courses for the serious chef are in French. Other addresses throughout the world and in the Loire Valley, at the Château des Briottières.

- École Lenôtre: 10 avenue des Champs-Élysées, 75008; tel: 01.42.65.97.60; website:http://www. lenotre.fr. Workshops and demonstrations for the amateur and a professional cooking school for serious chefs. Also in Cannes.

Libraries

There are hundreds of *bibliothèques* (libraries) in Paris; there is at least one public library in each *arrondissement*. Some libraries specialise in particular fields, there are even some for children only, such as L'Heure Joyeuse at 6 rue des Prêtres-Saint-Séverin, 75006. To obtain a library card, bring identification and proof of domicile. Some libraries may be open only from Tuesdays to Fridays; check before going. In addition, each University of Paris section has its own library for enrolled students, as does the American University of Paris.

- 4ᵉ: Bibliothèque Publique d'Information; Centre George Pompidou, second floor; tel: 01.44.78.12.33; http://www. bpi.fr. Extensive multilingual research library, periodicals, a video and music listening room, software library, Internet access. Open daily; hours vary.

- 7e: American Library in Paris: 10 rue du Général-Camou; tel: 01.53.59.12.60; website:http://www.americanlibraryinparis. org. Europe's largest subscription English-language library with fiction, non-fiction, periodicals, back issues, children's books. Readings, literary programmes, lectures, etc. are also organised. Research facilities available. Tuesdays–Saturdays; 10:00 am–7:00 pm.
- 13e: Bibliothèque Nationale de France, François Mitterand: 11 quai François-Mauriac; tel: 01.53.79.59.59; fax: 01.53.79.43.70; website:http://www.bnf. fr. Twelve million volumes (many in English), reading facilities. An exhibition centre, auditorium, conference room and restaurants also found on the premises. Bibliothèque Nationale at 58 rue de Richelieu, 75002 is the depository for manuscripts, engravings, maps, music scores, etc.; tel: 01.47.03.81.26.

> A complete list of public libraries—'Bibliothèques de la Ville de Paris'—should be available at your *mairie*.

HOUSING

If you are enrolled in a school for the fall semester starting in October, start your housing search in the summer. Do not come to Paris at the end of September and expect to find decent quarters when other students are also looking. If you are under 18, you may need a *garant* (guarantor), most often a parent, to guarantee financial responsibility and to sign the lease for an apartment. Inquire about housing at the resource organisations mentioned above, at the institution with which you will be affiliated and, perhaps, at the Paris Tourist Office, which can sometimes be helpful. The bulletin boards at the American Church and the American Cathedral often have notices of people looking for roommates or for sublets. See Resource Guide in Chapter 10 for addresses.

The Ville de Paris sponsors a major international housing campus, Cité Universitaire, at the southern edge of the city at 19 boulevard Jourdan, 75014; tel: 01.44.16.64.48; website:http://www.ciup.fr. Forty buildings of different national styles are spread across sprawling grounds that include housing for registered foreign students, as well as sports and cultural facilities. Countries have their own buildings and students usually stay in the hostel that corresponds with their nationality.

The Accueil Familial des Jeunes Etrangers at 23 rue du Cherche-Midi, 75006 is an au pair agency that also helps young men and women find rooms in a family home in exchange for work, or paying rooms; tel: 01.42.22.50.34; fax: 01.45.44.60.48; website: http://www.afje-paris.org).

Temporary Housing

Young people may stay inexpensively (and temporarily) at the *auberges de jeunesse* (youth hostels). The maximum stay is generally six nights. Hostels are crowded, so book in advance. Membership cards for Hostelling International can be purchased before departure at travel agencies that cater to budget travel, as well as at hostels themselves. Hostels have no facilities for ensuring the safety of valuables, so if you are bringing extensive baggage or a computer, staying in an inexpensive hotel might be better than in a hostel.

Fédération Unie des Auberges de Jeunesse (FUAJ) at 27 rue Pajol, 75018; tel: 01.44.89.87.27; fax: 01.44.89.87.10; website:http://www.fuaj.org, runs several hostels in the city centre. You can reserve and pay in advance at any hostel that is a member of Hosteling International (website: http://www.hihostels.com).

STUDENTS AND RATP

If you will be using the public transportation system regularly for school, investigate Imagine R, the RATP yearly pass for students that allows unlimited use of public transportation within Paris Zones 1 and 2 for a steeply discounted price.

THE WORLD CAPITAL OF FOOD

CHAPTER 6

'Eating in France is a ritual that
can reach religious proportions.'
—David Applefield

FRENCH CUISINE

Parisians love their restaurants. They love to eat in this capital of haute cuisine, and when they're not eating, they're talking about where to eat next. While Paris itself is not known for a particular cuisine, the city has, luckily, taken to its heart all the finest regional cuisines of France; what is served in the finest restaurants is called haute cuisine or *cuisine bourgeoise*.

Exploring the restaurants in Paris, each with its own approach to flavours and textures, will give you the unparalleled opportunity to participate in what is considered one of the world's great art forms. With some 10,000 eating establishments in Paris, ranging from casual cafés to world-renowned restaurants, dining within your budget is possible. Of course, the more refined the restaurant, the higher the price: a meal in a restaurant with Michelin 'stars' may cost about € 200 per person, wine not included, and even an average three-course dinner in a small bistro can cost about € 35, including a carafe of the *vin de la maison* (house wine). Although there is little that is truly cheap in Paris, prices are more reasonable in neighbourhood bistros and *brasseries* and in the interesting Asian and North African eateries where the food, although not as beautifully presented, can be delicious. Consult the restaurant guides and experiment with restaurants until you find those that please your palate—and purse. *Nouvelle cuisine*, an adaptation of traditional cooking that uses lighter foods, combinations of exotic ingredients and small portions, did not catch on in Paris, although many people are nonetheless eating lighter foods and smaller portions. This is partly because the portions served were usually already smaller than in restaurants elsewhere, especially in North America. *Cuisine de terroir*, which is currently popular, offers dishes in larger portions than *nouvelle cuisine* and combines regional ingredients with more traditional recipes. 'Slow food' offers leisurely meals that respect both the ecology and culinary traditions of the region and has its *passionnés* (fans) in Paris.

Many restaurants cater to the desire for lighter foods by cooking with olive oil rather than butter and cream. They are also experimenting with dishes to suit the tastes and budgets of a younger generation that is not willing to spend € 100 on one meal, a younger set that tends to frequent the more casual *brasseries* and bistros, wine bars, tearooms, and the inexpensive Asian restaurants. Fish restaurants and bistros are also increasingly attractive to people concerned about health and fitness. (Fish is freshest on Friday and some fish restaurants are closed on Monday.)

Paris has many restaurants offering the cuisines from the different regions of France or *cuisine de province/cuisine régionale*. These vary in quality and price, but it is possible to sample all the cuisines of France without leaving Paris, for example, the sausage and sauerkraut dishes of Alsace, tomato- and olive oil-based dishes of Provence, pork dishes from Lyon, cheese dishes from Savoy or the creamy specialties of Normandy. *Cuisine bonne femme* means home-cooked food, and a dish labelled '*maison*' means that it is a specialty prepared in-house.

THE MENU

First, note that in a restaurant, you will be brought *la carte* (the menu). Ordering *à la carte*, that is, from the standard *carte* is the most expensive way to dine, so it's best to check out the day's *menu*. In a French restaurant, *le menu* does not refer to the 'menu' as we understand it in English, that is, the list of offerings, but to a set meal of two or three courses. Restaurants of all calibres offer a *menu* (also called the *formule* or *prix fixe*), which is a fixed-price meal of a suggested combination of courses for that day. The price is determined according to the number of courses ordered. Sometimes the set menu is offered only at lunch (*midi*); sometimes it includes the house wine. Often a *plat du jour* (daily special) is written on a chalkboard or printed on a paper inserted into the menu. Aside from the lower price, another benefit of the *plat du jour* is that you'll be eating food that is at the height of its season. In autumn, for instance, game dishes such as boar, hare, pheasant and venison appear on menus, as well as wild mushrooms—*chanterelles*, *cèpes* and *girolles*. Spring and summer see *navarin d'agneau* (spring lamb stew), *morilles* (morels), asparagus, melons and other seasonal produce that make their appearance. Some of the finer restaurants offer a *menu dégustation*—a sampling of the chef's creations.

Your *serveur/serveuse* (waiter/waitress) is the best source for questions concerning the meal. The waiter profession is a respected one in France, and waiters, knowledgeable about ingredients and methods of preparation, take pride in what they serve. Waiters generally wear a similar uniform of black trousers, white shirt and often, a black bow tie. In better restaurants, they wear dinner jackets, while in cafés and *brasseries* they may wear a black, pocketed vest. Waiters are cordial, but they do not presume—as they sometimes do in America—to be your friends; you should not presume so either. Treat them pleasantly and with respect.

Do not hesitate to discuss with the *serveur* the ingredients in a dish you would like to order, to specify politely what you can and cannot eat, and to ask advice. Most often, the waiter will go back to the kitchen to discuss with the chef, but if he says that your request 'cannot be done', it could mean intransigence on his part; more likely than not, it means that the success of the dish requires a special method of preparation that cannot be altered. In such a case, order a different dish.

Start with an *entrée* (appetiser), then have the *plat* (main course). *Salade* (salad), heretofore served after the *plat*, is now usually served as an *entrée*. After the *plat*, a variety of cheeses may be offered; select a few of different textures. Then comes dessert and after that, café. If this all sounds like too much food, don't be concerned about ordering less. It is no longer frowned upon to order two courses instead of a three-course meal, and it is acceptable to share an appetiser or dessert, or to skip the cheese or dessert altogether. The French drink coffee after dessert, not with it, and except for breakfast, they do not drink *café crème* with meals, just small and potent café. Remember that 'doggy bags' do not exist in France.

How Do You Like Your Food?

When ordering, understand that the French generally like their food cooked minimally.

- *bleu* is hardly warm.
- *saignant* is browned on the exterior and warm on the inside.
- *à point* is medium.
- *bien cuit* is well done—although perhaps not well done enough for foreigners.

Specify in advance if you insist on having your meat well done. Veal may be *rosé* (pink) and poultry may also remain pink toward the bone. Also, if you like fish but hate the bones, ask to have it *préparé*, and your *serveur* will debone it for you.

THE AGREEABLE SEARCH

Bookstores carry an array of guides devoted to dining in Paris. The *Guide Michelin* awards up to three stars to the best restaurants; when a three-star restaurant loses a star, the scandal makes news all over the world. News of restaurants also appear in the daily newspapers and Parisians keep track of the opening and closing of restaurants, and when a famous chef leaves one establishment for another or opens his own.

Reading the descriptions and reviews of restaurants can become addictive. Start with your tourist guidebook. All guides recommend restaurants, rating them according to their readership—some concentrate on inexpensive establishments

In 2003, celebrated French chef Bernard Loiseau committed suicide, not long after the influential *Gault Millau* restaurant guide had downgraded his Côte d'Or restaurant in Burgundy.

catering to a budget traveller, while others may feature upmarket restaurants. The annually-updated *Zagat* guide rates restaurants according to readers' preferences, and the well-respected *Le Petit Lebey des Bistros Parisiens* lists bistros, *brasseries* and *bars à vin* (wine bars).

How to Choose

Categories of eating establishments overlap considerably, and what you might consider an upmarket restaurant with high prices, might consider itself a bistro. Even guidebooks differ in their particular categorisations. What an eating establishment is called matters less, of course, than the specialties of each, the quality of ingredients and their preparation, the service and the price. Good establishments of any category will be crowded, as Parisians love to eat out. Except in fine restaurants, do not expect to find a quiet corner for a private conversation.

Parisians eat outdoors whenever they can. If there is a spot of sun and a table, a Parisian will find it. Every café terrace will be crowded and restaurants that can do so, have tables outside, be it 20 tables with white parasols in an elegant courtyard or three small rickety ones on a too-narrow sidewalk. Some 4,000 cafés and restaurants have outdoor seating.

With so many restaurants and choices, recommendations from friends or your own exploration can be most helpful. All restaurants post their menus in their front windows, from which you can ascertain the type of cuisine, the specialties and the price range. When passing an inviting restaurant, step in and ask for a business card to take note of the location and telephone number, and look in at mealtimes to see whether a place seems filled with locals—people who already know what is good or bad, what is 'in' or 'out'.

Of course it is possible to get a bad meal in Paris, as it is anywhere. For instance, locals rarely frequent the establishments along the Grands Boulevards, for they generally cater to tourists, and although the food can sometimes be good, the service tends to be impersonal and prices high. (If a menu is printed in three or four languages with pictures of different flags, you can be sure it caters to tourists.) In Paris, if you heed recommendations of friends or the suggestions of a restaurant guide, disappointments will be rare.

It is most important to decide what you want for a particular meal. Do you want a formal meal in a restaurant or something light and fast? Do you want a warm welcome and friendly, casual service? Do you want to sample an innovative dish at a particular restaurant? Do you want to be guided by a knowledgeable waiter and sommelier to eating and drinking à la *française*? Do you want to celebrate a great occasion and take part in a gastronomic experience that you will always remember? Or on a particular day, do you just want your meat cooked to a crisp and some coffee with the main course (no matter how barbaric it seems to your waiter)? In the case of the latter, you should stick with restaurants that cater to many nationalities. In any case, respect each restaurant for what it is. A small, local bistro will not have refined, gourmet food and a two-star restaurant may not whip up a hamburger for your kids (although priding themselves on service, they may well do so).

Do not be hidebound. Experiment with dishes you have never heard of and foods not popular in your own country. France knows what to do with food. Even in restaurants of haute cuisine, expect to find beautifully prepared dishes made from inexpensive meats such as tripe, brains or kidneys—all considered delicacies by the French. After trying them, you might see why.

Some places advertise *à volonté*, meaning that for a particular dish, you may eat as much as you want for the price listed.

Business Hours

Restaurants and bistros open around noon and are busiest between 1:00 pm and 2:30 pm. They close after lunch and reopen for dinner. Lunch is a popular meal to eat out and restaurants are often full. When exploring an elegant restaurant, think about first trying it at lunch, when the portions served are smaller and less expensive than at dinner, but of the same quality. Dinner service starts at 7:30 pm and restaurants begin to fill up around 8:30 pm, taking their last order about 11:00 pm. *Brasseries* serve food all day, as do many of the *salons de thé*. Most restaurants close one day a week, and until recently it was hard to find a restaurant open on Sunday, except for kosher and Asian establishments.

Some establishments close around holidays and many, even those of haute cuisine, close for a *fermeture annuelle* (annual holiday) sometime in July or August. If they stay open, they may keep an irregular schedule, closing on the weekends or for lunch on Monday. In summer, it is best to double-check.

Dinner reservations at top restaurants can be made a month in advance. For the currently trendy restaurants, call several weeks ahead; for a restaurant in the neighbourhood, perhaps a day or two before the dinner. Lunch reservations are somewhat easier to obtain. *Maîtres d'hôtel* may ask for the number of *couverts* (table settings) rather than how many people. Some ask that confirmation be made on the day, and if they do not know you, may ask for your telephone number. You may request to be seated in an *espace non-fumeur* (no smoking section)—but it hardly makes a difference in crowded bistros. And don't forget that in making reservations, one usually uses the 24-hour clock: thus if you want to dine at 9:00 pm, ask for a reservation at 21 *heures*.

Cancel a reservation if you cannot make it, and do not arrive late, thinking mistakenly that you will just have to wait—seating is generally prompt, the *maître d'hôtel* having gauged when the previous party will vacate the table, and many of the best restaurants have one seating only. In the best restaurants men should wear jackets. Although dining out is more casual than heretofore, it is still best to dress appropriately for the establishment; it even heightens the sense of occasion. See *Restaurants* in the *Yellow Pages*.

Paying the Bill

L'addition (the bill) will not be brought to you automatically, for it would seem rude to presume you are finished if you are not. Signal the waiter by saying "*Monsieur*" or "*s'il-vous-plaît*" never "*garçon*" even though that is what you may have been taught in elementary French class. If the waiter is nearby, say "*l'addition, s'il-vous-plait*", or make the universal hand signal that he will recognise right away.

Almost all restaurants accept foreign credit cards. If using a credit card, do not include a *pourboire* (tip), which is already included in *l'addition*—this is indicated on the menu by *service compris*. Although the service is included one way or the other, the customer should leave a small amount on the table: perhaps five per cent in moderately-priced restaurants and more in elegant restaurants. Be sure to check the bill for accuracy.

RECOMMENDATIONS

One of the great pleasures of living in Paris is to collect restaurant favourites, noting on the back of business cards a memorable meal and filing them away, then passing on these *bonnes addresses* (good places) to friends. That's what I'm doing in this chapter by naming just a few eating spots. I like the ambience or the *accueil* (welcome) of some, but I respect the quality of the dishes prepared of all, regardless of the level of the establishment. *Voilà*, all my personal favourites below, representing a variety of culinary possiblities and categories.

Restaurants

A restaurant generally showcases refined dining at prices to match. Establishments run from the excellent to the world-famous, but in all, the presentation of the food and attentive service are part of the value of the meal. The patron of a small restaurant may personally supervise all dishes that come from the kitchen and make recommendations on wine, whereas the larger establishments have several *serveurs* dedicated to each table, plus a *sommelier* to discuss the wine. Service will be efficient but not rushed, and a full meal may take two or three pleasant hours. If you don't want to spend that much time (or money), there are excellent bistros to explore. What follows are some of my favourites:

■ 7e: Le Divellec; 107 rue de l'Université; tel: 01.45.51.91.96. Fish and seafood like you've never eaten before. Haute

Taillevent

8e: Taillevent; 15 rue Lamennais; tel: 01.44.95.15.01. Ooh-la-la! Some people think this is the best restaurant in Paris. I only know that for my birthday this is where I always hope to go. Haute cuisine at its finest with a formal yet intimate atmosphere and a wine list that is among the best. Closed on weekends.

cuisine of the seas, prepared with delicacy and elegance. Exquisite lobster dishes, the most seductive of oysters and even some spectacular desserts. Closed on weekends.

- 7e: Petrossian;18 boulevard deLatour Maubourg; tel: 01.44.11.32.32. Specialties in this one-star restaurant are its selections of imported caviars and mouthwatering fish dishes, presented in a beautiful and refined setting, with service to match. The best bargain is the € 38 lunch menu. The restaurant and its adjacent *traiteur* (takeaway delicatessen) are closed on Sundays.
- 8e: Flora Danica; 142 avenue des Champs-Elysées; tel: 01.44.13.86.26. If you love salmon, this is the place to go. And to go again. Salmon of all sorts—smoked, marinated, poached and roasted—but other equally delicious dishes if you don't fancy salmon.
- 16e: Hiramatsu; 52 rue de Longchamp; tel: 01.56.81.08.80. For special occasions, this one-star restaurant offers refined and imaginative French cuisine with a delicate Japanese attitude. With only 36 covers, this is an expensive but elegant experience. Closed on weekends.

Bistros

Some say that 'bistro' (alternatively spelt as 'bistrot') is a Russian word meaning 'hurry' and was introduced into France by Russian soldiers in 1815. Others claim it comes from the word *bistrouille*, which in certain northern regions is a mixture of coffee and *eau de vie*. The mention of 'bistro' once conjured up the image of hearty, home-cooked food in a casual, welcoming setting, but now bistros run the gamut from the small, family-run establishments to the extremely elegant and chic. The menu in casual bistros is often written on a blackboard and is changed daily according to what is in season, supplementing traditional dishes such as *bœuf bourguignon* (beef stewed in red wine) and *blanquette de veau* (creamy veal stew). Meals run from the modern and trendy, traditional and hearty, to old favourites imaginatively executed with a modern twist. Decent house wines are often sold by the carafe, but more impressive wines can also be found.

Try the bistros opened by younger chefs who have trained under the master chefs. Offering imaginative interpretations and reasonable prices, these establishments are among the most popular. Also, some of the noted chefs themselves have opened their own bistros, allowing people to savour their high-quality preparations at affordable prices. These are generally mentioned in guidebooks, featuring the name of the chef. Be sure to book in advance. My favourites:

- 1er: L'Escargot Montorgueil; 38 rue Montorgueil; tel: 01.42.36.83.51. In the market street, this old, staid-looking establishment on two floors has what I think are the best snails in Paris, with a sampler plate. Good dishes of all sorts. Closed on Sundays.
- 1er: Les Cartes Postales; 7 rue Gomboust; tel: 01.42.61.02. 93. Imaginative 'new French' cuisine, where it's also possible to sample multiple smaller plates with a definite Asian touch. Intimate ambience. Closed on Sundays.
- 6e: Le Voltaire; 27 quai Voltaire; tel: 01.42.61.17.49. Refined and elegant, intimate and welcoming, with toothsome dishes that are always perfectly prepared and presented. Make sure to reserve well in advance. Closed on Sundays.
- 6e: Le Mâchon d'Henri; 8 rue Guisarde; tel: 01.43.29.08.70. Tiny, smoky, crowded with locals and a lot of fun, offering good, hearty Lyon-inspired food. Chalkboard with the day's menu ensures the freshest of food. Friendly service and good prices.
- 15e: Chamade Café; 42bis avenue de Suffren; tel: 01.47.34.62.22. I like everything about this charming, upmarket neighbourhood place: the friendly welcome, the interesting dishes, especially the *magret de canard* (duck fillet) and the prices. In autumn, try the game dishes—wild boar, pigeon and duck.

- 17e: l'Huitrier; 16 rue Saussier-Leroy; tel: 01.40.54.83.44. Some of the best oysters in Paris, excellent fish dishes and good value for money in a little neighbourhood treasure. Hidden in a narrow street near the market at rue Poncelet.

Brasseries

Brasserie means 'brewery'. *Brasseries* began serving beer in the 17th century, and toward the end of the last century, started offering hearty Alsatian sausages and *choucroute* (sauerkraut), plus Alsatian Riesling and Gewurtztraminer wines. Current *brasseries* tend to serve simple, light meals and fresh fish, usually nicely presented and reasonably priced. Bright, lively and bustling, *brasseries* often remain open all day and stay open late. It is highly recommended to reserve in advance for the more popular ones. Pay attention to the decor: some look like traditional beer houses while others have an inviting Belle Epoque decor or Art Deco wood panelling and interesting glass and mirrors. See *Cafés, bars, brasseries* in the *Yellow Pages*. My favourites:

- 6e: Bouillon Racine; 3 rue Racine; tel: 01.44.32.15.60. A stunningly beautiful Art Nouveau *brasserie*, serving both Belgian and French specialties and a variety of interesting beers on tap. On some nights it can get crowded and hectic around 9:00 pm, so be prepared to wait; or go earlier.
- 7e: Le Petit Lutétia; 107 rue de Sèvres; tel: 01.45.48.33.53. Tourists may have found this charming *brasserie*, but the locals still come for the chalkboard specials, the *confit de canard* (preserved duck), the friendly *accueil* and the reasonable prices. Open till late.
- 12e: Le Train Bleu, located in the Gare de Lyon; tel: 01.43.43.09.06. It may be in a train station, but you'll wish the train would never come. A beautiful Belle Epoque dining room, with frescoes on the ceilings, murals on the walls and classic French cuisine. Certainly not cheap, but a worthwhile Paris experience, to be sure.
- 18^e: Wepler; 14 place de Clichy; tel: 01.45.22.53.24. Old-time Paris, modern oysters and seafood platters, crowded, noisy and fun. Stays open late.

International Offerings

France having been a major colonial nation, Paris has long-established North African and Asian restaurants throughout the city. Although Asian restaurants and *traiteurs* are found in most *arrondissements*, the 13ᵉ is known for its inexpensive Chinese and Vietnamese restaurants, as is Belleville in the 19ᵉ (also popular for its North African restaurants). Inexpensive Indian and Pakistani establishments are found in and around the Passage Brady in the 10ᵉ and Japanese restaurants around rue Sainte-Anne in the 2ᵉ. My favourites:

- (Chinese) 5ᵉ: Mirama; 17 rue Saint-Jacques; tel: 01.43.54.71.77. Lines spill out of the door for its excellent dumpling and noodle soups, as well as the roast duck and pork.
- (Italian) 12ᵉ: Sardegna a Tavola; 1 rue de Cotte; tel: 01.44.75.03.28. Authentic Sardinian specialties in an attractive Italian-style setting. Always crowded, reservations are necessary.
- (Lebanese) 16ᵉ: Noura; 21 avenue Marceau; tel: 01.47.20.33.33. Authentic Middle Eastern specialties such as hummus, tabouleh, marinated meat dishes and good Lebanese desserts. Other addresses. Open till late.
- (North African) 17ᵉ: Fradji; 42 rue Poncelet; tel: 01.47.54.91.40. Tunisian kosher restaurant with excellent couscous, welcoming service and a lively atmosphere. Moderate prices.
- (Pan-Asian) 13ᵉ: Tricotin; 15 avenue de Choisy; tel: 01.45.84.74.44. Crowded, noisy, cheap, fast and excellent. Pick and choose from Chinese and Vietnamese dishes, a wide choice available for soups and appetisers.
- (Tex-Mex) 16ᵉ: Susan's Place; 9 rue de l'Annonciation; tel: 01.45.20.8816. Probably the most well-known of the Tex-Mex places in Paris.
- (Thai) 7ᵉ: Le Petit Thiou; 3 rue Surcouf; tel: 01.40.62.96.70. Reasonably priced, modern restaurant serving excellent dishes. Lower-priced but of the same quality as its more upmarket, famous parent Thiou around the corner at 49 quai d'Orsay (tel: 01.40.62.96.70). Closed on Sundays.

- (Thai) 20ᵉ: Royal Bangkok; 4 rue du Cher; tel: 01.46.36.46.24). Perhaps off the beaten track, but authentic Thai specialties at reasonable prices. Worth making the trip.
- (Vietnamese) 5ᵉ: Kim Lien; 33 place Maubert; tel: 01.43.54.68.13. It's hard to choose among the many good Vietnamese establishments in Paris, but this one has a wide selection of dishes, well-prepared and interesting.

And of course, now there's sushi all around Paris, fresh and delicious. My favourites:

- 1ᵉʳ: Kinugawa; 9 rue du Mont Thabor; tel. 01.42.60.65.07. Expensive but first-class sushi in an upmarket setting. Generally crowded, so reserve in advance. Also at 4 rue St-Philippe-du-Roule, 75008; tel: 01.45.63.08.07. Closed on Sundays.
- 6ᵉ: Tsukizi; 2bis rue des Ciseaux; tel: 01.43.54.65.19. A tiny sushi bar in a short, narrow street. A few tables, a small counter, but delectable sushi. Reserve in advance. Closed on Sundays.
- 11ᵉ: Sukiyaki; 12 rue de la Roquette; tel: 01.49.23.04.98. Excellent sushi and other Japanese selections in a popular local restaurant near the Bastille.
- 16ᵉ: Matsuri; 2-4 rue de Passy; tel: 01.42.24.96.85; website:http://www.matsuri.fr. Good sushi on a conveyor belt allows you to have a fast lunch and choose only the dishes you wish. Reasonable prices. Two other addresses, home delivery also available.

Vegetarian Restaurants

Given the French reliance on meats, cream sauces and butter, it used to be difficult to find vegetarian, much less vegan, restaurants in Paris. This is no longer true and many restaurants will put together a platter of vegetables on request. Vegetarian fare is standard at Asian and Indian restaurants, and meatless dishes are common at Italian and *cacher* (kosher) restaurants as well.

- 5ᵉ: Les Cinq Saveurs d'Anada; 72 rue du Cardinal-Lemoine; tel: 01.43.29.58.54.

- 8ᵉ: Cine Città Café; 7 rue d'Aguesseau; tel: 01.42.68.05.03. Italian pastas and fish dishes in an upmarket kosher setting.

And the Unexpected...

Some places offer excellent food in interesting creations, others are offbeat and fun, yet others are just plain different. Paris always surprises and rarely disappoints. Below is a small selection:

- 4ᵉ: Chez Marianne; 2 rue des Hospitalières Saint-Gervais; tel: 01.42.72.18.86. Create your own plate of delicacies from a large variety of Middle Eastern and Central European specialties such as hummus, falafel, *foie de voillaie haché* (chopped chicken liver), etc. A popular and casual venue.
- 4ᵉ: L'As du Falafel; 34 rue des Rosiers; tel: 01.48.87.63.60. Down the street from Chez Marianne, this crowded kosher eatery serves the best falafel and *schwarma* (sandwich of shaved meat) in town. Order from the takeaway window or eat at tables jammed together. At lunchtime you may be rushed out before you've had your coffee in order to accommodate the people queuing—it's worth the wait.
- 5ᵉ: Breakfast in America; 17 rue des Ecoles; tel: 01.43.54.50.28. An American diner in Paris that serves real American breakfasts such as pancakes, H&H bagels, eggs and bacon, plus American burgers and cheesecake. Open daily; Sunday brunch available all day.
- 6ᵉ: Huîtrerie Regis; 3 rue de Montfaucon; tel: 01.44.41.10.17. This tiny modern place next to *métro* Mabillon serves only delicious oysters and prawns (*crevettes*) with their usual accompaniments. Open all day, Tuesday–Sunday.
- 6ᵉ: Le Relais de l'Entrecôte; 20 bis rue Saint-Benoit; tel: 01.45.49.16.00. At this fun steak restaurant, there's no choice except for dessert. You tell the waiter how you like your meat prepared, and the salad, steak and *frites* (fries)—all good—will come. Beware; they don't take reservations and there's always a line.
- 7ᵉ: Au Petit Sud-Ouest; 46 avenue de la Bourdonnais; tel: 01.45.55.59.59. Toast your own bread at your table for the delicious foie gras, served in this Southwestern

French restaurant tucked behind a small specialty shop. *Confit*, *cassoulet* and other excellent duck dishes. Closed on Sundays.

- 9ᵉ: J'Go; 4 rue Drouot; tel: 01.40.22.09.09. A play on the word *gigot* (roasted leg of lamb), this excellent restaurant specialises in lamb dishes from Quercy. Order chops for the individual diner or roasts for the entire group. Closed on Sundays.

- 12ᵉ: Le Baron Rouge; 1 rue Théophile Roussel; tel: 01.43.43.14.32. Ordinarily a wine bar adjacent to the lively Marché Aligre, the street is closed on Sundays and transformed into an oyster party. Bundle up in winter and be prepared to stand outside and eat dozens of oysters (or cold cuts) shoulder to shoulder with the crowd, downing your meal with glasses of crisp white wine.

Cafés and Bars

The café is an all-purpose eating establishment: you may linger over a breakfast croissant and coffee, dash in for a light lunch, stop for a cup of tea and a snack in the afternoon, or enjoy a drink in the evening. Ranging from the famous and expensive, to those catering to regulars from the *quartier*, cafés generally do not bother much about decor. Many have outdoor tables and are busy late into the night. Some cafés also double up as *bar/tabacs*, where you can buy items such as cigarettes, stamps, lottery tickets and telephone cards. Most importantly, some cafés are the community gathering places for friends. Each neighbourhood café has its own personality and loyal *habitués* (regulars), and can be a lot of fun.

Cafés are open all day and well into the night. Most neighbourhood cafés close around 10:00 pm; those in touristy areas stay open later. If a table at a café has a placemat and a table setting at mealtimes, it is reserved for those who come to eat; find a bare table if you just want to have a cup of coffee. For a quick coffee or a mineral water, stand at the *comptoir* (counter), where the prices are cheaper.

A bar has more to do with atmosphere than with

alcohol, and some daytime cafés are popular bars by night, serving drinks and simple meals until the wee hours. People go to their favourite bars at all times of the day: for a quick jolt of coffee in the mornings, for a simple lunch, for an apéritif before the theatre or drink after, or just to relax with a fruit juice in the afternoons. The 'happy hour' has become popular in early evening. Some bars have pleasant terraces, others are known for their music, and some are just popular as hangouts. Although there are trendy bars throughout the city, it is a local bar in your neighbourhood that will lure you in—and keep you coming back.

As for fruit juices, if you order an orange juice, you will most likely get something in a can; order, instead, an *orange pressée* or a *citron pressé* (lemonade) for a freshly squeezed drink served with a carafe of water to adjust the strength as you like. Cafés and bars are required to post their prices (*tarifs de consommation*) and distinguish between those for service at the *comptoir* and at tables. See *Bars, cafés* in the *Yellow Pages*.

Know Your Beverages

- *Café*: strong black coffee. Also *expresso, un express* or *un café noir*
- *Café serré*: double strength expresso
- *Noisette*: expresso with a dash of milk
- *Café allongé*: coffee with hot water to dilute it
- *Café filtre*: black coffee, less strong
- *Café au lait*: coffee with milk
- *Café crème*: coffee with steamed cream or milk
- *Décaféiné* or *un déca*: decaffeinated coffee
- *Thé nature*: plain tea
- *Thé citron*: tea with lemon
- *Thé au lait*: tea with milk
- *Infusion*: herbal tea
- *Chocolat chaud*: hot chocolate

Remnants of a visit to a Paris café.

Salons de Thé

Parisians drink tea but not with meals other than breakfast. If you order tea in a bar, you will get a tea bag or something already sweetened. Instead, Paris delights in its *salons de thé* (tea salons), which serve exotic teas, coffees and light meals, often in a lovely ambience. Tearooms tend to stay open all day, many opening at breakfast and closing around 7:30–8:00 pm. Well-known salons offer formal high teas, including those of hotels such as the Ritz, Crillon and Meurice, but these can be more expensive and less friendly than the independent salons. Many of the local establishments sell teas to take home, including *tisanes/infusions*. See *Salons de Thé* in the *Yellow Pages*.

- 1er: Angélina; 226 rue de Rivoli; tel: 01.42.60.82.00. The most famous in Paris. Teas, light meals and unforgettable *chocolat chaud*, a wintertime favourite of Parisians.
- 1er: Jean-Paul Hévin; 231 rue Saint-Honoré; tel: 01.55.35.35.96. This could be what some people claim is 'the world's best *chocolatier*' with unbelievably delicious pastries, teas, *chocolat chaud*, plus light lunches and snacks. Closed on Sundays.

- 4e, 6e and 8e: Mariage Frères, 30 rue du Bourg-Tibourg; tel: 01.42.72.28.11; 13 rue des Grands-Augustins tel: 01.40.51. 82.50
  260 rue du Faubourg-Saint-Honoré; tel: 01.46.22.18.54
  Celebrated, elegant *salon de thé*, offering dozens of teas, light meals and lovely pastries.
- 5e: La Mosquée; 39 rue Geoffroy Saint-Hillaire; tel: 01.43.31. 18.14. An interesting salon in a mosque.
- 8e: Ladurée; 16 rue Royale; tel: 01.42.60.21.79. Fashionable, always crowded and famous for its macaroons. Full meals are excellent as well. The salon at 75 avenue des Champs-Elysées stays open until 1:00 am (tel: 01.40.75.08.75). Also found at 21 rue Bonaparte (tel: 01.44.07.64.87).

The Wine List

Wine has been produced on French soil since the time of the Romans 2,000 years ago. Currently, about a quarter of the world's annual wine production originates from France, amounting to almost two billion gallons, culled from some three million planted acres. Despite the seemingly large selection in wine shops around the world, most French wines are not exported, so living in Paris affords the best opportunity to taste and learn about wine.

The French love wine and are knowledgeable about their country's wine-growing regions and offerings. They generally understand which wines go best with which type of meal, enhancing both the appreciation of the meal and the wine. This can be easily—and pleasantly—learned by tasting wines at any of the city's many wine bars, taking every opportunity to explore the *cartes des vins* (wine lists) in Paris restaurants and by asking advice of a knowledgeable *sommelier*. You might also explore the Musée du Vin at rue des Eaux/5 square Charles Dickens, 75016, and try its restaurant and wine tastings (tel: 01.45.25.63.26; website:http://www. museeduvinparis.com).

It is not necessary to order an entire bottle of wine, and many people do not. Although the French have a reputation for great alcohol consumption, most people consume alcoholic beverages, primarily wine, only at mealtimes, sipping for the taste but drinking water to quench the thirst—this brings out the flavour of the wine and lessens the effect of the alcohol. Even some of the better wines are now available in half-bottles, and restaurants are beginning to serve wine by the glass. In neighbourhood restaurants, the house wine is generally a decent *vin de table* and comes in several sizes: *un carafe* is a litre, *un demi* is half a litre and *un quart* is a quarter of a litre. *Un pichet* (a pitcher) can be had for a *demi* and a *quart*. Regional restaurants offer a selection of wines that compliment their cuisine. Order, too, some water, either *un carafe d'eau*, which is tap water and provided free, or mineral water, either sparkling (*gazeuse*) or still (*plate*).

Drinking hard liquor such as whisky before dinner is thought to deaden the taste buds. Instead, try an *apéritif*, such as vermouth, porto, *pastis*, *kir* (white wine with a drop of blackcurrant liquor or *crème de cassis*) or *kir royal*, made with champagne. After dinner, a *digestif* would be a subtle *cognac*, the fuller *armagnac*, *calvados* or any fruity *eau de vie* such as *poire William* (pear).

Learn about French regional wines by frequenting the city's ubiquitous *bars à vin* (wine bars). Each has its particular emphasis on both wines and food. Open for lunch and early evening meals, wine bars are similar to cafés, but the offerings tend to be more interesting. Wine bars can be wood-panelled and staid, or modern and noisy. The food also varies, but in general includes light foods and salads. Wine bars are popular as much for their sociability as their fare, and people linger after work or late in the evening. Prices are determined by the wines sampled, and these range from the ordinary to the excellent. L'Ecluse is a well-known, popular wine bar with five locations.

Many wine shops have tastings (see pages 228–229). My favourites (in addition to Le Baron Rouge, mentioned above):

- 1er: Juvéniles; 47 rue de Richelieu; tel: 01.42.97.46.49. Casual wine bar where English is spoken. A large selection of French and imported wines, by the glass as well as the bottle. Choose from hearty fare or tapas-style smaller plates. A fun place. Closed on Sundays.

- 1er: La Taverne Henri IV; 13 place du Pont-Neuf; tel: 01.43.54.27.90. On the Île-de-la-Cité, this old wine bar has been remodelled and updated. Closed on Sundays.

Beer

Parisian beer houses sell their brews in an entirely Gallic ambience. *Bière à la pression* is draft beer and comes in three sizes: the most common *demi* (8 oz), *sérieux* (16 oz) or *formidable* (about a litre). France produces a few bottled beers, Kronenbourg and Stella Artois being the best known. If you order a *bière*, you would have asked for a bottled beer. For draft beer, order *un demi* or whatever size you want.

Currently it is the pub—Irish, Australian, British and Scottish —that has hit the city hard, and more are springing up. They host special events for their country's holidays, play sporting events on large television screens, arrange dart competitions and offer just about anything to be found in a traditional pub, including the food. *Funky Paris* (http://www.funkymaps.com), distributed free, has current information on the pub scene. See *Bars, pianos-bars, pubs* in the *Yellow Pages*.

- The Frog is a popular chain of pubs with locations all around the city, serving fresh-brewed ales from imported British ingredients, and other draft beers:
  The Frog & Rosbif; 116 rue St-Denis 75002
  Frog & Princesse; 9 rue Princesse 75006
  The Frog at Bercy Village; 25 cour Saint-Emilion
  The Frog & British Library; 114 avenue de France
- 5e: Café Aussie; 184 rue Saint-Jacques; tel: 01.43.54.30.48. Happy hour, special events and televised sports matches in an Aussie stronghold.
- 6e: The Highlander, 8 rue de Nevers; tel: 01.43.26.54.20. Two floors of activities with a Scottish flavour—televised sports matches, weekly events. Open until 5:00 am.
- 6^e: The Moose; 16 rue des Quatre Vents; tel: 01.46.33.77.00. Canadian bar and grill and good beer on tap.

Ice Cream

La glace (ice cream) has traditionally been consumed in summer, but with international chains opening shops

throughout Paris, it is becoming popular year round. Parisian *glaciers* (ice cream makers and parlours) often make their creations on the premises using fresh ingredients. What makes French ice cream so delicious is that the flavours taste so real. Moreover, with smaller portions and less butterfat than the imported ice creams, a dish or cone of French *glace* is not overwhelming. Despite the popularity of ice cream, Paris' most celebrated *glacier*, Berthillon, closes for most of the summer, but some groceries and eating establishments carry their ice cream. Häagen-Dazs has more than a dozen outlets throughout Paris and is available at supermarkets. See *Glaciers* in the *Yellow Pages*. My favourites:

- 4^e: Berthillon; 31 rue St-Louis-en-l'Ile; tel: 01.43.54.31.61
- 6^e: Ben and Jerry's; 1 rue du Four; tel: 01.43.25.10.63
- 7^e: Martine Lambert; 192 rue de Grenelle; tel: 01.45.51.25.30
- 14^e: Glacier Calabrese; 15 rue d'Odessa; tel: 01.43.20.31.63

Restauration Rapide

For quick meals, it is easy to find a *casse-croûte* (sometimes called *le snack*). Bars offer pre-made sandwichs, bakeries make their own and *traiteurs* can be found in all neighbourhoods. It is also easy to stop at a café for a *croque-monsieur* (grilled ham and cheese sandwich) or a *croque-madame* (the same sandwich but with a fried egg on top), or to pick up a crêpe at a sidewalk *crêperie*. Some places offer items *sur le pouce* (on the go) for people on the run.

The Italian *panino* (sandwich), made on fresh, warm bread, has become popular. Toastissimo is a small chain selling good *panini*, as is Pomme de Pain. Other eateries advertise sandwiches made with the bread of the famous baker Poilâne. Lina's makes sandwiches to order on the bread of your choice, including Poilâne bread. See *Restaurants: restauration rapide et libre-service* in the *Yellow Pages*.

- 6e: Cosí; 54 rue de Seine; tel: 01.46.33.35.36. The best sandwiches! You choose from a wide choice of fillings to stuff bread steaming hot from the wood-fired oven. Friendly welcome. English spoken.

Student Restaurants

Resto U (*restaurant universitaire*) is a chain of low-priced restaurants for registered students, operated by Centre Régional des Oeuvres Universitaires et Scolaires (CROUS). Some are cafeterias and others are *brasseries-grilles*. The food is plentiful and nourishing. Students with a valid student card may buy tickets at any Resto U during lunch and dinner hours. Tickets may be bought individually or more cheaply in a carnet of 10. For a list of the restaurants, inquire at CROUS at 39 avenue Georges-Bernanos, 75005 (tel: 01.40.51.36.00; website:http://www.crous-paris.fr).

EATING IN
Knowing How

Knowing how and when to shop for food is the key to eating well at home in Paris, whether you intend to cook or not. Wide-ranging options include buying fresh ingredients and starting from scratch, or buying the artistically prepared, ready-to-cook meats from the butcher and adding already cleaned potatoes and vegetables. You can also buy entire, freshly cooked meals from a *traiteur* that advertises *vente à emporter* (takeaway), or even high-quality frozen meals. For times when even these easy options are not appealing, you can order a meal by telephone for *livraison à domicile* (home delivery), from Japanese sushi to Italian pizza and Indian curries.

The quality of fresh ingredients in Paris is extremely high, as food for sale is regulated by law. Butter, cheese, poultry and vegetables must conform to the standards set for the region from which they come, and the label *appellation d'origine contrôlée* monitors the quality of both food products and alcoholic beverages. Thus, food at outdoor markets, neighbourhood *traiteurs* and supermarkets conveniently located in every *quartier*, are of a certain standard. *Agents de conservation* (preservatives) are rare, so food will taste better and be fresher but may spoil quickly. Look for the *date de péremption* (expiration date) on packaged foods, indicated by '*vente jusqu'à*' or '*consommer avant*' followed by the expiration date. (North Americans should remember that the date is written in the order of day, month and year.) If you have bought an expired product, take your receipt and the product back to the shop, and it will be exchanged in most cases.

Groceries are open from about 8:00 am until 7:30 pm, although neighbourhood shops may take a lunch break. Supermarkets stay open all day, some until 10:00 pm. *Traiteurs* and bakeries are open on Sunday mornings to supply the traditional Sunday lunch, as are outdoor markets. Most shops are closed on Monday, except supermarkets. In the summer, small shops will post signs announcing their *fermeture annuelle* (annual closure) for the entire month of July or August. Supermarkets stay open, but some outdoor markets have a reduced number of stalls and some groceries close altogether until *la rentrée* (the return—to school and work—after the long summer vacation) in September.

Europe is on the metric system (see Resource Guide in Chapter 10 for a conversion guide). Thus, people used to ounces and pounds will have to convert to grams and kilograms when looking at a food package. (1,000 milligrams = 1 gram and 1,000 grams = 1 kilo = 2.2 pounds.) With fresh produce, however, it is common to ask for *une livre* (a pound).

The Markets

Shopping at the *marché* (food market) is one of the most pleasant aspects of French life. Vendors sell fish, meat and the freshest vegetables, and quality is generally high. Most also sell candies and some offer clothes and gadgets. The markets listed directly below are *couverts* (covered) and permanent. They are open daily, except on Monday. Generally, they close for lunch, open again around 4:00 in the afternoon and close around 7:00 pm. Covered markets usually have only food items and flowers. Not all markets are equal in their range of merchandise, quality or price. These market buildings can be quite charming, depending on their age and upkeep.

Remember that it is usually the *commerçant* (vendor) who selects the produce, and vendors do not take kindly to customers pawing through the merchandise, although it is

Where to Get What

- *Alimentation générale*: grocery
- *Boucherie*: butcher's; *boucherie chevaline*: horse-meat butcher
- *Boulangerie*: bakery; *pâtisserie*: pastry store
- *Brûlerie/torrefaction*: coffees and teas
- *Charcuterie*: delicatessen meats
- *Confiserie–chocolatier*: candy, handmade chocolates
- *Épicerie*: small grocery
- *Fromagerie*: cheese store
- *Poissonnerie*: fish market
- *Rôtisserie*: spit-roasted meat and chicken
- *Traiteur*: prepared foods for takeaway
- *Triperie*: tripe and innards
- *Volailler*: poultry shop

permitted at some stalls. After meeting your order, the vendor may ask, *"avec ceci?"* ("what else would you like?") If you need nothing more, say *"ça sera tout, merci"* ("that's all, thanks").

- 3e: Marché des Enfants-Rouges; rue de Bretagne
- 3e: Marché du Temple; rue Perrée
- 6e: Saint-Germain; rue Mabillon (the old Marché Saint-Germain, now inside a shopping mall)
- 8e: Marché Europe; rue Corvetto
- 8e: Marché de Castellane; between rue Tronchet and rue de l'Arcade
- 10e: Marché Saint-Quentin; boulevard de Magenta
- 12e: The inexpensive, international Marché Beauvau; Place d'Aligre
- 16e: Marché Saint-Didier; rue Mesnil
- 16e: Marché de Passy; rue Bois-le-Vent
- 19e: Rue Secrétan; near *métro* Bolivar

Some 65 open-air markets (*marché volant*) float around the *arrondissements*, appearing on certain days in one location and moving elsewhere on others. Markets are generally open from 8:00 am–1:00 pm; many areas have several open on different days or a different selection of vendors. Each market has its own personality, and some have an international flavour to match their surroundings. For a complete list of all the markets with their opening days and hours, access the city's website: http://www.v1.paris.fr/EN/Living/markets/markets.asp. For the ultimate in market experiences, visit Le Potager du Roi, the charming vegetable garden of Louis XIV at Versailles (http://www.potager-du-roi.fr). Still a working garden, run by the National Horticultural School, it holds a market shop that sells freshly picked produce.

Market Streets

A *rue commerçante* is a street lined with food shops. Most are open on Sunday mornings and closed on Mondays, and many are pedestrian streets, creating a festive atmosphere. In small shops that are not *libre-service* (self-service), you may be asked to pay at the *caisse* (cashier) after ordering your food, then to bring the receipt back to the counter to receive the packages.

When paying, always count your change.

- 2ᵉ: Rue Montorgueil: pedestrians only. Charming old street of shops and cafés.
- 5ᵉ: Rue Mouffetard: Paris' most famous.
- 7ᵉ: Rue Cler at avenue de la Motte-Picquet: high-quality, two-street-long *rue commerçante*.
- 14ᵉ: Rue Daguerre: in a residential neighbourhood near Denfert-Rochereau.
- 17ᵉ: Rue de Lévis: pedestrians only, an old-time village atmosphere prevails.
- 17ᵉ: Rue Poncelet: beginning at avenue des Ternes, an upmarket market street.
- 18ᵉ: Rue Lepic: a famous market street at the foot of Montmartre.

Supermarkets
Supermarket chains ensure convenient one-stop shopping in just about every *quartier*; they are all *libre-service*. They range from the reliable and well-stocked Monoprix, to the mid-level Franprix and G-20, down to the unadorned Leader Price and ED L'Epicier—the original cheap supermarket chain with its

Shops lining market streets present beautifully arranged seasonal produce.

sometimes sparse stock. Most city supermarkets close on Sunday; some are open on Sunday mornings, depending on the neighbourhood.

People with cars often head for the *banlieue* where gigantic *hypermarchés* offer a wide selection and low prices; they also carry electronics and household items. These include Auchan, Casino, Intermarché and Carrefour, which has one outlet in the city in the 16ᵉ. Small shopping baskets are found by the entrance to each supermarket. Wheeled *caddies* (carts) may be linked together by a lock, requiring the insertion of a one euro deposit, which is returned when the cart is reinserted into the rack. As of this writing, plastic *sacs* (bags) are provided. (Some supermarkets had tried to terminate this service on ecological grounds but quickly reinstated the service, at least temporarily.) Others now charge a few cents for the bags. In any case, expect to bag the groceries yourself. The charge for home delivery depends on the amount spent. See *Supermarchés et Hypermarchés* in the *Yellow Pages*.

Food Halls

In addition to the supermarkets, food halls (usually in department stores) offer upmarket, international and often costly selections. Both food halls below have excellent products of the highest quality, lovely prepared foods for takeaway and an impressive international selection. They are closed on Sundays.

- 7ᵉ: La Grande Épicerie de Paris; 38 rue de Sèvres; tel: 01.44.39.80.00.
- 9ᵉ: Galeries Lafayette Gourmet; 40 boulevard Haussmann; tel: 01.42.82.34.56.

Ordering Groceries Online

You can order groceries online for home delivery from supermarkets, as well as from Picard, the frozen food specialist described on page 216, and Telemarket, a long-established grocery ordering service. See also the section on 'Eating Out at Home' below.

- Auchan; website:http://www.auchandirect.fr
- Carrefour; website:http://www.ooshop.com
- Picard; website:http://www.picard.fr
- Telemarket; website:http://telemarket.fr
- Monoprix; website: http://www.monoprix.fr

Groceries for Homesick Anglophones

Don't Americans need an Oreo once in a while and don't the English pine for Hobnobs? The shops below specialise in items from Anglophone countries. Make sure the products have not expired, although packaged goods can last longer than the date indicated. Supermarkets and food halls also carry international packaged goods, but the selection changes, so buy several of an item you particularly like when you chance upon it.

- 3ᵉ: The Bagel Store; 31 rue de Turenne; tel: 01.44.78.06.05. Small café selling bagels, cream cheese, spreads, salads and a few packaged American goods.
- 4ᵉ: Thanksgiving; 20 rue Saint-Paul; tel: 01.42.77.68.29. American grocery and restaurant with some homemade foods for takeaway. Open on Sundays, closed on Mondays.

- 7e: The Real McCoy; 194 rue de Grenelle; tel: 01.45.56. 98.82. A small American grocery. McCoy Café around the corner at 49 avenue Bosquet also has some products.
- 10e: Saveurs d'Irlande; 5 cité Wauxhall; tel: 01.42.00.36.20. Irish, English and Scottish products at reasonable prices, from smoked salmon to whisky, haggis, bacon and cheeses.
- 15e: Merry Monk; 87 rue de la Convention; tel: 01.45.75.88.41. British packaged products such as teas, marmalades, biscuits, coffees, teas and cakes. Pastries are made daily and traditional items for holidays are also available.
- 16^e: The English Shop; 10 rue du Mesnil; tel: 01.45.53.11.40. Small shop selling British delicacies, teas, excellent cheddars and biscuits, as well as china and a selection of magazines in English. Less expensive than some of the other shops.

International Offerings

International shops are sometimes clustered around *rue commerçantes*—the entire area of Belleville, for example, is international in flavour. Asian, African, Middle Eastern and Japanese food shops are also found in the 2e, around rue Sainte-Anne, while the 13e is a focal point for the Asian community. Indian groceries can be found in the Passage Brady in the 10e and a smaller selection of Indian packaged goods at the Grande Epicerie of Le Bon Marché. Supermarkets carry some lines of international foods such as Old El Paso, Häagen Dazs and Ben and Jerry's ice cream, as do both the food halls already mentioned.

- 2e: Kioko; 46 rue des Petits-Champs; tel: 01.42.61.33.65. Two-level Japanese supermarket, selling everything you could want, including freshly-made sushi. Closed on Mondays.
- 4e: Israël; 30 rue François-Miron; tel: 01.42.72.66.23. A wonderful bazaar-like hodgepodge, including spices from around the world and fixings that you never thought you would find in Paris.
- 8e: Jabugo Ibérico; 11 rue Clément-Marot; tel: 01.47.20.03.13. Interesting emporium that sells all sorts of Spanish hams.

- 13ᵉ: Tang Frères; 44-48 avenue d'Ivry; tel: 01.45.70.80.00. Large Asian supermarket. Open on Sundays, closed on Mondays. Other addresses.

Traiteurs

Almost every neighbourhood has small *traiteurs* offering *plats à emporter* (prepared dishes for takeaway). *Charcuteries*, particularly known for their variety of smoked and salted pork products, also have prepared dishes, and the two categories overlap slightly (see Meat Markets on pages 221–223). As one would expect in Paris, the selection is mouthwatering, from stewed rabbit and guinea fowl *fricassée*, to roasted chicken and veal or beef loin, with potatoes, rice, vegetables, salads on the side, and desserts rounding off the meal. Dishes change according to the season. Monoprix has a serviceable takeaway department and the *traiteurs* at the food halls are excellent. The Asian *traiteurs* are the least expensive, but are uniform in their offerings.

Some elegant *traiteurs*, such as those below, are known for their artistic and flavourful creations, with prices to match. They have addresses throughout the Paris region, so it's best to check the Internet or the phone book for the ones nearest you. See *Traiteurs* in the *Yellow Pages*.

- Fauchon; website: http://www.fauchon.fr
- Dalloyau; website:http://www.dalloyau.fr
- Hédiard; website:http://www.hediard.fr
- La Comtesse du Barry; http://www.comtessedubarry.fr

EATING OUT AT HOME

Just about any type of cooked meal can be delivered *à domicile* (to the home). Generally, if a business' name starts with '*Allô...*' (hello), it probably offers home delivery of products or services. See *Restauration à domicile* in the *Yellow Pages*.

- http://www.alloresto.fr is a website that represents dozens of restaurants throughout Paris, organised by specialty and location. There are establishments of all grades, prices and ethnic specialties. Order directly on the Internet for delivery to your home or office. You pay according to what the restaurant accepts—cheque, cash or *tickets restaurant* (vouchers given to employees by their companies that are the equivalent of cash and can be used as payment at some restaurants). Look for the catalogue *Guide des Resto d'Or*, issued annually.

- Matsuri has three Japanese restaurants in Paris specialising in sushi that is delivered to your home. Order by phone or online (tel: 01.40.26.11.13; website:http://www.matsuri.fr).

Frozen Food

People who work late cannot always get to the stores in time to buy the appropriate ingredients for a meal. Thus, frozen food (*les surgelés*) is handy. In addition to prepared dishes ready to cook or just to reheat, frozen ingredients such as herbs, crème fraîche and sauces, fish fillets, meats, cleaned vegetables and desserts are available.

The high-quality chain Picard has some 50 outlets in Paris. A monthly catalogue details special offers (info tel: 08.01.13.12.11; http://www.picard.fr). See *Surgelés: produits alimentaires* in the *Yellow Pages*.

BAKERIES

A *pâtisserie* specialises in desserts and often sells breads; a *boulangerie* sells bread and simple desserts as well. The distinctions overlap—indeed, you will see many B*oulangerie-Pâtisserie*—and good cakes may be found in many bakeries; nonetheless, the *pâtisserie* has more refined and beautifully decorated offerings. Neighbourhood bakers also sell sandwiches and *quiches*.

Bread is always fresh in Paris. By law, *boulangeries* must choose their own flour, and knead and bake the bread on their premises; otherwise they may not call themselves *boulangeries*. Bakeries—*boulangeries* or otherwise—may carry a sign that says '*tradition française*' or '*pain maison*' meaning that the *baguettes*, the staple for most French, are baked on the premises. Another popular bread is the *pain de campagne*, a more substantial bread made by blending different flours. Most bakeries sell *pain à l'ancienne*, which is generally made with unbleached flour and non-chemical leaven. A current favourite is the *boule*, a round dark-coloured country-style bread with a crunchy crust.

The weight and price of *baguettes* are government-regulated; those of specialty breads are not. Some bakeries get around this by sprinkling the bread with flour and calling it a *baguette campagnarde*. Not all breads are equal and certainly not all *boulangeries*. With more than 1,000 in Paris, just shop around for those that suit your taste.

For breakfast, *baguettes* are sliced lengthwise and buttered and/or spread with jam. At lunch, the bread is often used for sandwiches, and at dinner it is torn off in chunks. This is all done immediately before eating, as *baguettes*, made with no fat, tend to dry out quickly. Bread is baked early in the morning, late in the afternoon and on Sunday mornings, so it's easy to buy bread just before you want to eat it. Everyone else is doing the same, so on Sunday mornings, for example, expect to wait in line at the most

Bread, Glorious Bread!

- *Baguette*: a long, thin loaf made from flour, water, yeast and salt. *Demi-baguette*: half a *baguette*. *Ficelle*: a thin and crispy *baguette*
- *Bâtard*: similar to a *baguette* but thicker
- *Brioche*: sweet, buttery roll or bread made with eggs
- *Croissant*: crescent-shaped pastry rolls, eaten at breakfast: '*nature*' is without butter, '*au beurre*' is with butter
- *Pain au chocolat*: flaky chocolate-filled pastry, also eaten at breakfast
- *Pain*: a bread loaf
- *Petit pain*: a roll
- *Pain de campagne*: country-style bread, comes in various shapes
- *Miche*: a large country bread
- *Pain au levain*: sourdough
- *Pain de mie*: sandwich bread, which can be bought *tranché* (sliced).

popular shops. Supermarkets carry both fresh and packaged breads. Note also that *baguettes* are generally not wrapped but are, instead, handed to the customer with a small paper square to hold while transporting home.

Pâtisseries specialise in exquisitely decorated *gâteaux* (cakes) and *tartes* (fruit pies or tarts). Some are particularly known for their elegant creations and there is some overlap with chocolate shops (see below), such as the elegant multi-store Lenôtre and Dalloyau.

Each *quartier* has its *boulangeries* and *pâtisseries*, and although many close in August, at least one bakery in each neighbourhood stays open. Supermarkets and some *traiteurs* also offer well-made desserts, but the food halls have the most imaginative (and expensive) creations. Small bakeries generally close for lunch and reopen until 8:00 pm. See *Boulangeries or Pâtisseries* in the *Yellow Pages*. Kayser, with outlets around the city, is very popular. My favourites:

- 6ᵉ and 15ᵉ: Poilâne; 8 rue du Cherche-Midi; tel: 01.45.48.42.59. One of the most celebrated bakeries in

Paris offering country-style breads. Also at 49 boulevard de Grenelle; tel: 01.45.79.11.49.

- 7ᵉ: Poujauran; 20 rue Jean-Nicot; tel: 01.43.17.35.20. Look out for the organic *baguettes*, nut and fruit breads, and chocolate cake.
- 15ᵉ and 1ᵉʳ: Max Poilâne; 87 rue Brancion; tel: 01.48.28. 45.90. Sourdough and other specialty breads. Also at 42 place du Marché-Saint-Honoré; tel: 01.42.61.10.53.
- 2ᵉ: Stohrer; 51 rue Montorgueil; tel: 01.42.33.38.20. Founded in 1730, one of the city's best. Its specialty is a creamed cake called *puit d'amour* (well of love).
- 6ᵉ: Gérard Mulot; 76 rue de Seine; tel: 01.43.26.85.77. Outstanding *pâtissier*, chocolatier and *traiteur*.
- 12e: Moisan; 5 place de'Aligre (tel: 01.43.45.46.60). Organic bread, delicious tarts, crowded on weekends.

Indulging Your Sweet Tooth

- *Baba au rhum*: *brioche* dough baked in small molds and soaked in rum
- *Charlotte russe*: ladyfingers (oval pieces of dry sponge cake) placed around whipped cream
- *Dacquoise*: meringue of nuts, sugar and shaved chocolate, layered with whipped cream
- *Éclair*: small, rectangular *choux* pastry filled with cream and topped with icing
- *Financier*: almond cake
- *Madeleine*: small almond tea-cake with characteristic scallop markings
- *Merveille*: hot sugared doughnut
- *Millefeuille*: literally 'thousand layers', layers of puff pastry filled with cream and dusted with sugar
- *Palmier*: sugared, crisp cookies shaped like palm leaves
- *Sablé*: shortbread, variously flavoured with chocolate or almond, sometimes with jam in between layers
- *Savarin*: molded cake of baba dough, sprinkled with rum and filled with cream

FISH

A delectable selection of *poisson* (fish) and *fruits de mer* (seafood) is readily available, some of which, such as shrimp, may be precooked. Fish is sold fresh at supermarkets and at the *poissonnerie* (fish market) daily, except on Mondays, and at outdoor markets and the *rues commerçants*. The food halls also have exceptionally good fish every day.

The *poissonnier* (fishmonger) will price a whole fish by its weight and clean it too. Fish also comes in fillets or *darnes* (steaks), priced by weight by the piece. Almost all *poissonneries* make fish soups. In supermarkets, soups and fish preparations are found in refrigerators near the fish counters. Inspect the packing and expiration dates on the packages. See *Poissonneries* in the *Yellow Pages*.

Smoked fish and caviar are also popular, and the food halls mentioned above have the widest variety. Comptoir du Saumon and Caviar Latian have several addresses. Those below have excellent selections of caviar, smoked fish and snails.

- 7e: Pétrossian; 18 boulevard de la Tour-Maubourg; tel: 01.44.11.32.22. With a one-star restaurant above.
- 8e: Caviar Kaspia; 17 place de la Madeleine; tel: 01.42.65.33.32.
- 8e: La Maison du Caviar; 1 rue Vernet; tel: 01.40.70.06.39. Restaurant at 21 rue Quentin-Bauchart; tel: 01.47.23.53.43.
- 15e: La Maison de l'Escargot; 79 rue Fondary; tel: 01.45. 75.31.09.
- 15e: Paris Caviar; 130 rue Lecourbe; tel: 01.55.76.69.20.

SPECIALTY FOODS

Paris abounds with kosher groceries, *traiteurs*, butchers and bakeries. Look around rue des Rosiers in the Marais, especially, and the market street rue Cadet in the 9th arrondissement. The same is true of halal restaurants and food stores, which are more found in the northeastern quartiers, especially around Belleville. Most groceries now carry organic foods, and there are several *bio* (*biologique*) shops and a popular *bio* market on boulevard Raspail on

Kosher, halal, and other specialty cuisines are plentiful in Paris. This kosher pizza place is at 11 rue des Rosiers in the Marais.

Sunday mornings. The food halls mentioned on page 213 also have specialty products.

Most supermarkets also carry kosher and halal products, especially at seasons of religious events. Although the famous Jo Goldenberg in the Marais has closed, Finkelsztajn's at 27 rue des Rosiers (tel: 42.72.78.91) has good deli products and probably the best rye bread in the city. Note that the kosher establishments close on Friday afternoon and open again Saturday evening or Sunday.

MEAT MARKETS

Meats in France are excellent. French lamb is world-famous, and beef, pork and veal are all available at the *boucherie* (butcher's). Cuts may be unfamiliar to you, but if you describe to the *boucher* (butcher) what you want, he can provide it. All meats except horsemeat are sold at the *boucherie*.

That few hormones are used in raising cattle means that the meat may not be particularly tender and will require longer cooking time or thinner cuts. Meat is not aged very long, so its texture may be different from what you are used to. Chopped or minced meat is usually ground to order and should be cooked and eaten the day of purchase. In fact, butchers generally cut meats to order, rather than prepackage them, and some are known for specialty cuts and artistic creations.

Although butchers are often closed on Mondays, the supermarkets have fresh meat every day, either packaged or freshly cut. Food halls have excellent cuts and some rolled or otherwise nicely prepared. Butchers are found in the outdoor markets and in the *rues commerçantes* as well. There are several chains of reliable butchers—both Chevy and Roger have shops around the city. For butchers in your own neighbourhood, see *Boucheries, Boucheries-Charcuteries* in the *Yellow Pages*.

Some meat shops are more specialised. Flavourful, lean horsemeat, less popular than heretofore, is sold in all cuts at the *boucherie chevaline* and at most *marchés*. *Marchands de volaille* or *volaillers* specialise in poultry. Some sell hot, cooked poultry and other meats, such as pork ribs or rabbit, cooked on the *tournebroche* (rôtisserie). Most shops make a distinction, both in quality and price, between the *poulet fermier* (free-range chicken) and the traditional chicken. See *Volailles et Gibiers* in the *Yellow Pages*.

Ham and fresh pork products can be bought at both the *boucherie* and *charcuterie*, although the latter is traditionally known for its pork products and has a wider range of sausages and *pâtés*, as well as a larger selection of prepared takeaway foods and salads. Both supermarkets and *charcuteries* also have a selection of thinly sliced *jambons de pays* (hams) from different regions of France, the most famous being the *jambon de Bayonne* (ham from Bayonne). The kosher *charcuteries* sell the same types of products, but made with beef or turkey.

- 6ᵉ, 7ᵉ, 13ᵉ: Charles Traiteur
  10 rue Dauphine; tel: 01.43.54.25.19
  135 rue Saint-Dominique; tel: 01.47.05.53.66
  26 rue Duméril; tel: 01.43.31.97.87.
  Prize-winning *boudin blanc* (white pudding or sausage with milk), *andouillette de Troyes* (intestines from Troyes) and *boudin noir* (black pudding or blood sausage)—three

of the most popular French sausages (www.roiduboudin. com). House-smoked salmon, terrines, salads, cheeses and dishes to take home and reheat.

- 7ᵉ: L'Ambassade du Sud-Ouest; 46 avenue de la Bourdonnais; tel: 01.45.55.59.59. Small shop carrying regional specialty products, with a restaurant behind. Sells *foie gras*, *canard confit*, *cassoulet*, wines and tinned products.
- 8ᵉ: Granterroirs; 30 rue de Miromesnil; tel: 01.47.42.18.18. Lovely specialty shop for *foie gras*, truffles, cheeses and jams. Communal tables for a light lunch.

FROMAGERIES

Cheese is an important part of French cuisine and an interesting conversation point at any table. Cheese is grouped into families according to their production, texture, flavour and nutritive value. They can be made from the milk of a *vache* (cow), *brebis* (sheep) or *chèvre* (goat), each with its own flavour; aged or not; made from whole or skim milk; pasteurised or non-pasteurised (*lait cru*); hard, semi-soft, soft, or one of the various stages in between. They may be white, creamy yellow, orange or brown, and come in large wheels or small disks that are sliced, cut or whole, sometimes with edible moulds and rinds. Many are seasonal. This vast variety of cheeses means, in fact, that most have not been exported. Newcomers from countries in which cheeses are pasteurised may not have tasted the most exquisite of the French cheeses, and a very pleasant education is in store.

Cheese generally finishes its ageing on the premises of the *fromagerie* (cheese shop) but not at the *crémerie*. For same-day eating, ask for soft and semi-soft cheeses that are *bien fait* (perfectly ripe); for consuming later, they should be *pas trop fait* (not quite ripe). Every *quartier* has its own cheese shops, each carrying a slightly different variety.

Charles de Gaulle famously said: "How can you be expected to govern a country that has 246 kinds of cheese?" When he asked his rhetorical question some 50 years ago, there were at least 250 kinds of cheese. Now there are more than 400, ranging from the ancient Roquefort (said to have been a favourite of Charlemagne), to Boursin, an invention of the 20th century.

Fromage de chèvre or goat cheese—but one of the numerous varieties of cheese available from the *fromageries* of Paris.

Cheese is served between the *plat principal* and the dessert, and it should be served at room temperature. Some people do not refrigerate their cheeses, keeping them instead in a special layered cheese container and eating them soon after purchase. If you refrigerate, keep each cheese wrapped separately, so as not to mix flavours. Some cheeses keep longer than others, and uncut cheeses continue to age.

At dinner, serve cheeses of different textures and flavours. A *plateau de fromage* (cheese platter) generally offers at least one mild and one strong cheese, a blue and a variety of soft, semi-soft and hard. Begin with the mildest and move on to the strong.

Supermarkets and food halls carry packaged, pasteurised cheeses, as well as freshly cut, unpasteurised cheeses, which are more flavourful. The best cheeses are found at the *marchés*, *fromageries* and *crémeries* that also sell butter, eggs and milk. Milk from supermarkets often comes in containers marked *Ultra-Haute Température/UHT* that may be kept unrefrigerated for many months before opening. Butter is most flavourful when cut fresh from a large slab (*beurre à la motte*): it comes *demi-sel* (lightly salted) or *doux* (sweet). See *Fromageries* in the *Yellow Pages*.

- 7e: Barthélémy; 51 rue de Grenelle; tel: 01.45.48.56.75
- 7e; Crémerie Quartrehomme; 62 rue de Sèvres; tel:1.47.34.33.45
- 14e; Boursault; 71 avenue du Général Leclerc; tel: 01.43.27.93.30
- 15e; Fromagerie Laurent Dubois; 2 rue Lourmel; tel: 01.45.78.70.58
- 16e: Fromager Lillo; 25 rue des Belles-Feuilles; tel: 1.47.27.69.08
- 17e: Alléosse; 13 rue Poncelet; tel: 01.46.22.50.45

TEA AND COFFEE

Supermarkets and food halls sell international brands of packaged teas and coffees, as well as fresh coffee beans. Beans are also sold at *brûleries/torréfactions*, many of which are known for particular selections. Some even work with the customer to determine his/ her preferred blend and keep the recipe on file. *Torréfactions* generally also offer a selection of fresh teas. Le Comptoir Richard has several shops in the city; for shops in your neighbourhood, see *Café (torréfaction)* in the *Yellow Pages*.

- 1er: Cafés et Thés Verlet; 256 rue Saint-Honoré; tel: 01.42.60.67.39
- 2e: Brûlerie San José; 30 rue Petits-Champs; tel: 01.42.96.69.09
- 5e: Brûlerie Maubert; 3 rue Monge; tel: 01.46.33.38.77

Tea lovers should try salons dedicated to tea: Mariage Frères, with several locations (http://www.mariagefreres.fr) is the most outstanding, specialising in teas and herbal *tisanes* (infusions). Le Palais des Thés also has several addresses and a website for ordering teas (http://www.palaisdesthes.com). For inexpensive Asian teas, try Tang Frères. See *Thé (importation, négoce)* in the *Yellow Pages*.

- 5e: La Maison des Trois Thés; 1 rue Saint-Médard; tel: 01.43.36.93.84. Closed on Mondays.
- 8e: Twining's; 76 boulevard Haussmann; tel: 01.43.87.39.84 English teas.

- 13ᵉ: L'Empire des Thés; 101 avenue d'Ivry; tel: 01.45.84.62.15. 69 rue du Montparnasse, 75014; tel:01.42.18.10.18; Open on Sundays.

CHOCOLATES

Chocolat is not just appreciated in Paris, it's almost a cult. People talk about chocolate in almost the same way they talk about wine, from the *chocolat chaud* found in tearooms and the delicious creations of famed *chocolatiers*, to the simple *tablettes* (bars) sold at supermarkets. Chocolates in France are so delicious because they contain a high percentage of cocoa—sometimes more than 70 per cent—and the higher the quantity of cocoa, the richer the confection; even chocolate bars in supermarkets display the percentage of cocoa in each bar. Look for chocolate in the form of fish just before April Fool's Day ('April Fool' is '*poisson d'avril*', and *poisson* means 'fish'), hearts before Valentine's Day, bunnies and chickens before Easter, and even chocolate mushrooms in autumn. See *Confiseries, chocolateries* in the *Yellow Pages*.

Some of the best *chocolatiers* have several locations. Try the following:

- Maison du Chocolat, which some people consider as the best in Paris.
- Cacao et Chocolat. Exotic fillings, with Latin overtones.
- Lenôtre. Remarkable and exquisitely presented candies.
- Debauve & Gallais, one of the city's oldest and most venerated.
- Dalloyau, which is mentioned above as a *traiteur*

The excellent Belgian *chocolatiers* Godiva, Jeff de Bruges, Daskalidès and De Neuville all have stores in Paris.

Chocolatier nonpareil

There's little to say about the two boutique *chocolatiers* below, because even superlatives aren't good enough. Once you try their extraordinary confections, you may never go anywhere else. Be prepared to pay handsomely for perfection.

- Patrick Roger; 108 boulevard Saint-Germain, 75006; tel: 01.43.29.38.42.
- Pierre Hermé; 72 rue Bonaparte, 75006; tel: 01.43.54.47.77.

WINE

When choosing a wine, it helps to describe the meal to be served with the proprietor of the *cave* (wine shop). Be clear as to the desired price range of the wine, and he will suggest the most appropriate wine. Discuss too, the temperature at which the wine should be served. White wines are served chilled, as are some red wines. It is interesting to note that the shape of the bottle varies according to the type of wine and the region. The percentage of alcohol varies as well and must be indicated on the label.

In general, French wines (and other Old World, European wines) are classified by the *terroir*—the interplay of the soil and climate upon the vines. Thus, what is indicated on the label is the area of the château. This is unlike the wines of the New World (non-European wines), which are often labelled by the type of grape.

In addition to local *caves*, there are reliable chains with wines of all categories and prices. Nicolas, a franchise operation with more than 200 shops in Paris, has at least one shop in each *arrondissement*. The advice of the *caviste* (wine merchant) is only as good as the owner of each franchise, but most are fairly knowledgeable. Repaire de Bacchus, another franchise, has more than 20 shops throughout the city. Most shops will deliver wines depending on how much is bought.

Supermarkets also have extensive selections of domestic wines, and during the Foire aux vins (Wine Fair) in October, the supermarkets offer an even broader selection and knowledgeable sales personnel. Some, such as Carrefour, bottle wines under their own label. Galeries Lafayette Gourmet Food Hall and Le Bon Marché have interesting selections, occasional promotional sales and opportunities for tasting. *Traiteurs,* such as Fauchon and Hédiard, are often interestingly well-stocked and helpful in their advice. See *Vins* in the *Yellow Pages*.

- 6e: La Dernière Goutte; 6 rue de Bourbon-le-Château; tel: 01.43.29.11.62. Wine tastings on Saturdays and stays open on Sundays. The American proprietor specialises in estate-bottled wines.

Wine shops where one can find the myriad regional wines of France.

- 2^e and 13^e: Legrand Filles & Fils; 1 rue de la Banque; tel: 01.42. 60.07.12. Lovely shop in the Galerie Vivienne, with well-priced *vins de pays*, vintage wines, *eaux de vie* and other brandies. Wine bar, books, accessories and some food products.
- 7e: Ryst-Dupeyron; 79 rue du Bac; tel: 01.45.48.80.93. Known for its family-produced *armagnac,* aged *calvados*, and wines from Bordeaux. Catalogue available.
- 8e: Les Caves Taillevent; 199 rue du Faubourg Saint-Honoré; tel: 01.45.61.14.19. A vast assortment of excellent wines, plus regular Saturday morning wine tastings.
- 8e: Les Caves Augé; 116 boulevard Haussmann; tel: 01.45.22. 16.09. Prestigious shop with old wines and some reasonably priced younger ones.
- 14e and 16e: Les Caves du Savour; 120 boulevard du Montparnasse; tel: 01.43.27.12.06. Wines of all qualities and price ranges. Wine tasting and catalogue for telephone orders. Home delivery available.

CHAMPAGNE

Although vines have been growing in the northern Champagne region of France since Roman times, the second fermentation that produces the delicious bubbly that people revere didn't come into being until the 17th century. And lucky for connoisseurs, its refinement and prestige have increasingly grown. Today, only wines grown in this region and produced by the *méthode champenoise* may be called Champagne. All others are generally called "sparkling wines."

There are many varieties and producers of Champagne. Work with your *caviste*, pay attention to the tastings when they're announced, and you might even take a weekend up in Reims or Epernay and visit the tasting rooms of the *grandes marques*. Learn which Champagnes you like and then you'll appreciate the words of the great English economist John Maynard Keynes: "The only regret in life is that I did not drink more Champagne."

ENJOYING PARIS

CHAPTER 7

'When I dream of an afterlife in heaven,
the action always takes place at the Paris Ritz.'
—Ernest Hemingway

PARIS, ANY TIME OF THE DAY

There's always something to do in Paris, any time of the day or night. From cultural opportunities to shopping, from sports to educational courses in just about anything you might want to know, Paris does not disappoint. It's a city of some 50 museums; a place where classical music is as important as popular music, where 300 films are shown each week in a variety of languages and where discos start to swing at 1:00 am. Two hundred and fifty theatres show anything from plays to the naughtiest revues in late-night cabarets. In fact, cultural activities of all sorts are important to the French and are allocated about one per cent of the country's annual budget—more than what most other nations spend. The *mairie* also subsidises cultural festivals throughout the year, some offered free of charge.

People who do not speak French should have few problems finding where and when everything is. The city of Paris has an extremely detailed website (http://www.paris.fr), as does the Paris Tourist Office (http://www.parisinfo.com). The *mairie* (town hall) of your own *arrondissement* will have information on all aspects of the district, from shopping to sports, and just about anything you could want. It's up to you to figure out what suits you best.

FINDING OUT WHAT'S NEW

Parisians eagerly await the publication of the weekly events guides. Available each Wednesday morning at news-stands, both *Pariscope* (€ 0.40) and *L'Officiel des Spectacles* (€ 0.35) provide detailed descriptions of the week's activities, from sporting events, special exhibitions at museums and art galleries, theatre, concerts and films, to recommended restaurants, bars and discos. *Figaroscope*, also published on Wednesday, is the events supplement of the daily newspaper, *Le Figaro*. *Zurban* is an events magazine that offers full articles in addition to weekly schedules, as well as reviews of restaurants and interesting areas of the city. *Nova*, a lively monthly magazine that is increasingly popular with young people, details all the events in Paris. You can also check online at such addresses as http://www.pariscope.fr or http://www.culture.fr. There are several others.

PARIS ITSELF

Start by getting to know the city. There are many multilingual guided tours available, whether through a guide or a recording. For opportunities offered by the city of Paris and RATP, access the RATP website http://www.ratp.com. Click on *se deplacer*, and then on *Plans des lignes de bus touristiques*. This will include the most popular Open Tour bus (info tel: 01.42.66.56.56). You may buy a one- or two-day ticket at any one of the stops and get on and off the buses at any of the stops.

- Paris Walks; tel: 01.48.09.21.40; website: http://www.paris-walks.com. Guided walks in English for various parts of the city. Daily two-hour tours (rain or shine) may include a walk through Hemingway's Paris, Île-de-la-Cité, Montmartre, the Latin Quarter, the Marais and more. Reservations not required.
- Fat Tire Tours; tel: 01.56.58.10.54; website: http://www.fattirebiketoursparis.com. Bicycle tours in English around Paris, starting at the Eiffel Tower. Motorised Segways are available for those who want less strenuous outings. There's also a Friday night *randonnée* (outing) that starts at the place d'Italie. Reserve in advance.
- Not a Tourist Destination Tours; tel: 01.40.27.82.11; website: http://www.notatouristdestination.com. Multilingual (English, French, Spanish, Chinese, etc.) guided tours off

the regular routes. Food tours (pastry shops, cheese and wine shops, etc.), fashion tours for both men and women and an evening-out tour that will help you discover the most fashionable bars and clubs in Paris. Groups are small and tours can be customised to your needs.

- Cityrama; 4 place des Pyramides, 75001; tel: 01.44.55.61.00; website:http://www.cityrama.com.
  A wide variety of minibus tours in and around the city, and throughout France, including an excursion to the La Vallée Outlet Shopping Village for a day of discount shopping.
- Paris Vision; 1 rue Auber, 75009; tel: 01.47.42.72.31; website:http://www.parisvision.com and 214 rue de Rivoli, 75001; tel: 01.42.60.30.01. Coach or minibus tours of the city, plus tours to Disneyland Paris, Versailles, Giverny, Mont Saint-Michel and other parts of France.
- Paris Story; 1bis rue Scribe, 75009; tel: 01.42.66.62.06; website:http://www.paris-story.com; http://www.exploreparis.fr. A multi-media tour of the 2000-year history of Paris.

MONUMENTS AND MORE

As you're out and about. you'll see monuments throughout the city that are history lessons in themselves. Knowing something about them in advance will allow you to better appreciate the city's beauty and pride. The Paris Tourist Office issues a handy multilingual brochure *Paris en 6 Monuments* that describes in detail l'Arc de Triomphe, la Sainte-Chapelle, la Conciergerie, le Panthéon and la Basilique Royale de Saint Denis. The website http://www.monum.fr also has information on monuments in both French and English.

There's also lots to discover the history of Paris that has little to do with just monuments and streets. Climbing to the top of the Eiffel Tower or Cathédral de Notre Dame are always popular, but think of these other activities as well:

- Batobus; tel: 01.44.11.33.99; 08.25.05.01.01; website: http://www.batobus.com. Run by the Port Autonome of Paris, the Batobus is a seasonal tour of the city by boat. Running on a limited schedule in winter but with a regular timetable from April to October, it makes eight stops, including at the Eiffel Tower, Louvre and Notre Dame. Prices vary, depending on how far you want to go, whether you want a one- or two-day pass or whether you are an adult or child. With the passes, you can get on and off at will to visit museums or monuments near to the stops.

- Canauxrama; tel: 01.42.39.15.00; website: http://www.canauxrama.com. Cruises on the canals of Paris, the Seine and the Marne. Enjoy learning about Paris through its canals and going through the locks—an experience not to be missed.

- Les Catacombs; 1 avenue du Colonel Henri Rol-Tanguy 75014; tel: 01.43.22.47.63; website:http://www.parisinfo. fr. In 1785, the cemeteries in overcrowded Paris were becoming a health problem, so many remains were dug up and transported into a former quarry. See six million bones and skulls lined up along a path of about 1.5 km, all arranged according to the cemetery from whence they came. Both macabre and fascinating.

- La Tour Montparnasse; tel: 01.45.38.52.56; website:http://www.tourmontparnasse56.com. The 56th floor of the

Montparnasse Tower offers an exceptional 360-degree view of Paris, with interactive terminals, historical photos, a media presentation and explanations of the viewpoint from where you are. There is even a bar/café for a snack. Open every day until late at night.

- Père-Lachaise Cemetery; 16 rue du Repos, 75020. The 'Westminster Abbey of Paris' where thousands of famous people who lived in Paris have been buried. Parisians go to what must be the most visited cemetery in the world for a Sunday afternoon stroll, walking along the landscaped aisles and stopping at the graves of the famous or loved. They also admire the interesting sculptures and pay homage at the memorials to the deported of World War II or to the heroes of the Paris Commune who were lined up and shot at the Mur des Fédérés. Get a map from a stand outside the cemetery and find the tombs of famous people such as Edith Piaf, Gertrude Stein, Oscar Wilde, the famous 12th-century lovers, Abélard and Heloïse, and even Jim Morrison of The Doors, who died in Paris in 1971.

- Les Égouts de Paris; Pont de l'Alma, across from 93 quai d'Orsay, 75007; tel: 01.53.68.27.81; website: http://www.parisinfo.fr. Open Monday–Thursday, Saturday–Sunday, from 11:00 am–5:00 pm, closes at 4:00 pm in winter. Many people take a guided tour of the sewer and water management system of Paris. Smells can be... peculiar... and sometimes in the rainy season, flooding causes closure of the area. Nonetheless, it's an interesting experience.

THE GREATEST ART

Paris, of course, has some of the most well-known museums in the world. They range from 'the greats' such as Le Louvre to the educational such as the Musée du Vin (Museum of Wine), down to the truly offbeat such as the Musée d'Eventail (Museum of Fans). Check the city and tourist office websites, and also the Museums of Paris website (http://www.museums-of-paris.com) for details on museums and exhibitions.

Many of the city's museums only charge entry for their special exhibits; their permanent collections are free, for example, at the Musée du Petit Palais, Musée Carnavelet, Musée

Actually, if you spent 30 seconds in front of each piece of art at the Louvre, 24 hours a day, it would take you more than seven months to view it all.

Cernuschi and Musée Cognacq-Jay. In addition, the national museums generally have reduced rates for people over 60 years old and under 18, and all are free (for the permanent collections) on the first Sunday of each month. If you are in Paris for just a short visit (or if you have friends coming to Paris for a visit), there are three museum passes to consider: one-day, three consecutive days or five consecutive days. Passes are sold at museums, monuments, *métro* stations and the Paris Tourist Office. City museums are usually closed on Monday, and national museums are closed on Tuesday.

Do not think that once you've seen the Louvre, the Musée d'Orsay and the Pompidou, you've seen everything worth seeing. There are dozens of other spectacular art museums, as well as science museums, not to mention the new museum that took years to build—the Musée du Quai Branly, which specialises in the arts and civilisations of Africa, Oceania and the Americas. There's also the Musée de la Poupée (Doll Museum), Musée de la Magie (Museum of Magic) and there's even a little museum at the apartment where Vladmir Lenin lived while he was in exile just before the Russian Revolution. So, given that it could take a month or more just to grasp the Louvre, there's certainly enough in Paris to edify you for quite some time.

TICKET PURCHASE

Billets (tickets) to events are sold at the box office about two weeks in advance, and for some events, up to a month before. Box offices are generally open for ticket purchase from 11:00 am to 7:00 pm. Most accept telephone reservations although lines are often busy, and credit cards are accepted. Pick up tickets at least an hour before the performance, and be prepared to stand in line when purchasing tickets and picking them up at the venue before the event.

Major events, however, sell out quickly, especially those with big-name performers, so buy tickets as early as possible. It is often best to go well in advance of an event to an agency that handles cultural, entertainment and sporting events, with the most current information on dates and locations. They charge a small commission, but it is worth paying for the convenience. The Fnac stores have ticket agencies: you can also order by telephone or online (tel: 08.92.68.36.22; website:http://www.fnac.com). Virgin Megastore has the same type of service (tel: 08.25.12.91.39; website:http://www.virginmega.fr). The shopping centre Le Bon Marché also has a *billeterie* (ticket agency) in the basement. For ticket agencies, see *Théâtres et Spectacles location de places* in the *Yellow Pages*.

Most ticket agencies take reservations over the phone with a credit card guarantee. Some send the customer a voucher for picking up the actual ticket at the event before the performance. Arrive early to pick up your ticket, as there is no guarantee that it will be held for very long.

As in any major city, tickets to cultural events are expensive. Yet, season tickets are sometimes available at preferential prices, and there are inexpensive performing arts and film festivals, as well as free year-round church concerts. Some theatres sell reduced-price tickets just before a performance, but to have access to a wide choice of half-price tickets on the day of a performance, it's worth checking the Kiosque, either at 15 place de la Madeleine or on the Esplanade of the Tour Montparnasse. If you do get tickets from the Kiosque, make sure the tickets do not say *sans visibilité*, meaning that at least a part of the stage will not be visible from your seats. On the other hand, some people accept such tickets and take a chance on moving to a better seat if someone doesn't show up or leaves at the *entr'acte* (intermission).

If you have no ticket at all, try standing at the entrance before the event is to begin with a sign saying '*CHERCHE UNE PLACE*' ('ticket wanted')—people sometimes sell their extra tickets.

Students and young people under 26 may also visit one of the Kiosques Paris Jeunes for reduced prices to events, and check the website http://jeunes.paris.fr
- Kiosque le Marais: 14 rue François Miron 75004
- Kiosque Goutte d'Or: 1 rue Fleury 75018
- Kiosque Champ-de-Mars: 101 quai Branly, 75015

THEATRE

Parisians have been flocking to the theatre since the 17th century, when the Comédie Française was founded under Louis XIV (http://www.comedie-francaise.fr). Performances ranged from classic tragedies and political satire, to slapstick and farce. Some productions were so risqué that Louis XIV finally censored what could or could not be performed. But Parisians loved all the offerings, and when they didn't, they let their displeasure be known with catcalls, whistles and generally rowdy behavior, becoming part of the spectacle themselves.

Although audiences are better behaved these days, Paris is still a city that appreciates live performances and has more theatres than any other city in the world. No matter what you wish to watch, you'll probably find it, from international classics in elegant and historical surroundings to offbeat performances in funky, non-mainstream storefronts. The Comédie Française itself now performs at three venues (see its website), with an expanded repertoire ranging from the classics of Molière, Racine and Corneille to works by playwrights such as William Shakespeare, Samuel Beckett and Anton Chekhov. These are performed in French of course, although there are performances in the original language from time to time. For current and upcoming productions at some 60 theatres in all parts of the city, access www.canaltheatre.com.

- La Cartoucherie in the beautiful Bois de Vincennes at the eastern edge of Paris is a complex of eight theatres, staging an imaginative range of international works, both classics and avant-garde.
- L'Odéon, Théâtre de l'Europe in place de l'Odéon, 75006; http://www.theatre-odeon.fr. After a 30 million-euro renovation, this venerable theatre glows with beauty. Its mission is to 'bring to life the artistic heritage of Europe', and it does so by staging international productions, often in their original languages.
- Le Bouffes du Nord: 37 boulevard de la Chappelle, behind the Gare du Nord 75010 (tel: 01.46.07.34.50; http://www.bouffesdunord.com) was "rediscovered" in 1974, after

having been abandoned decades before. Now renovated (although its rather dilapidated look has been deliberately maintained), it is the base of famous director Peter Brook, whose experimental productions—often in English—are consistently sold out.

English-language theatre troupes are sparse but do turn up from time to time. In addition to the weekly events guides, check the free English-language tabloids that can be found in bookshops: *Fusac*, *Paris Voice* and *Irish Eyes*. And note that Word for Word, an experimental theatre group from San Francisco, performs each spring at the American Library in Paris (http://www.americanlibraryinparis.org).

CINEMA

Since the Lumière brothers presented the first 'moving pictures' in 1895, the French have regarded cinema as an art form like any other, and it receives much the same attention. Hundreds of films are shown each week in theatres across the city, either in French (*version française—vf*) or in the original language (*version originale—vo*) with French subtitles.

The selection is outstanding: *films nouveaux* (recently released films) and *exclusivités* (films on general release) are plentiful, film festivals showcasing certain directors or types of films are popular, and *reprises* (older films brought back) are often shown once a week.

New films open on Wednesday. Check the weekly events which list the week's films by subject and by theatre in each *arrondissement*. The listings state the time of the *séance* (projection), which usually starts off with advertisements and trailers, and how many minutes later the film itself starts. Allô Ciné has a very useful website (http://www.allocine.fr) and also has recorded information on all films (tel: 08.92.89.28.92).

Arrive early for popular films and be prepared to queue for tickets and to enter. Doors usually open about 10 minutes before the *séance*. Occasionally an *ouvreuse* (usherette) will show you to a seat; tipping is not required, but it is customary to give € 1.00. Most theatres now have vending machines or snack counters in the lobbies; in others, an *usherette* comes into the *salle* just before the show and sells snacks from a basket. In summer, theatres are *climatisés* (air-conditioned).

The Salles

Gaumont, UGC and Mk2 are major first-run, citywide cinema chains with multiplexes. Generally each chain shows a particular set of films at all its theatres but at slightly different times, making it convenient to see any film. Some have a late-night show on weekends, and they all show films in *vo*. The Champs-Elysées has several cinemas on both sides of the avenue. Art house films are shown across the city, with the greatest concentration of *salles* in the 5e and 6e. Action is a small chain that specialises in the screening of old films, and look for cinemas such as L'Arlequin, Saint-André-des-Arts, and Quartier Latin. See *Cinéma: salles* in the *Yellow Pages*.

Cinema Prices

Although prices may seem high for the cinema, they are generally in line with cinemas in other capital cities. The major cinemas offer *cartes privilège* (discount cards) and theatres at the Forum des Images (http://www.forumdesimages.net/fr/) have discount programmes. Some theatres also offer loyal customers a *carte de fidélité*, rewarding multiple ticket purchases with a free film. Some of the major cinema chains have done away with senior discounts, but others have reduced prices for the first showing of the day, which is usually just before noon. There are also cut-price film festivals, and in summer, La Villette hosts the free-admission *Cinéma en Plein Air* outdoors in the park. Rent a chair or bring a blanket and a picnic dinner. Forum des Images also organises a similar *Cinema au Clair de Lune*, screening films around a chosen theme outdoors at selected spots in each *arrondissement*. These free outdoor screenings usually attract a large crowd.

MUSIC

Music of all kinds, music at all hours, music everywhere—that's Paris. Look for seasonal offerings of classical music, performances by visiting artistes and church concerts, etc.

Classical music is publicly supported at national and local levels, and Paris boasts symphony orchestras, chamber groups and church ensembles. There are also performances by international guest orchestras, chamber groups and visiting soloists on tour, as well as regular concert performances by museums and churches.

The main concert season is from October to June. Get tickets early, for concerts sell out quickly, especially those with famous conductors or soloists. Subscriptions to concert series are available, and subscribers have first choice for seats. Some *salles de concerts* (concert halls) offer student discounts just before performances.

Classical festivals are held throughout the year—pleasantly outdoors in summer. See the listing of annual festivals at the end of the chapter. Those in the nearby suburbs and accessible by public transportation are listed in the weekly events guides. Look out too for religion-oriented music at holiday times, such as the Festival d'Art Sacré, and church music around Christmas and Easter.

Radio-France organises the most concerts in Paris and is the sponsor of the Orchestre National de France and the Orchestre Philharmonique (tel: 01.42.30.15.16; http://www.radiofrance. fr). The Cité de la Musique at 221 avenue Jean-Jaurès, 75020 (tel: 01.44.84.45.00; http://www.cite-musique.fr) has a very varied repertoire and is home to the contemporary chamber group, Ensemble InterContemporain. (http://www. ensembleinter.com) Adjacent is the Conservatoire National Supérieur de Musique et de Danse de Paris.

Free Concerts

Paris has a long tradition of free concerts. In May and June, classical and jazz concerts are held at the Parc Floral of the Bois de Vincennes, and free concerts are held in public gardens throughout the summer. No admission is charged to attend performances by students at the École Normale de Musique and the Institut National des Jeunes Aveugles or rehearsals at the Cité de la Musique or Maison de Radio-France.

Along with their paid concert season, many churches offer free concerts of sacred music throughout the year (especially Eglise Saint-Roch on rue Saint-Honoré), although generally not in August. In winter, it's wise to bundle up, for some of the churches are unheated.

The Opera

The Paris Opera is one of the pillars of the Parisian musical scene, attracting international stars to its major season, which runs from September to mid-July. The Opéra Bastille at Place de la Bastille, 75012, opened in 1989, is one of François Mitterrand's *Grands Projets* and is the largest opera house in the world (tel: 08.92.89.90.90; http://www.opera-de-paris.fr). The Bastille offers opera performances in the Grande Salle, and other concerts and performing art festivals in the smaller Amphithéâtre and Studio. It generally stages 16 operas per season with a varied repertoire. Although the opera is always an elegant occasion, formal dress is not required, except perhaps for opening nights.

When the Opéra Bastille was built, it was originally intended that the beautiful Opéra Garnier at Place de la Opéra,

75009 be used only for ballet and other dance concerts. Now, however, it also hosts opera, putting on smaller works and special programmes. Schedules and reservations can be obtained through the numbers and website above.

The best seats are, of course, expensive. The box office sells tickets two weeks prior to a performance; it is best to go on the first day that tickets are available and wait in line. Although the box office opens at 11:00 am, some people arrive by 7:00 am for tickets to the most popular performances.

DANCE

The Ballet de l'Opéra National de Paris performs primarily at the Opéra Garnier, integrating some contemporary works into its classical repertoire; use the same channels to get information as you would for operas. The Bastille also hosts international productions.

You can catch contemporary dance performances at the Théâtre de la Ville at 2 place du Châtelet, 75001 (tel: 01.40.28.28.40), which was founded by Sarah Bernhardt. There are also regularly scheduled ballet performances at the Palais des Congrès and the Théâtre des Champs-Elysées at 15 avenue Montaigne, 75008 (tel: 01.49.52.50.50; http://www.theatrechampselysees.fr).

Currently, however, it is the offbeat theatres that are staging the most interesting performances. Look for Asian and Middle Eastern dance troupes at the Centre Mandapa at 6 rue Wurtz, 75013 and contemporary dance at L'Etoile du Nord, 16, rue Georgette-Agutte, 75018 (tel: 01.42.26.47.47). Check *Pariscope* for other venues.

NIGHTLIFE

From blues, jazz and the hottest rock to the most mellow *chansons* (songs); in music bars, discotheques and enormous stadiums, there is not an evening in Paris when something is not going on. If you have patience, your favourite group will eventually come to Paris, for they all do at one time or another.

Au Lapin Argile, a famous cabaret in Montmartre. In its vicinity is the world-renowned Moulin Rouge. In addition to traditional revues, Paris also boasts the trendiest clubs and bars, making for a bustling nightlife.

The major stadium for big musical events is the Palais Omnisports de Paris-Bercy (http://www.bercy.fr). Another large venue is Zénith at 211 avenue Jean-Jaurès, 75019 at La Villette (http://www.le-zenith.com). In addition to its classical repertoire, the Cité de la Musique puts on jazz and other concerts depending on the seasons and festivals. And the Olympia at 28 boulevard des Capucines is an old-time music hall that still attracts the crowds for both retro and modern sounds (http://ww.olympiahall.com). In fact, different styles oberlap throughout Paris, especially for Latin and African music, which can now be found just about everywhere.

Fortunately, resources are plentiful to learn what's current. And since venues change and concerts get sold out quickly, stay up-to-date by picking up at your newsstand the weekly *Pariscope, l'Officiel*, or *Les Inrockuptibles*. Inquire at the ticket offices of La Fnac or Virgin Megastore. And listen to Radio Nova (101.5FM), and TSF (89.9FM). The city and tourist office websites can be helpful, and there are several others, including http://www.parisbouge.com, and the English-language site http://www.parisvoice.com.

In Paris, the truly *branché* (plugged in) crowd changes its preferences seemingly with the wind, but whichever the wind, it does not start blowing until late. *Boites* (discotheques) are popular, but not before midnight, and dancing can last until dawn. Many clubs impose a cover charge, often including the first drink (*consommation*). If not, the first drink can be expensive. Occasionally entrance fees are waived and some clubs distribute free-entry coupons around town.

- New Morning; 7–9 rue des Petites-Ecuries, 75010; tel: 01.45.23.51.41; website:http://www.newmorning.com. Ever popular, hosts jazz, salsa, world music, blues and just about anything interesting that is passing through Paris.
- Bataclan; 50 boulevard Voltaire, 75011; tel: 01.43.14.00.30; website: http://www.bataclan.fr. A beautiful old theatre, hosts French and international rock performances and dance concerts
- L'International: 5-7 rue Moret 75011; tel: 01.49.29.76.45. No entry fee for this varied bar and concert venue. Its detailed website lists the upcoming concerts: http:www.linternational.fr.

AND ALL THAT ...

Parisians have loved jazz since World War I, when American black soldiers first introduced it to the city. The Banlieues Bleues jazz festival held here in spring draws internationally known jazz performers.

- Le Caveau de la Huchette at 5 rue de la Huchette, 75005; tel: 01.43.26.65.05. Most famous for traditional jazz.
- Duc des Lombards; 42 rue des Lombards, 75001; tel: 01.42.33.22.88. One of the coolest jazz spots in the city.
- Le Petit Opportun; 15 rue des Lavandière-Sainte-Opportune, 75001; tel: 01.48.72.16.95. Small basement club frequented by top jazz groups.
- Cithéa Nova; 114 rue Oberkampf 75011; tel: 01.40.21.70.95; website: http://www.citheanova.com.
- Les 7 Lézards; 10 rue des Rosiers, 75004; tel: 01.48.87.08.97. Interesting visiting jazz performers play to an always lively, appreciative crowd.
- Les Sunset/Le Sunside; 60 rue des Lombards, 75001;

tel: 01.40.26.46.60. A perennial favourite, this double venue hosts both electric and accoustic big-name groups and soloists.

THE GAY AND LESBIAN SCENE

To find the most up-to-date information on the gay and lesbian scene in Paris, access http://www.legayparis.com and http://wwwdykeplanet.com. The magazine *Tetu* keeps tabs on Paris happenings, as does the website of radio station *Fréquence Gay*, which carries information on resources (http://www.radiofg.com). For social and activist groups and networking, see the Resource Guide in Chapter 10. Here are a few well-known venues:

- Men's club: Le Club 18; 18 rue de Beaujolais 75001 (tel: 01.42.97.52.13). Timeless and still going strong, with music and dancing until dawn on weekends.
- Men's bar: Le Duplex; 25 rue Michel-le-Comte, 75003; tel: 01.42.72.80.86. One of Paris' oldest gay bars, still going strong, still cruising. Eclectic music, good drinks. Open daily from 8.00 pm–2.00 am.
- Men's bar: Quetzal; 10 rue de la Verrerie, 75004; tel: 01.48.87.99.07. Completely redone and modernised, this cruising bar has a dancing area and terrace. Open daily from 5:00 pm–5:00 am.
- Men's café: Open Café: 17 rue des Archives, 75004; tel: 01.42.72.26.18. Great summer terrace at this trendy café that is always packed, especially early evenings. Open daily from 10.00 am–2.00 am.
- Mixed bar: Le Mixer; 23 rue Sainte-Croix-de-la-Bretonnerie, 75004; tel: 01.48.87.55.44. A mixed crowd hangs out at this popular Marais club-bar. Everyone is welcome daily from 5:00 pm–2:00 am.
- Women's bar: Unity Bar; 176–178 rue Saint-Martin, 75003; tel: 01.42.72.70.59. Lively billiards bar with a definite atmosphere—cruising, excellent drink and fun and games.
- Women's disco: Le Rive Gauche: 1 rue du Sabot 01.40.20.43.23. A glittery dance hall from the '70s just off boulevard St-Germain. Still popular, but weekends only.

- Women's bar: La Champmeslé; 4 rue Chabanais, 75002; tel: 01.42.96.85.20. One of the original lesbian bars, now a classic. International beers on tap, good cocktails, plus readings, cabaret shows, art exhibitions and charity nights. Open from 3:00 pm; closed on Sundays.

DAY TRIPS THROUGHOUT THE PARIS AREA
Some of the most celebrated historical French sites are within the Paris region and can usually be reached in less than an hour by the national SNCF trains or the commuter RER trains—both inexpensive. However, if you're interested in guided tours in English, try a tour bus company that offers comfortable coach rides not only to spectacular sites near Paris, but also those further afield: south to 'chateau country'—the Loire Valley, 'champagne country' near Reims, and even as far north as Mont Saint-Michel and the walled city of Saint-Malo in Brittany. Most Paris hotels display brochures of these tour companies; otherwise, contact one of these:

- Cityrama; tel: 01.44.55.61.00; website:http://www.pariscityrama.com
- Paris Vision; tel: 01.47.42.27.40; website: http://www.parisvision.com
- Paris Trip; tel: 01.42.12.86.72; website: http://www.paris-trip.com

Basilique Royale de Saint-Denis
Although this exquisite basilica is in the northern Parisian suburb of Saint-Denis, it isn't exactly an 'out-of-town' trip, for it's easily reached by *métro* line 13. Construction of the basilica began in 1122 and many of the kings of France are entombed here, from Dagobert in the 7th century to Louis XVI and Marie-Antoinette, both guillotined in 1793 during the French Revolution. Sometimes called the 'Westminster Abbey of France', this masterpiece of Gothic architecture was built on the spot where Saint Denis is said to have been buried in the 3rd century. Legend goes that the patron saint of France walked to this spot carrying his own head after having been decapitated by the Romans.

La Défense

Just a few minutes west from central Paris and lying on the RER Line A, La Défense is a 750-hectare major business complex in France, headquarters to the country's most important corporations. Completed in the 1970s, more than 100,000 people work in some 100 modern skyscrapers and more than 30,000 people live in residential high-rise buildings that are linked by landscaped gardens and walkways dotted with sculptures and a large pool with musical water displays. There's a small train that gives a tour of the area. Don't miss the Quatre-Temps shopping mall, one of the largest in France. Take the glass elevator to the 35th floor of La Grande Arche for a spectacular view of Paris.

Château de Versailles

Approximately 20 km southwest of Paris, about half an hour away by RER Line C, the Chateau de Versailles is the most spectacular and famous palace in France, if not the world. It was built by Louis XVI who had engaged the same architects and landscapers used by the unfortunate Fouqet for his Château Vaux-le-Vicomte (see below). With some 700 ornately decorated and furnished rooms that hold 6,000 paintings and 2,000 sculptures, plus some 800 hectares of gardens, fountains, and woods, it's best to put aside an entire day for Versailles. (Check its website below for the schedule of fountain displays during summer.) Adjacent is the Petit Trianon, a palace designed for Mme de Pompadour in 1768 and later given to Marie Antoinette by Louis XVI. Not far is the Potager du Roi, the 'kitchen garden' of Louis XIV, now run by the National Horticultural School. The Grande Écurie (Big Stable) houses a museum of coaches (http://www.chateauversailles. fr). For detailed information on all attractions in the town of Versailles, contact the Office de Tourisme de Versailles at 2bis avenue de Paris, Versailles (tel: 01.39.24.88.88; http://www. versailles-tourisme.com).

Château de Chantilly

Less than a half an hour from Paris by train from the Gare du Nord or 45 minutes by RER Line D, lies the entire domain of Chantilly, a bequest to the Institut de France. The palace is called Musée Condé after the former owners—princes who were cousins to the French kings. The cream-coloured Renaissance palace, rebuilt after it was destroyed during the French revolution, is surrounded by a lake and houses an extensive collection of paintings and books. Here too, is the Hippodrome racetrack that sponsors the annual Prix de Diane Hermès, one of the most fashionable equestrian events of the Parisian season. The 15,000-acre forest is popular for hiking and cycling (http://www.chateaudechantilly.com).

Château de Fontainebleau

A 45-minutes train ride from Gare de Lyon to Fontainebleau-Avon and a short bus ride will take you to this exquisite 16th-century Renaissance palace built by François I and expanded by later kings, even Napoleon, who bid farewell from its courtyard as he went into exile. The palace is sumptuously decorated and adorned with tapestries, paintings and frescoes. Once the hunting grounds for French kings, the Fontainebleau forest that surrounds the town is now a popular weekend outing for Parisians (http://www.musee-chateau-fontainebleau.fr).

Cathedral of Chartres

About 95 km southwest from Paris and accessible by train from Gare Montparnasse, the charming town of Chartres is famous for the stained glass windows of its cathedral, built between 1145–1220. One of the greatest French Gothic cathedrals, Notre Dame de Chartres is noted for its magnificent 'Chartres blue'-and-red windows. Stroll through the preserved medieval streets of the town to the 13th-century Église Saint-Pierre, which also has stained glass, visit the museum and see some particularly fine old houses as you walk down to the banks of the river Eure. In the summer months, there is a local tourist train that makes a round of the town. See http://www.chartres.com.

Château de Vaux-le-Vicomte

Only 25 minutes from Gare de Lyon to Melun by train or by the RER Line D2, this exquisite 17th-century country chateau (http://www.vaux-le-vicomte.com) was built by Nicolas Fouquet, Finance Minister to Louis XIV. To celebrate the completion of the magnificent chateau, the unfortunate minister invited His Majesty to a lavish fête that included a display of Chinese fireworks, bejewelled elephants, a musical composed by Lully and a play written by Molière. Consumed by jealousy and anger at the extravagance of his Finance Minister, the king had Fouquet arrested for embezzlement and sentenced to life imprisonment. He then proceeded to hire Fouquet's architect and landscaper to build his Château de Versailles!

Giverny

It's easiest to use one of the tour bus companies mentioned above to tour the charming home and gardens of Impressionist painter Claude Monet (http://www.fondation-monet.com), located some 76 km northwest of Paris. Take time, too, to visit the Musée d'Art Américain (http://www.maag.org), which holds a collection of works of American Impressionists, many of whom studied or resided in France. If you take the train, it's about an hour from Gare Saint-Lazare to Vernon, where a bus then takes you to Giverny. Monet's lovely garden and pond with its Japanese bridge have been immortalised in his paintings, especially in his paintings of water lilies.

Auvers-sur-Oise

Some 30 km to the northwest of Paris, Auvers-sur-Oise (http://www.auvers-sur-oise.com) was the final home of Dutch Impressionist Vincent Van Gogh. Take the train from Gare du Nord to Cergy-Pontoise, then the local train in the direction of Creil.

In addition to visiting the Auberge Ravoux where Van Gogh lived and died, a stroll through the town will provide a well-documented tour of the buildings that have become so familiar through Van Gogh's paintings, including the Église Notre Dame. There are several museums to visit and the atelier of the painter Daubigny, and you can also walk up the hill to the cemetery where Van Gogh and his brother Theo were buried. Linger over lunch at the elegant Hostellerie du Nord before heading back to Paris.

Brussels, Belgium

It takes only a little more than an hour to get to downtown Brussels (http://www.visitbelgium.com) from Gare du Nord by the Thalys train (make reservations through SNCF). Imagine lunching on *moules frites* (mussels and French fries) with a refreshing Belgian beer in a restaurant on the beautiful Grand Place, then browsing for a few hours at the Royal Museum of Art, before taking the train back to Paris. All in all, an easy and lovely afternoon well spent.

Disneyland Resort Paris

The European Disney theme park can be reached in less than an hour by RER Line A, or directly by bus from Charles de Gaulle airport. The Disney Village offers hotels, restaurants and shops for those who want to stay more than one day to visit the Disneyland Park and its five differently-themed attractions. Golf Disneyland has three 9-hole courses (which may be combined into 18-holes) and is open year-round. There is also the Walt Disney Studios, which exhibits films and animation productions. Add water activities, tennis courts and year-round entertainment, and Disneyland isn't just for the kids. (See http://www.disneylandparis.com.)

KEEPING FIT
Becoming Fitness-Conscious

The French, although passionate sport spectators, have not been known for being extremely *sportifs* (sporty) themselves. This is changing however, as younger people are becoming fitness-conscious. They are smoking and drinking less while exercising more. Gymnasia are opening all across Paris, jogging is popular, rollerblades are seen on the streets and in the *métro*, and some main city streets have bicycle paths. Paris offers an extensive system of public sports facilities, including tennis courts, swimming pools, gyms and running tracks, all increasingly crowded.

The daily sports newspaper *L'Equipe* has information on all current sporting events. The weekly events guides— *Figaroscope*, *L'Officiel des Spectacles* and *Pariscope*—are issued

on Wednesdays. They list all the sporting events for that week and some individual sporting possibilities.

Spectator Sports

The main indoor public arena is the Palais Omnisports Paris-Bercy at 8 boulevard de Bercy, 75012. It holds football, tennis and volleyball matches; ice-skating competitions; equestrian events and rock concerts. The Parc des Princes, located at the southern tip of the Bois de Boulogne, at 24 rue Commandant-Guilbaud, 75016, is a 50,000-seat stadium where football (soccer to Americans) and rugby games are played, as well as the French Open at Roland Garros. Then, there is the 80,000-seat Grande Stade de France, constructed in the late 1990s just beyond the northern edge of the city in Saint-Denis, where the finals of the World Cup matches in 1998 were held. In addition to sports matches, it currently hosts large musical events. The stadium is easily reached by RER and *métro*.

Like most Europeans, the French are avid football fans. The football season runs from the end of July to the following April. The Paris team is Paris Saint-Germain (http://www.psg.fr), which plays at Parc des Princes. Season tickets are available and single tickets may be purchased online, at the stadium or at ticket agencies. Buy tickets well in advance, for the important matches sell out early.

Horse races are also popular. The Hippodrome d'Auteuil and Hippodrome de Longchamp are in the Bois de Boulogne, and each has its particular racing season and events. The Hippodrome de Vincennes in the Bois de Vincennes is known for its trotting meets. Bets may be made at the track or off-track through the Pari Mutuel Urbain (PMU) at many *tabacs*. For information, see *Paris Turf*, a racing magazine (http://www.paris-turf.com).

The Two Largest Parks

The Bois de Boulogne is at the western edge of Paris, 846 hectares that run the length of the 16^e down to the suburb of Boulogne-Billancourt. Parisians go there to *pique-niquer* (picnic) or *se promener* (stroll). Located in the Bois are the racecourses mentioned above and Roland-Garros, the tennis stadium that is home to the French Open 'Grand Slam' tournament held each spring. Here too are running tracks, a workout course, artificial lakes, rowboat and bicycle rentals, as well as swimming pools. The Parc de Bagatelle has an old castle and lovely rose gardens. The Jardin d'Acclimatation has a children's playground and amusement park, zoo, donkey rides and puppet shows.

The Bois de Vincennes stretches east from the 12^e. Larger than the Bois de Boulogne, it is more wooded, less built up and often more tranquil. Jogging paths, rowboat rentals on two lakes, baseball and football fields, and a large tennis facility are some of the park's attractions. In addition, at Le Parc Floral there are playgrounds, ping-pong tables, a theatre for children and a working farm. The city's largest zoo is here. The office of your *mairie* should have the booklet *Jardins et Environnement* with details about the city parks and their facilities.

Resources

Access the city's website for the online *Guide du Sport*, which lists many of the municipal sport centers and federations of the sports disciplines. The *mairie* in each *arrondissement* should also have detailed information about the facilities available in that district. And the Fédération Sportive Gaie et Liesbienne Ile-de-France is an umbrella association fostering amateur sports for gays and lesbians (http://www.fsgl.org).

Running

Parisians do not often practise *le footing* (jogging) around city streets, for traffic and pollution can be unpleasant, but people do jog along the quais with their broad sidewalks and lovely views. Many runners head for the Bois de Boulogne and its 35-km paths that wind through meadows and around lakes; or to the Bois de Vincennes and its outer circuit of almost 11 km or inner circuit of 8 km. In the city centre, people run in the Tuileries, the Champ-de-Mars, Parc Monceau, Parc des Buttes-Chaumont, Parc de Montsouris and the Jardin du Luxembourg.

Some 24 of the city's *centres sportifs* (sports centres) have running tracks; eight are indoors. Buy a subscription ticket, which allows entrance to the track, showers and locker rooms. Tracks are closed to the public when schools or the organised running clubs have reserved them.

Bicycling

Bicycling is a popular sport and there are clubs and special events for cyclists. If you don't have a bike of your own, you can rent one, although buying one second-hand is not expensive. For rentals, see *Location de cycles, motos et scooters* in the *Yellow Pages*. For detailed information on cycling, contact the Fédération Française de Cyclisme at 5 rue de Rome, 93561 Rosny-sur-Bois Cedex (tel: 01.49.35.69.00; http://www.ffc.fr). Also, ask at your *mairie* for *Paris à Velo*, a booklet which details everything you need to know about cycling in Paris.

The RATP rents bicycles at its Maison Roue Libre, with branches at the Bastille and near Les Halles (http://bus38.online.fr/rouelibreeng.html). It's best to check their website for current information. The companies listed below both rent and sell bicycles; the first two also offer city tours. And, of course, the *vélib* bicycles are docked all around the city for short trips.

- 11e: Paris à Vélo, C'est Sympa; 22 rue Alphonse Baudin; tel: 01.48.87.60.01
- 5e: Paris Vélo; 2 rue du Fer-à-Moulin; tel: 01.43.37.59.22
- 11e: Bicloune; 7 rue Froment; tel: 01.48.05.47.75; website: http://www.bicloune.fr.

Some of the SNCF trains have bike racks and many do not charge extra for transporting bikes. Bicycles are also available for rent at many SNCF train stations in the countryside.

Les Centres D'Animation

In the municipal sports system, some 30 *centres d'animation* train adults and children in a wide variety of activities. Among the cultural activities offered are lessons in music, dance, language and the performing arts. There are also dozens of sports courses, including martial arts, tennis, fencing, golf, basketball and other ball games, water sports and even *pétanque* (a traditional game using metal balls). A small enrollment fee is charged. Inquire at your neighbourhood sports facility and ask at the *mairie* for the booklet, *Centres d'Animations*, which details the offerings.

Aquaboulevard

One of the most extensive sports complexes in the Paris area is Aquaboulevard de Paris, at 4–6 rue Louis-Armand, 75015 (tel: 01.40.60.10.00; http://www.aquaboulevard.com). It is part of the Forest Hill chain of sports and tennis clubs, and seems to have everything. It has both indoor and outdoor facilities, including 11 tennis courts, six squash courts, practice and miniature golf, gym and aerobics programmes and a huge swimming complex with a tropical lagoon. There are shops and restaurants as well.

Gyms

More than 100 gymnasia exist throughout the city, with different facilities and programmes. Both public and private gyms are crowded, and they all vary in amenities and services, so look around before joining. Private clubs are opening at a rapid rate in each neighbourhood. The *Yellow Pages* have several sections concerning fitness: *Clubs de forme* and *Gymnastique: Salles et Leçons*. See also the *Guide du Sport*.

- Les Cercles de la Forme; website: http://www. cerclesdelaforme.com. Seven centres around Paris offering a full range of fitness courses, dance classes and cardio training.

- Club Med; website: http://www.clubmedgym.com. A chain of 22 full-service gyms throughout the city, some with swimming pools.

- 3ᵉ: Espace Vit'Halles; A chain of ten clubs in Paris and Ile de France, with high-tech equipment, classes, swimming, sauna and steam facilities; website: http://www.vithalles.fr. High-tech equipment, aerobics classes, swimming and sauna and steam facilities.

- 5ᵉ: Club Quartier Latin; 19 rue Pontoise; tel: 01.55.42.77.88; website: http://www.clubquartierlatin.com. Full-service gym with cardio and aerobic training, weights, squash, various classes, etc.

Tennis

There are some 44 public tennis centres in Paris with more than 170 courts. To join the public system, residents must obtain the *Carte Paris-Sports*, with an identification number to use when reserving a court. Applications may be obtained from tennis centres or your *mairie*. The card takes about four weeks to process (info tel: 01.47.43.48.00; website: http://www.fft.fr). Bring identification and two photos.

Courts are always crowded. Reserve them in advance online (http://www.tennis.paris.fr). Charges are by the hour and are reasonable. It costs more to play in the evening when the courts are lit. You can also join tennis clubs, which themselves have arrangements with courts around the city. See *Tennis courts et leçons* in the *Yellow Pages* and *Tennis* in the *White Pages*. The French Open (known in France as Roland-Garros) begins in the last week of May at Stade Roland-Garros. The Paris Open takes place at Bercy in November. Tickets are difficult to obtain except for early rounds.

For information and inquiries regarding membership in private clubs, call the Fédération Française de Tennis at Stade Roland-Garros, 2 avenue Gordon-Bennet, 75016 (tel: 01.47.43.48.00; website: http://www.fft.fr).

Swimming Pools

There are more than 30 municipal swimming pools sprinkled around Paris. They are well maintained, and many are quite attractive. Swimming is one of the most accessible sports and pools are crowded year round. This means that most pools are heavily chlorinated, so to keep bathing suits from falling apart too quickly, you should rinse them out thoroughly after each use. Men must wear trunks, not boxer bathing suits, and in theory women must wear a one-piece suit, although this rule is sometimes broken. A swimming cap is required for both sexes.

During the school year, students have priority and pools are closed to the public, except for a few hours early in the morning, during lunchtime and in the evenings. Inquire at your pool for its schedule, especially during vacations when public access is increased. In the public pools, check how your clothes and valuables will be kept, because some facilities are more secure than others.

You may buy a single-day entry, but a 10-visit card or a three-month pass is more economical and allows access to any public pool. Inexpensive, this is one of the true bargains of Paris. Ask for the foldout card *Nager á Paris*, which lists all the public pools. See *Piscines (établissements)* in the *Yellow Pages*. Also, for a treat, visit the brand new Piscine Joséphine Baker, which floats in the Seine just below the Bibliothèque Nationale, off Quai François Mauriac. The pool is large enough to accommodate some 500 swimmers and has a retractable glass roof over its man-made 'beach'.

Golf

Golf is increasingly popular in France, but it is expensive, especially on weekends. To play golf regularly or to obtain a handicap, you must have a permit, which may be issued on a daily, trimester or annual basis. Inquire at the Fédération Française de Golf at 68 rue Anatole-France, 92309 Levallois-Perret cedex (tel: 01.41.49.77.00; website: http://www.ffg.org). Ask also for information about golf tournaments in the Paris area.

There are no full-sized *parcours* (golf courses) in Paris itself, but there are almost 100 throughout Île-de-France. Don't miss Golf Disneyland, part of the enormous Disneyland Paris Resorts, about 32 km east of Paris: Allée de la Marc Houleuse, 77700 Magny le Hongre (tel: 01.60.45.68.90; website: http://www.disneylandparis.com). Some of the private clubs, such as the exclusive Golf de Saint-Cloud, have waiting lists of several years, and most require recommendations. Fortunately, many are open to non-members certain days of the week. In general, you must bring the membership card to your own club and proof of your handicap. See *Golf terrains et leçons* in the *Yellow Pages*, *Golf* in the *White Pages*.

Rollerblading and Skating

Rollers (rollerblades) are enormously popular. Pari Roller (http://www.pari-roller.com) organises a Friday night *randonnée* (outing) that sees up to 10,000 bladers cruising the streets of Paris. Pari Roller staff guide bladers along the routes and police, also on rollerblades, patrol traffic, protecting the participants. Routes change and starting points are announced in advance. The *randonnée* starts around 9:30 pm at the Montparnasse tower and usually follows a 25-km course. Although it moves quickly, the route is long and the event lasts until the wee hours of the morning.

The Sunday afternoon *randonnée* is a family-oriented and beginners event, run by Rollers et Coquillages (http://www.rollers-coquillages.org), starting near place de la Bastille. You can also access the website of the Roller Squad Institute (http://www.rsi.asso.fr).

For ice skating, try the place de l'Hôtel de Ville, which is flooded and frozen in winter, making a pleasant rink.

Oriental Arts

Some 18 of the municipal sports centres offer yoga, and almost all of them, some kind of martial arts training, including aikido, jiu-jitsu, judo, karate and taekwondo. For information, see the *Guide du Sport*. The Fédération Française d'Hatha-Yoga at 50 rue Vaneau, 75007 offers information on

Even the policemen are equipped with rollerblades to patrol the mass rollerblading events regularly organised in Paris—a real treat for rollerbladers and fun to watch, too.

yoga in Paris. (tel: 01.45.44.02.59; http://www.ff-hatha-yoga.
com). The Fédération Karaté et Arts Martiaux is at 122, rue
de la Tombe-Issoire, 75014 (tel: 01.43.95.42.00; http://www.
ffkama.fr). See *Arts martiaux divers (salles et leçons)* in the
Yellow Pages.

Boules
Fun to watch or play is the classic French *pétanque* (commonly
called *boules*), in which metal balls are thrown toward a small
spherical target. It can be played wherever there is a level
surface and is played in town squares all over France, with
onlookers commenting on every throw. To play, you need
a set of *boules* (balls), which are available at most sporting
goods stores. In Paris there are a dozen *boulodromes* (bowling
pitches), including in the Arènes de Lutèce and the Bois
de Vincennes.

Sports Clothes and Equipment
Active wear can be found in department stores and at some
of the discount shops. The upmarket international chains Fila
and Lacoste have shops in the city, as do the sports footwear
chains Foot Locker and Adidas; sizes are consistent in these
stores. See *Sport et loisirs: articles et vêtements (détail)* in the
Yellow Pages.
- Au Vieux Campeur; 48 rue des Ecoles 76005; tel:
  01.53.10.48.48; website: http://www.auvieuxcampeur.fr.
  Chain of specialised stores offering high-quality camping,
  climbing and diving equipment, hammocks, sleeping bags,
  travel books, accessories, etc.
- Courir; website: http://www.courir.com. Chain of sports
  shoe stores selling internationally known brands at very
  good prices. Also at Aquaboulevard.
- Decathlon; website: http://www.decathlon.fr. Several stores
  selling sporting clothes and equipment, including for
  bicyling. Good prices and service.
- Go Sport; website: http://www.go-sport.com. Chain of
  sporting equipment stores. Extensive selection of clothes
  at reasonable prices.

SHOPPING
Haute Couture

Paris is, of course, the capital of haute couture. Haute couture may affect only a few men and women who can afford thousands of euros for a handmade suit or dress; nonetheless, the fashion industry occupies a prominent position in Paris and the world. Paris has always been known for its couturiers—Dior, Chanel, Givenchy, Hermès, Lanvin and Saint Laurent—but is now also feeling the presence of international designers such as the German Jill Sander, the Italian Giorgio Armani, the Japanese Issey Miyake and the Americans Ralph Lauren and Calvin Klein.

The famous Parisian haute couture fashion shows take place in February and July, but unless you are a celebrity, a fashion editor at a prominent magazine or newspaper, or a particularly heavy spender, do not expect to be invited. Just one outfit, intricately hand stitched, perhaps festooned with glittering ornaments and cut drastically up the middle or down the side, can cost more than most of us spend on our annual budget for clothes! And beautiful as the creations are, they have little to do with the experience of shopping in Paris.

Many of the couturiers have, however, *prêt-à-porter* (ready-to-wear) salons, selling clothes and accessories under their *griffe* (designer label). Their *prêt-à-porter* may not be hand-stitched, but are of a high quality and expensive too. Many are housed in what is known as the 'Golden Triangle' near the Rond-point (roundabout) des Champs-Elysées, in streets such as avenue Montaigne or rue François 1er and rue du Faubourg Saint-Honoré. Others are scattered around the city and some have branches in the fashionable parts of town. The Paris Tourist Office has a list of addresses for the major designers, which are also listed in most guidebooks. If you are really interested in exploring a couturier's line of *prêt-à-porter*, do not let the sometimes frigid attitudes of the salespeople intimidate you or dissuade you from looking around.

Top designers who are not couturiers are called *créateurs*. Their *prêt-à-porter*, also of the highest quality, can be quite costly, but somewhat below the range of those of the couturiers.

Haute couture aside, clothes are, in general, expensive in France, although prices remain relative to their quality: a man's suit may cost over US$100 more than in the United States but hundreds of thousands of yen less than a comparable suit in Japan. Tax on clothes (included in the price) may be above 20 per cent. Until recently there were few outlets for imported inexpensive labels, thus Parisians traditionally purchased fewer items but of high quality, especially classic items that would not quickly go out of style. This is why style has always been more important than fashion and why Parisian women so often seem so carefully put together, with a scarf tossed over the shoulders of a classic white blouse or a pin at the collar of a tailored dress.

Today, however, the revitalisation of Paris, the inclination of tourists to spend money on clothes and the new welcome extended to foreign business mean increased imports at all levels of quality and price. The presence of international chains such as Gap, Zara and Levi's is offering new options for inexpensive yet durable clothing, especially for young people. Shopping in Paris is becoming much like shopping in any other city, but you can still find areas of Parisian character if you try.

Where to Shop

This section does not pretend to be exhaustive in terms of clothing stores—there are so many individual boutiques that it would take a telephone book to list them all. Tourist guides have sections on shopping, and there are several dedicated to shopping in Paris. However, while these guides include a range of shops—both in category and price—and they often offer some unique, offbeat ideas, they are often geared toward the tourist who has discretionary funds to spend in a limited amount of time.

Most of the inner *arrondissements* have their own shopping areas, in keeping with the character and economic level of the neighbourhood. In addition to the fashionable streets noted above, Place des Victoires on the Right Bank is a designer nucleus, as is the area around Place des Vosges. At the top of the 16ᵉ is avenue Victor-Hugo, leading down toward the

aristocratic rue de Passy, both known for their upmarket flavour.

On the Left Bank, shops on boulevard Saint-Germain and along rue de Rennes are increasingly fashionable. Some international top designers have opened their own boutiques to the dismay of the longtime residents who would like to keep the village atmosphere of the area intact—they won't succeed. Nearby but slightly out of the tourist scene, streets around place Saint-Sulpice, rue de Grenelle and rue de Sèvres are lined with boutiques of all categories and prices, from established and upcoming designers down to the most basic shops—they just take exploring to find.

Inexpensive shops can be found throughout the city. The department store Tati (see page 267) always has interesting merchandise—if you can ferret it out, and the streets around place de la République and the huge Paris garment district at Sentier and Place du Caire are good places to look for bargains. For shops that are deemed good value for money, including discount shops, see the guidebook *Paris Pas Cher*. (http://www.guideparispascher.com).

When to Shop

Although Parisians may be interested in the *nouveautés* (new collections), many wait for the biannual *soldes* (sales) to buy clothes, when all shops, including the most fashionable, offer reduced prices. During the *soldes*, the line around the block at designer boutiques can be daunting, as clever shoppers may have inspected the merchandise in the stores prior to the opening sale date. About half of all consumer purchases are made during the January and June sales. Sales are regulated by the government: they are allowed only after Christmas and in a six-week summer period, and merchandise must have been in the store for at least 30 days, to ensure that inferior merchandise is not brought in solely for a sale. Toward the end of the sales, some stores will advertise *deuxième démarque* or *dernière démarque*, indicating further markdowns in price. Many shops also have promotions throughout the year, when items on the sales floor are marked for clearance or special items are brought in for a particular promotion.

Shops are generally open from 10:00 am–7:00 pm. Some of the smaller shops close for a few hours at lunchtime and may stay open until 8:00 pm. Department stores are open all day and generally stay open slightly later one evening a week. With only a few exceptions, shops are closed on Sundays, and some shops stay closed on Monday. August can make for difficult shopping, as many of the smaller shops close for the month. The department stores, fortunately, are open all day, six days a week, all year round. In December, shops are generally open on Sundays.

The Customer

If you come from a society where the customer is always right, then you'll be surprised in Paris that this is not the case. Sometimes, it even seems like the salesperson is doing you a favour by just waiting on you, and you may have to wait for her to finish her conversation with another salesperson to be even noticed. Just wait where you can be easily seen, make eye contact when you can and don't show any impatience.

Inspect all items before you purchase them. In many stores you will not be able to return or exchange items once they are purchased.

Size Conversions

Basically, you have to try on clothes and shoes until you see what size fits and not simply rely on the size shown on the label. Some companies use several factories to make their clothes, which means that different dresses or suits of the same designer may not actually fit the same, despite showing the same size. And, of course, different designers have different sizing policies. In general, an American woman should add 30 to her dress size to find the comparable size. Thus a size 12 woman would look for a 42. British women should add 28. For men, a size 'small' shirt translates to about a 37–38 and a 'medium' is about 40. For a chart, see the Chapter 10.

Sizing policies may begin to change as the French woman herself is changing. With better nutrition and exercise, the French woman's waist is said to be 10 cm wider than the average post-World War II size, and manufacturers may well be forced to modify the cut of their creations, so women won't have to buy larger sizes.

Department Stores

As in any large city, the department stores in Paris vary in their approach to the merchandising and pricing of their goods. The most prestigious department stores such as Galeries Lafayette and Printemps are called *grands magasins*, each with its own personality and branding. Although they may cater to tourists and be staffed with English speakers, they basically sell what appeals to the French. To cater to the endless flow of tourists, the *grands magasins* provide services such as currency exchange, ticket and travel agencies, as well as tourist information. The *grands magasins* also have weekly fashion shows and offer discounts to tourists.

In some department stores, as in some food shops, it is common to select the merchandise, get the bill from the salesperson, take it to the *caisse* to pay, and only then take the validated receipt back to the salesperson to pick up your order. In some, it is possible to get one overall bill (*carnet d'achats*) and to pay for all selections at one time.

Department stores participate in the biannual sales, but since there are periodic promotions on clearance merchandise, the sales prices are sometimes not much lower. See *Centres Commerciaux et Grands Magasins* in the *Yellow Pages*.

- 1ᵉʳ: Madelios; 23 boulevard de la Madeleine; tel: 01.53.45.00.00. Men's upmarket department store, featuring the most fashionable designers in formal, street and casual wear.
- 3ᵉ: Tati; 4 boulevard Rochechouart; tel: 01.55.29.50.50. Sprawling shops with merchandise at low prices. Other addresses.
- 4ᵉ: BHV (Bazar de l'Hôtel de Ville); 40 rue de Rivoli; tel: 01.42. 74.90.00. Known for its wide variety of home-improvement items, including artists' materials, household items, etc.
- 7ᵉ: Le Bon Marché; 24 rue de Sèvres; tel: 01.44.39.80.00. Another *grand magasin*, the city's oldest and still one of the best. Elegant merchandise, beautifully presented, for the family and for the home. In the basement (*sous-sol*) are a bookshop, ticket agency, toys and games, CDs and DVDs and a good stationery department.
- 9ᵉ and 14ᵉ: Galeries Lafayette; 40 boulevard Haussmann; tel: 01.42.82.57.87. A *grand magasin* comprising several large buildings offering just about everything—designer wear, exquisite lingerie, hairdressers, a gourmet food emporium, household items, etc. Other services such as currency exchange, a ticket agency and a shoemaker are available too. A much smaller branch at Centre Commercial Maine Montparnasse; tel: 01.45.38.52.87.
- 9ᵉ, 13ᵉ and 20ᵉ: Printemps: 64, boulevard Haussmann; tel: 01.42.82.50.00. Another *grand magasin* with services to rival that of Galeries Lafayette, located just next door. Men should look especially at Printemps de l'Homme, a separate six-floor emporium dedicated to them. Try the *brasserie* located under a beautiful Art Nouveau dome. Open until 10:00 pm on Thursdays. Also at Centre Commercial

Italie 2; tel: 01.40.78.17.17 and 21 cours de Vincennes; tel: 01.43.71.12.41.

- 16e: Franck & Fils; 80 rue de Passy; tel: 01.44.14.38.00. Department store for women with an elegant refurbished ambience.

- Monoprix: Chain of basic merchandise stores and supermarkets, with branches in most *arrondissements*. Good prices, many products under the store's own label. Hours vary according to the location.

Shopping Centres

Many of the *centres commerciaux* (shopping malls) have entrances/exits linked to the *métro*, making shopping convenient in inclement weather. An easy *métro* ride to La Défense leads directly into Les Quatre Temps, the largest shopping complex in France, with hundreds of clothing and shoe shops, household stores, restaurants, services and the *hypermarché* Auchan.

Lying outside the city, but easily reached by car and public transportation, La Vallée Outlet Shopping Village is a complex of some 100 upmarket and designer stores selling clothing, shoes, leather goods and housewares at discount prices (http://www.lavalleevillage.com). You can catch a shuttle bus from the RER station Val d'Europe at Marne-la-Vallée, or take the train to the station Marne-la-Vallée-Chessy-Parc Disneyland.

- 1er: Carrousel du Louvre; 99 rue de Rivoli. A mall attached to the Louvre. Two underground levels filled with an assortment of upmarket shops. Open on Sundays.

- 1er: Forum des Halles; 101 Porte Berger. Enormous mall, with hundreds of shops of all sorts and levels, including a large FNAC.

- 1er: Les Trois Quartiers; 23 boulevard de la Madeleine. Multi-level upmarket fashion mall with a perfume store, hairdressing salon, plus many boutiques, including some top designers.

- 14e: Maine Montparnasse. Near the Tour Montparnasse, at place du 18 juin 1940. Large mall that includes Galeries Lafayette and C&A.

Look up from the tempting wares while shopping at Printemps to admire the beautiful glass dome above. The decor changes according to the seasons and festivities, but it's never less than eye-catching, especially at Christmas time.

- 16ᵉ: Plaza Passy; 53 rue de Passy. A small, popular, modern mall with international shops and a supermarket in the heart of the fashionable Passy district.
- 17ᵉ: Boutiques du Palais des Congrès; Porte Maillot. Upmarket fashion shops, excellent food shop, tea room, etc.

Discount/Second-Hand Clothes

Paris swarms with discount clothing shops, which are extremely popular with Parisians. There are several types: some shops sell new but out-of-season designer clothes, while others, known as *dégriffé*, sell clothes with the labels taken out or mutilated. The *dépôts-vente* (consignment shops) sell slightly used clothes of fashionable ladies who may have worn them only once. Look out too for shops that advertise *vêtements d'occasion* (second-hand clothes) or have the word '*troc*' in their names (this could mean that clothes may be exchanged for others after inspection by the shops). *Fripe* means the shop specialises in retro clothes, while *solderies* refers to shops where there is a permanent sale.

Some designers maintain discount shops for their out-of-season designs. If the word '*stock*' is in the name, it means the shop sells new clothes from a designer or factory. (Designers often contribute overstock to the crowded biannual *braderies*, or jumble sales at the Porte de Versailles.) See *Dépôts-vente: vêtements* in the *Yellow Pages* and *Paris Pas Cher*.

- 1ᵉʳ: Didier Ludot; 24 galerie Montpensier at Palais Royal; tel: 01.42.96.06.56. Haute couture and accessories. Prices may not be inexpensive, but they are certainly significantly lower than the original prices.
- 1ᵉʳ: Les Ciseaux d'Argent; 156 rue de Rivoli; tel: 01.42.61.09.44. Men's clothes and shoes. Good brands with the labels removed and good value for money.
- 6ᵉ: Le Mouton à Cinq Pattes; 138 boulevard Saint-Germain; tel: 01.43.26.49.25. Vintage clothes and previous season's stock. A popular shop, so you have to buy what you fancy right away or it will be gone. Several addresses in the 6ᵉ.

- 16ᵉ: Reciproque; 95–123 rue de la Pompe; tel: 01.47.04.30.28. Specialised upmarket discount stores in one street. Open from Tuesday–Saturday.

Catalogue Shopping

Catalogue shopping is increasingly popular and companies such as La Redoute (http://www.laredoute.fr), which also has shops in Paris, and 3Suisses distribute thick catalogues which are eagerly pored over by many. Prices are generally fair, returns are accepted (with the appropriate paperwork), and occasionally there are special sales.

International catalogue companies will ship to France. Duty on merchandise imported from outside the EU can be high, so check to see whether the company has an online service within the EU, where shipping between countries does not entail duty fees. For instance, at Lands' End in the UK (http://www.landsend.co.uk), prices may be higher than in the United States, but since there is no duty charged for shipment to France and postage is at domestic rates, the price you ultimately pay may be similar, depending on the amount of your order .

Flea Markets

Inexpensive clothes can be found at some of the city's flea markets. See page 282, Products and Services, for a list of the city's best flea markets.

Children's Clothes

All department stores carry a variety of children's clothes; some *dépôts-ventes* selling children's clothes.

Du Pareil au Même, Jacadi and Natalys are French chains for children's clothing, and Le Petit Bateau, with several stores, sells colourful, comfortable and reasonably priced items. The international chains Benetton, Baby Gap and Gap Kids also have shops throughout the city. See *Paris Pas Cher* for well-priced children's clothes.

For traditionally French elegant clothes, the stylish Bonpoint is at 15 rue Royale (tel: 01.45.66.52.40; http://www.bonpoint. fr), and for the more fashionable, try Tartine et Chocolat at

24 rue de la Paix (tel: 01.47.42.10.68; http://www.tartine-et-chocolat.fr). Both have several branches.

For one-stop shopping, try Bonton at 82 rue de Grenelle, 75007; tel: 01.44.39.09.20; website: http://www.bonton.fr. Kids' furniture, toys, books, clothing and accessories. Closed on Sundays.

- 6e:Chercheminippes: various addresses in rue du Cherche Midi 75006 (tel: 01.42.22.33.89). Good discounts on children's clothes; women's and men's clothing and decorations, in different shops in the same street.
- 12e: Bambini Troc; 26 avenue du Bel Air; tel: 01.43.47.33.76. Dépôt-vente for children an expectant mothers, plus other items for children.
- 13e: Troc Lutin; 6 rue des Cinq-Diamants; tel: 01.45.81. 44.57. *Dépôt-vente* for designer clothes for kids up to 14 years old, plus a sports and games section.

For children's shoes, try the chain Petits Petons with four shops in Paris; Six Pieds Trois Pouces, which sells shoes under its own label at three outlets; as well as some international brands such as Reebok.

Shoes

Shops such as Charles Jourdan, Christian Louboutin, Walter Steiger or Stéphane Kélian offer meticulous workmanship in styles both fashionable and classic—with prices to match. Department stores offer a wide selection of brands and prices, and discount shoe stores that sell end-of-the-line models and overstock can make purchasing fashionable shoes much more affordable. This holds true for children's shoes as well.

Look for shoe shops clustered in rue du Dragon and rue du Cherche-Midi. Rue Meslay, near Place de la République, has several discount shoe stores, as does boulevard Magenta. For retail stores, see *Chaussures* in the *Yellow Pages*. For shoes at particularly good prices, including discount shops, see *Paris Pas Cher*.

Shoe sizes are in centimetres. Shoes are basically sold in one width (medium), but each brand has its own sizing standards, so you have to check out different brands until you find the one whose sizes best fit your feet. You can start with the department stores, which gather many brands under one roof. In general, an American woman's size 6–7.5 would correspond to sizes 37–39 and a British woman's size 6–7.5 would be sizes 38–40. A man's shoe size 9 would be about a size 42 for both American and British men.

- La Halle Aux Chaussures: Chain of inexpensive self-service shoe stores with shoes for the entire family.
- Arche: Chain of trendy women's shoe shops, selling colourful and modern—and very comfortable—shoes.
- Mephisto: Popular French chain selling comfortable, supportive shoes. Not cheap, but much cheaper than buying them in North America

Cordonneries (shoe repair shops) can be found in any *arrondissement* and BHV has a repair service. Some *métro* stations also have shoe repair and polishing booths—look for signs near the WC that indicate '*cireur*'. The Talons Minute shops offer fast repair service.

Products and Services

No matter what you need (or want), it can no doubt be found somewhere within the city's confines. The brand names might not be the same and the exact item might have some minor differences, but globalisation—a source of worry to the French—means that many imported items are found here, from food brands to computers, clothing and cosmetics to children's games. Prices for these items, once quite high, are now fairly reasonable, owing to worldwide competition and 'e-tail' on the Internet. For appliances, utilities and home repair resources, see Chapter 5.

Unfortunately, the French idea of 'customer service' still revolves around the old Latin saying: "*caveat emptor* (let the buyer beware)." First of all, always count your change; mistakes can be made, and cashiers can be harried. But you're also a foreigner, so you have to be somewhat more careful about the rare dishonest person taking advantage of someone unfamiliar with the currency. Look at any order form carefully before you sign it. Ask all your questions in advance, for afterwards if something isn't to your liking, you may not be able to exchange it.

But this is beginning to change, at least in the larger stores. If you need to exchange damaged merchandise (which for some reason, you could not have noticed before purchase), make sure you have all your receipts and the original packaging before you set off. When negotiating with the salesperson, be extremely polite, don't indicate that the shop did anything wrong, and don't raise your voice; if anything will work, it's *politesse* (politeness). Also, if you, as you begin exploring your new neighbourhood, let it be known to shopkeepers that you have just moved to the *quartier* and are not a tourist, they'll understand that you are asking for good service.

Some shops offer a *carte de fidelité*, meaning that after you spend a certain amount, you are entitled to a discount on your next purchase. A *carte d'adhérent* means that as a cardholder you are entitled to discounts and rewards for shopping. Some bookshops and cleaners offer these rewards, as do a few of the supermarket chains and Fnac.

BOOKSHOPS

Parisians love to read, so there are *librairies* (bookshops) in every neighbourhood, and all department stores carry books. Some, especially those in the tourist areas, carry English-language books, and both Fnac on rue de Rennes and Virgin Megastore on the Champs-Elysées (open on Sundays) stock foreign-language titles. There are also several well-stocked shops devoted to English-language books. You can expect to pay about 20 per cent more for a new book than you might at home. Shops that buy, sell and trade used books are cheaper. Shops generally place special orders if the books are on the computer inventory. To order books online, try http://www.amazon.co.uk. Some shops are open on Sunday afternoons; most organise readings by authors.

You may also borrow books from the American Library (see page 182), which houses some 120,000 titles in English, current periodicals and DVD/videocassettes. The library also

Darty

The one major shop that prides itself on its *service après-vente* (after-sales service) is Darty, the nationwide chain of appliance, electronics and household stores (see Chapter 5), where repair service is rapid and efficient. http://www.darty.com

organises author evenings and other events. Membership rates are reasonable. Check out, too, the *bouquinistes*—the small open-air stalls that line the *quais* on both sides of the Seine from the Musée d'Orsay to Pont de Sully, selling old books of all sorts. On weekends, it's fun to browse at the Marché aux Livres (book market) at Square George-Brassens, 75015 for bargains. The Salon du Livre (Paris Book Fair) that takes place in late spring is open to the public.

- 1er: Galignani: 224 rue de Rivoli ; tel: 01.42.60.76.07. Books in English and French; specialises in art books.
- 1er: W.H. Smith; 248 rue de Rivoli; tel: 01.44.77.88.99. British book chain; open on Sundays, 1:00–7:30 pm. Readings and meet-the-author events.
- 4^{e}: Red Wheelbarrow; 22 rue Saint-Paul; tel: 01.48.04.75.08. Literature and non-fiction.
- 5^{e}: Abbey Bookshop; 29 rue de la Parcheminerie; tel: 01.46. 33.16.24. The 'Canadian' bookshop.
- 5^{e}: Shakespeare & Company; 37 rue de la Bûcherie; tel: 01.43. 25.40.93. Famous shop packed with new and used books.

The famous Shakespeare and Company bookshop in the Latin Quarter, revered hangout of book lovers and well-known—and would-be—writers.

- 6^e: Berkeley Books of Paris; 8 rue du Casimir Delavigne; tel: 01.46. 34.85.73. Second-hand books.
- 6^e: San Francisco Book Co; 17 rue Monsieur-le-Prince; tel: 01.43.29.15.70. Second-hand books.
- 6^e: Tea and Tattered Pages; 24 rue Mayet; tel: 01.40.65.94.35. Used books; also has a small tea room.
- 6^e: Village Voice; 6 rue Princesse; tel: 01.46.33.36.47. Popular author's evenings.
- 11^e: Attica; 106 boulevard Richard Lenoir; tel: 01.55.28.80.14. Books in many languages.

COMPUTERS

Although *ordinateurs* (computers), *imprimantes* (printers) and associated *informatique* (IT) products have traditionally been expensive, prices are now more competitive—at least in the new megastores and the *hypermarchés* in the nearby surburbs and along the *périphérique*. Prices vary somewhat from store to store, so it pays to shop around. Check magazines such as *PC Direct* at news-stands for prices. To locate shops, see *Informatique and Micro-informatique (vente-maintenance)* in the *Yellow Pages*.

Several chains sell small electronic goods, computers, *logiciels* (software) and associated items. Fnac and Virgin Megastore carry everything hi-tech, including computers, software and accessories. Software is, of course, in French; if you need software in other languages, bring your own. Think also of the keyboard, for the French *clavier* (keyboard) does not use the Qwerty format; you can change the language of your system, but the actual keyboard remains the same.

If you bring your own computer to France, bring proof of purchase with the serial numbers of the computer (or printer) just in case customs officers ask you to prove that the equipment is yours.

- La Fnac; tel: 01.53.10.44.44; website: http://www.fnac.com. Chain with an extensive offering of CDs, cassettes, videos, computers, peripherals, software and books. Fnac Digitale at 77–81 boulevard Saint-Germain, 75006 specialises in high-tech products of all sorts: computers, printers, software, personal organisers, etc.

- Virgin Megastore. International chain with several addresses in Paris. Music, videos, books, computer hardware, software, printers, radios, stereo equipment, etc. Open until midnight daily and 1:00 am on Saturdays; store at 52 avenue des Champs-Elysées, 75008 is open on Sundays (tel: 01.49.53.50.00).
- Surcouf; 139 avenue Daumesnil, 75012; tel: 08.92.70.06.00; website: http://www.surcouf.com. Multi-storey bazaar selling computer hardware, software (some in English), peripherals, etc. Also offers technical support and repair.
- Anglo Computers; tel: 08.11.00.72.39; website: http://www.anglocomputers.com. English-language software and qwerty keyboards are hard to find in France. If these are important to you, contact Anglo Computers, which offers everything that an Anglophone could want.

Technical Support
Power outages are rare, but to suppress the occasional power surges, buy a *parasurtenseur* (surge protector) at computer shops and hardware stores.
- Micro King; 33 rue Dautancourt, 75017; tel: 01.53.06.65.10; website: http://www.micro-king.com. On-site emergency repairs, Internet and network installations, upgrades and repairs.
- Sourys; tel: 01.40.82.90.92 or 06.25.05.64.70 (mobile); http://www.sourys.com. On-site emergency computer repairs for Mac and PC, networks, Internet, ASDL, Wi-Fi, Palm Pilots; training in hardware and software usage.

COSMETICS/PERFUMES
Department stores sell international brands of perfumes and cosmetics, and some carry their own brand names. Hypoallergenic beauty products can be found in pharmacies, and parapharmacies have an even wider selection. Fashion houses such as Chanel and Dior develop their own perfumes, and a few parfumeries, for example, the well-known Annick Goutal, create their own fragrances.

For cosmetics, product name, colours and numbers differ from country to country, so a shade you bought at home may not exist in Paris, or it may exist under a different name. If possible, bring along your old product for comparison. Inexpensive chains and supermarkets such as Monoprix also carry internationally known products.

FLOWERS/PLANTS

Fleuristes (florists) are found in every district and many are open on Sunday mornings. Selections vary according to the season. When purchasing flowers, you will be asked if they are '*pour offrir*' (to offer as a gift): if so, the flowers will be trimmed and wrapped. Most florists deliver and those that advertise 'Interflora' can wire flowers abroad (toll-free tel: 08.10.35.38.77; website: http://www.interflora.fr). Aquarelle and Monceau Fleurs are chains of well-priced shops, as is Au Nom de la Rose, which does lovely arrangements with roses. Food markets sell inexpensive flowers and the markets listed below are dedicated to flowers. See *Fleuristes* in the *Yellow Pages*.

- 4e: Île-de-la-Cité. Closed on Sundays, when a bird market takes over.
- 8e: Place de la Madeleine. Open on Tuesdays–Sundays.
- 17e: Place des Ternes. Closed on Mondays.

Truffaut at 85 quai de la Gare, 75013 is an excellent, well-priced supermarket for plants and flowers (tel: 01.53.60.84.50). It carries plants of all types and sizes, and offers landscaping services for your garden or balcony. Open on Sundays, it offers home delivery.

HOME FURNISHINGS

In addition to the furniture stores listed below, the major department stores carry large selections of home furnishings, all in keeping with the overall style and quality of that particular store. With all shops, however, ask about the delivery policy—some charge extra for delivery. See *Meubles* in the *Yellow Pages*.

For home improvement items, the basement of BHV is a

haven for the *bricoleur*. It is a warren of aisles and byways, filled with stacks of merchandise large and small—just about anything you need for home improvement and repair. This is also true of the well-stocked Leroy Merlin nearby, at 52 rue Rambuteau (tel: 01.44.54.66.66; website: http://www.leroymerlin.fr). To find specific addresses and opening hours of chain stores, access their websites.

If you need to buy a new mattress, check out the variety available at department stores, or call Matelsom, which sells mattresses by phone or online (tel: 08.00.00.30.30; website: http://www.matelsom.com). Specify what you are looking for and they will deliver within 48 hours. (Note that bed sizes are slightly different from those in North America.)

Marché Saint-Pierre at 2 rue Charles Nodier, 75018 is a discount warehouse for fabrics, linens, curtains and other such items (tel: 01.46.06.92.25). Closed on Sundays and Mondays in August. There are other similar shops in the area.

- Habitat; website: http://www.habitat.fr. International chain with inexpensive furniture, household items and tableware.

- Ikea; website: http://www.ikea.fr. Huge international chain selling inexpensive home furnishings, with several stores in the Paris region.

- Pier Import; website: http://www.pier-import.fr. Chain carrying colourful, inexpensive housewares and furniture.

- Compagnie Française de l'Orient et de la Chine; website: http://www.cfoc.fr. Small, upmarket chain for Oriental furniture, table linens, fabrics, clothing, etc.

- 7e: Reveblanc: 155 rue de Grenelle; tel: 01.47.05.93.13. Linens outlet shop, with brand-name, high quality merchandise. Bilingual staff.

- 7e: Roche-Bobois; 193–197 boulevard Saint-Germain; tel: 01.45.48.46.21; website: http://www.roche-bobois.com. Several upmarket shops offering modern, stylish furniture, including Galeries Lafayette.

- 6e and 8e: Maison de Famille
  29 rue Saint-Sulpice;   tel: 01.40.46.97.47
  10 place de la Madeleine; tel: 01.53.45.82.00.
  Everything for the home in attractive, multi-storied shops.

- 7e: The Conran Shop; 117 rue du Bac;
  tel: 01.42.84.10.01; website: http://www.conran.com.
  Well-known British firm selling modern furniture and
  kitchen accessories.
- 9e: Lafayette Maison. Across from the main Galeries
  Lafayette stores on boulevard Haussmann, a multi-storied
  10,000 sq m annex devoted to everything you could need
  for the home.

Used Furniture

Used furniture is available from a variety of sources,
including the *marchés aux puces* (flea markets) listed below.
See *Dépôts-vente: meubles, équipement pour la maison* in
the *Yellow Pages*, and see *FUSAC* for ads. You'll find well-
maintained antiques, just as you'll see furniture that is
simply well-used—you'll have to scout. The shops below
are popular with a quick turnover of merchandise.

- 14e: Dépôt Alésia; 117 rue d'Alésia; tel: 01.45.42.42.42
- 19e: Dépôt Flandre; 63 quai de la Seine;
  tel: 01.40.35.40.29
- 20e:Le Grand Dépôt Vente de Paris; 81 rue Lagny; tel:
  08.90.71.17.77

Antiques

Stores specialising in antiques cluster in various parts of
the city. Several of these 'villages' are open on Sundays and
closed early in the week. There are also periodic antique
markets, usually in spring and summer, mentioned in the
weekly events guides.

- 1er: Le Louvre des Antiquaires; 2 place du Palais Royal.
- 4e: Le Village Saint-Paul; at the intersections of rue Saint-
  Paul and rue Charles V. Closed on Sundays.
- 7e: Carré Rive Gauche; along rue des Saints-Pères and rue
  du Bac.
- 15e: Le Village Suisse; avenue de la Motte-Piquet at avenue
  de Suffren.

Kitchen and Dining Equipment

Department stores sell kitchen and dining equipment, and small kitchen appliances are sold in *drogueries* (general stories) and some *quincailleries* (hardware stores). Shops on rue de Paradis specialise in tableware. See *Articles de ménage et de cuisine* in the *Yellow Pages*.

- 1er: Dehillerin; 18–20 rue Coquillière; tel: 01.42.36.53.13. Famous two-level, kitchen equipment emporium.
- 1er: Mora; 13 rue Montmartre; tel: 01.45.08.19.24. Kitchen supplies, utensils, dishes, paperware. In business for more than 150 years.
- 2e: A. Simon; 48 & 52 rue Montmartre; tel: 01.42.33.71.65. Long-established supplier of kitchen equipment, dishes, glasses, utensils, pitchers and other gadgets.
- 6e and 16e: Culinarion; 99 rue de Rennes; tel: 01.45.48. 94.76. Practical kitchenware shops. Also at 24 rue de Passy; tel: 01.42.85.21.51.
- 6e and 14e: Geneviève Lethu; 95 rue de Rennes; tel: 01.45. 44.40.35. Chain of upmarket tableware shops with a range of styles and prices. Other addresses.
- 15e: Kitchen Bazaar; 11 avenue du Maine; tel: 01.42.22.91.17. Modern implements; other addresses.

Outdoor Markets

The outdoor street markets described in Chapter Six usually carry non-food kitchen items, clothes, umbrellas, some cosmetics and sometimes even furniture. For an interesting artisans' market, try:

- Marché Parisien de la Création; boulevard Richard Lenoir at Place de la Bastille. In Montparnasse, at the entrance to the Edgar Quinet Métro (Line 6), some 120 artisans display their creations in this art and design market. Open Sunday, 10:00 am–7:00pm.

Flea Markets

- 1er: Marché aux Puces d'Aligre; Place d'Aligre. Good flea market selling mostly household odds and ends, but ther are also good discounted clothing shops. Open from Tuedays–Sundays.

- 14e: Les Puces de Vanves; avenue Georges Lafenestre, at Porte de Vanves and Porte Didot. Furniture, odds and ends, paintings, etc. sold in the mornings; used clothes in the afternoons. Open on weekends, from 7:00 am–7:30 pm.
- 18^e: Les Puces Saint-Ouen/ Clignancourt; between Porte de Saint-Ouen and Porte de Clignancourt. Huge flea market, divided into several mini-markets. The most famous of all the flea markets, selling antiques, clothes, shoes, books, records, etc. Open on Saturdays, Sundays and Mondays, from 7:30 am–7:00 pm
- 20^e: Les Puces de Montreuil; avenue de la Porte-de-Montreuil. Appliances, old furniture, used clothing, crockery. Open on Saturdays, Sundays and Mondays, from 7:00 am–6:00 pm.

HAIR AND BEAUTY SERVICES

When it comes to hairdressers or barbers, it's always best—no matter where you live—to ask your friends for recommendations. You can start off by shopping around. Look into the windows of *coiffeurs* and see which are busy and what kind of clientele they serve. Hair salon chains offer reliable services, as do the hotels and department stores, often charging less than the small neighbourhood *coiffeurs*—a source of increasing consternation among the independent operators. Although a *shampooing et brushing* (wash and blow-dry) or a *coupe* (cut) at the chains may cost less, the quality varies according to the stylist—as is the case anywhere—and turnover of stylists tends to be higher than in neighbourhood salons. Salons have their prices posted in the windows.

If you use hair dye, bring a few bottles with you until you find a comparable colour, as brands and colours are not the same as what is found at home. Tips are not included in the price, and everyone who attends to you—shampoo person, hair stylist, cloakroom attendant—gets a tip based on the level of service. Most shops close on Mondays. Get recommendations from your friends, see *Paris Par Cher* or *Coiffeurs* in the *Yellow Pages*. The chains listed below are well known and reliable—depending, of course, on the expertise of each *coiffeur*—and they have shops throughout Paris. Many *coiffeurs* serve both men and women.

- Jacques Dessange
- Jean-Claude Biguine
- Jean Louis David
- Maniatis
- Saint-Algue

Paris is also known for salons where hairdressers undergo *formation* or training, and these offer low-cost cuts to customers willing to take a chance on a (well-supervised) student's ability. *Salons de perfectionnement* give established stylists the opportunity to update their techniques. These salons are often open on Mondays, when regular salons are closed. Some salons perform both hair and beauty services (*coiffure & esthétique*), but most are separate. An *institut de beauté* (beauty treatments) performs manicures, pedicures, waxing, facials, massages and makeup applications, and sells its products. Some *parapharmacie* also offer *soins de beauté* (beauty treatments).

LAUNDRY AND DRY CLEANING

Fortunately, *laveries automatiques* (self-service laundromats) are found in every area, for unfurnished apartments are often not equipped with *lave-linges/machines à laver* (washers) or *séche-linge/séchoirs* (dryers), and apartment buildings do not have laundry rooms. Some furnished apartments come with washers but no dryers.

Washers in the laundromats take one *jeton* (token) per load. Bring your own soap, bleach and softener to avoid paying for them at laundromat rates. The *super-essorage/essoreuse* (spinner machine) removes moisture, saving money on dryers. Some laundromats also have facilities for inexpensive, self-service dry cleaning. See *Laveries pour particuliers, Laveries en libre-service* in the *Yellow Pages*.

Most dry cleaners (*nettoyage à sec/pressing*) are also *blanchisseries* (laundries) for washing and pressing items. Cleaning and laundry are expensive because much of the finishing work is done by hand, not machines. Less costly options are either to press washed clothes, or to have clothes cleaned but not pressed. Some dry cleaners ask for payment in advance, and most accept cheques and cash only. *Teintureries* offer high-quality cleaning at high prices but are worth it for your most elegant outfits, since the quality of cleaners can vary considerably. Home pickup and delivery is sometimes available. See *Pressing* in the *Yellow Pages*. The cleaners listed below are especially known for their work on fragile items:

- 7e: Pressing de la Bourdonnais; 29 avenue de la Bourdonnais; tel: 01.45.51.86.91. The 'American Dry Cleaner in Paris'.
- 16e: Pouyanne, 'Le Médecin de la Robe' ('The Dress Doctor'); 31 rue Longchamp; tel: 01.47.27.11.62.
- 8e: Parfait Elève de Pouyanne; 57 boulevard Haussmann; tel: 01.42.65.34.23.

OPTICAL SERVICES

Eye glasses and contact lenses are expensive, and most chains of *opticiens* (opticians) are no less expensive than the independent shops. Alain Afflelou, Lissac Frères and La Générale d'Optique are chains with reasonably priced products. See *Opticiens* in the *Yellow Pages*.

When coming to France, bring an extra pair of glasses with you and an up-to-date prescription. SOS Optique is a home repair service for eyeglasses (tel: 01.48.07.22.00). If you have an eye emergency and cannot get to the Hôpital Hôtel Dieu or Hôpital des Quinze-Vingts, call SOS Oeil for a house call (tel: 01.40.92.93.94). The Fondation Ophtalmologique Adolphe de Rothschild at 25 rue Manin, 75019 is a major eye clinic (appointment tel: 01.48. 03.65.68 or 01.48.03.65.30; website: http://www.fo-rothschild.fr).

ANNUAL FESTIVALS AND HOLIDAYS

There's something going on somewhere in Paris almost every day of the year, be it a military parade, a display of antiques, a poetry weekend, a neighbourhood fair, an outdoor concert, a film or theatre festival, a sporting event, or even a public wine tasting. The city regularly sponsors periods of reduced-price theatre or cinema tickets and, in summer, endless free outdoor events.

Everyone loves a holiday, and Parisians are no exception. If a national holiday (*jour férié*) falls on a Tuesday or Thursday, they are likely to '*faire le pont*' (make a bridge) to the long weekend by closing shop on the Monday prior to the holiday or the Friday following the public holiday. This is common practice for most offices and some businesses, even banks.

In addition to the national holidays (listed in bold below), there are dozens of cultural festivals. Many of these are listed below, but others crop up and dates change; it's best to keep yourself informed. Check the website of the Paris Tourist Office at 25 rue des Pyramides 75001 (http://www.parisinfo.com) or the city of Paris itself (http://www.paris.fr). Also consult the weekly events magazines *Pariscope* or *l'Officiel des Spectacles*, issued on Wednesdays.

January

- 1 Jan: **Jour de l'An (New Year's Day)**—A national holiday. Basically a day for family visits and leisurely meals at home, sometimes with the exchange of gifts.
- 6 Jan: Epiphanie—La Fête des Rois. A traditional pastry—*la galette des rois*—is baked with a little figurine (*la fève*) inside. *Galettes* are eaten at home and at friends' homes. The person who gets the slice with *la fève* is the 'king' or 'queen' for the day.
- Two weeks in January: La Mairie de Paris Vous Invite au Concert. Two concert tickets for the price of one.

February

- Early Feb: Chinese New Year. Festivals and parades, especially in Chinatown in the 13e.
- Late Feb: Foire à la Ferraille de Paris. Amusing fair in Bois de Vincennes with antiques and knick-knacks.

March

- Early March: Salon International de l'Agriculture. World's largest agriculture exposition at Parc des Expositions, Porte de Versailles. Food and wine from the provinces, prize-winning livestock, farm equipment, etc.

- Mid-March: Salon de Mars. Antique fair in Place Joffre, in front of the École Militaire.
- Mid-March: Musicora. International salon of classical music at Porte de Versailles.
- Mid-March: Printemps du Cinéma. Three days of films at only € 3.50 during this popular annual event.
- Palm Sunday: Prix du Président de la République. Horse race at the Auteuil racetrack, Bois de Boulogne.
- Late March: Banlieues Bleues. Suburban jazz festival with world-renowned musicians.
- March/April: Foire du Trône. Amusement park on the Reuilly lawn at Porte Dorée, at the edge of the Bois de Vincennes.
- March/April: Festival du Film de Paris. Previews of international films, held at various theatres around the city. Often attended by directors and actors.
- March/April: Paris Festival of Sacred Art. Easter concerts at churches around Paris. Also in November.

April

- 1 Apr: April Fool Day. Pastries and chocolates in the shape of fish, as 'April's Fool' translates to '*poisson d'avril*', '*poisson*' meaning 'fish'.
- Pâques: Easter Sunday
- **Lundi de Pâques (Easter Monday)**—a national holiday
- Mid-April: Paris Marathon
- Late April: Salon du Livre. Book fair at Porte de Versailles
- Late April to May: La Foire Internationale de Paris. fair at the Parc des Expositions with everything from furniture to food, gardening equipment and wine-tasting.
- Late April/Early May: La Mairie de Paris Vous Invite au Théâtre. Two theatre tickets for the price of one.

May

- **1 May: Fête du Travail (Labour Day)**—a national holiday. A parade near the Bastille; people give each other sprigs of *muguets* (lily of the valley) for happiness and good luck.

This is the one day of the year when the Tourist Office on the Champs-Elysées is closed.

- **8 May: Victoire 1945 (V-E Day)**—a national holiday. Celebrates the World War II victory in Europe in 1945 with a parade on the Champs-Elysées.
- Mid-May: Les Cinq Jours de l'Objet Extraordinaire. Many antique shops on the Left Bank hold open houses.
- **Sixth Thursday after Easter: Ascension (Ascension Day)**—a national holiday.
- **Second Monday after Ascension Day: Pentecôte (Pentecost)**—a national holiday. Pilgrimages to Sacré-Coeur.
- Late May: French Open Tennis Championships. Two-week tennis tournament, one of the four annual 'Grand Slams', held at Stade Roland Garros in the Bois de Boulogne.
- Late May: Festival de Paris. Dance, theatre and music at various locations.
- Mid-May to July: Festival de Jazz de Paris. Jazz concerts throughout the city.
- Last Sunday: Fête des Mères. The same commercial hype for Mother's Day as anywhere else.

June

- All month: Foire Saint-Germain. Held at place Saint-Sulpice, this varied fair features poetry readings, music, lectures and more. One of the most popular of the year.
- All month: Festival de Saint-Denis. Several weeks of classical music at Saint-Denis, a suburb to the north.
- Early June, odd numbered years only: Salon International de l'Aéronautique et de l'Espace. Paris Air Show with displays of aircraft and air shows, held at the Parc des Expositions du Bourget, which is at the Le Bourget airport.
- Mid-June, on a Sunday some weeks after Mother's Day: Fête des Pères (Father's Day).
- Mid-June/July: Festival du Marais. Music, dance and theatre in the historic *hôtels particuliers* (townhouses) in the Marais.

- Mid-June: Grand Steeplechase de Paris. Annual steeplechase at the Auteuil racetrack in the Bois de Boulogne.
- Mid-June to mid-July: Festival Chopin à Paris. An annual Chopin festival held in the Orangerie de Bagatelle of the Bois de Boulogne.
- 21 June: Fête de la Musique. A vibrant welcome of summer with music played in all parks and many squares and street corners. The Champ de Mars, the esplanade leading to the Eiffel Tower, sometimes welcomes half a million music lovers until the wee hours of the morning, with major programmes and performers.
- Late June: Course des Garçons de Café. Waiters run an 8-km course around the Hôtel de Ville, carrying trays with full glasses of beer.
- Late June: Grand Prix de Paris. Horse race at Longchamp racecourse, in the Bois de Boulogne.
- Later June: Lesbian, Gay, Bi and Trans Pride March. Held near the Bastille, this is one of the happening events of the year, with floats and wild costumes.

July

- July/August: Le Cinéma en Plein Air. Free films on a big screen in the park at La Villette. They start when it gets dark, which can be quite late. Bring a blanket or deck chair for the grass and make yourself comfortable.
- Early July: Foire Internationale d'Art au Grand Palais. International art exhibition at the Grand Palais.
- 13 July: Bastille Day Eve. Festivities to open Bastille day, including Les Bals des Pompiers—balls organised by the Fire Department in various districts. They take place in the streets, attracting numbers who dance for hours.
- **14 July: Le 14 Juillet**—a national holiday. Impressive military parade on the Champs-Elysées and fireworks after sunset (that is, quite late) at the Trocadéro. Get to the Champ de Mars early—half a million people come to picnic and enjoy the evening. If there is a theatre production that interests you, national theatres are free on 14 July.

A crowd eagerly awaits a concert during the Fête de la Musique, held annually on 21 June, the longest day of the year.

- Mid-July/Mid-August: Paris, Quartier d'Eté. Music and dance festival in various venues.
- Mid-July/Mid-August: Paris Plage. For several years, the city of Paris has been importing sand and creating a 3-km beach along the Seine. Chairs, cafés, showers, fountains, palm trees and three million visitors—sunbathers or strollers—enliven the *quais* in summer.
- July/August: Musique en l'Île. Concerts in the Eglise Saint-Louis, on the Île Saint-Louis.
- Mid-July/Mid-September: Festival Estival de Paris. Classical music in churches and museums.
- Late July: Arrivée du Tour de France Cycliste. The end of the Tour de France on the Champs-Elysées.

August
- **15 Aug: Assumption Day**—a national holiday

September
- Mid-Sept: Opera season opens.
- Mid-Sept: Jazz at La Villette. One of the best jazz festivals, featuring international groups.
- Mid-Sept: Fête de l'Humanité. Workers' festival at La Courneuve, a northern suburb. Sponsored by *L'Humanité*, the independent (formerly Communist) newspaper. Stands of international communist parties offer crafts and foods of their countries, plus music and a lively atmosphere.
- Mid-Sept: Journées du Patrimoine. Long lines form one weekend each year when the major buildings and palaces of France are opened to the public. In Paris, this includes the Palais de l'Elysée (the President's official residence), the Matignon (the Prime Minister's official residence), the Palais du Luxembourg (the Senate) and hundreds of other buildings.
- Mid-Sept to December: Festival d'Automne. Major performing arts festival.

October
- First Sunday: Prix de l'Arc de Triomphe. Horse race at Longchamp.

- Mid-Oct: Foire Internationale d'Art Contemporain (FIAC). International fair of contemporary art.

November

- **1 Nov: Toussaint (All Saints Day)**—a national holiday. Parisians visit the graves of their loved ones in advance of Jour des Morts (All Souls Day), placing chrysanthemums on their graves. On this one day, the oldest cemetery in Paris, the Cimetière du Calvaire, which dates from the 13th century, is open to visitors. Toussaint follows Halloween, which has caught on in Paris.
- 2 Nov: Jour des Morts (All Souls Day).
- 1–7 Nov: Paris Open. Tennis championships at the Palais Omnisports de Paris-Bercy.
- Early Nov: Salon d'Automne. Art salon in the Grand Palais.
- **11 Nov: Armistice 1918**—a national holiday. Veterans Day, celebrating the World War I Armistice.
- Mid-Nov: Trophée Lalique de Patinage Artistique. Figure skating competition at the Palais Omnisports de Paris-Bercy.
- Mid-Nov: Paris Festival of Sacred Art. Concerts in churches around the city.
- Third Thursday: Arrival of the Beaujolais Nouveau. Always a great source of conversation among wine lovers and critics.
- Late Nov: Salon du Chocolat. Great chocolate fair and market at the Carrousel du Louvre, 99 rue de Rivoli, 75001. More than 100 European chocolate-makers display and offer their products, and give demonstrations of chocolate recipes.

December

- All Month: Christmas in Paris. Animated *crèche* (nativity scene) outside the Hôtel de Ville. Main shopping streets are illuminated and store windows in the department stores are beautifully decorated. Stores are generally allowed to remain open on Sundays in December.
- Early Dec: Festival du Cinéma Gay et Lesbien de Paris. Week-long gay and lesbian film festival, held at the Forum des Images, at Forum Les Halles.

- Early Dec: Salon Nautique International. International boat show.
- Early Dec: Nocturne des Boutiques du Comité Vendôme. Some of the expensive boutiques around Place Vendôme stay open late to encourage Christmas shopping.
- 24 Dec: Réveillon (Christmas Eve). Feast at midnight, with traditional offerings such as oysters, foie gras, truffles, *marrons glacés* (glazed sweet chestnuts) and, of course, the *bûche de Noël* (log cake). Midnight mass at city churches.
- **25 Dec: Noël (Christmas)**—a national holiday. Turkey with chestnuts is a specialty.
- 31 Dec: Midnight festivities on New Year's Eve.

PARLEZ-VOUS FRANÇAIS?

CHAPTER 8

'In Paris they simply stared when I spoke to them
in French; I never did succeed in making those idiots
understand their own language...'
—Mark Twain

THE FRENCH ACADEMY

The French are convinced that theirs is the most beautiful language in the world. This is not new—almost 400 years ago in 1635, under the reign of Louis XIII, Chief Minister Cardinal Richelieu founded L'Académie Française, expressly to watch over the French language and ensure its purity. It was also meant to unify a country that was still divided by dialects, from the north to the south. Today, the Academy is still going strong, its primary mission being to set the rules and standards on usage, vocabulary and spelling. It continues to update and publish the definitive dictionary of the French language, first issued in 1694; oversees works on grammar, logic and other such subjects; and it administers several prestigious literary prizes.

Although the Academy has ruled that words—even those associated with newly evolving technological developments—should be French and not imported from English (or other languages), this rule is not always abided by in common usage. For example, many people use 'franglais' (français-anglais) terms, such as '*uploader*', '*le chewing gum*' and '*le software*' (instead of the approved French term, '*logiciel*')—a corruption of the language, the French pronunciation notwithstanding. English words such as 'weekend' and 'snack' have also made their way into daily usage, producing '*le weekend*' and '*le snack*'. And a bus driver who drives too quickly is routinely called '*un cowboy*'.

L'Académie Française

To be elected as one of the '40 immortals' of the French Academy is one of the highest honours a person can receive. Among the approximately 300 former Academy members are Jacques-Yves Cousteau, Voltaire, Victor Hugo, Alexandre Dumas (the son), Honoré de Balzac, François-René de Chateaubriand, Eugène Ionesco, Alexis de Tocqueville and, surprisingly, the French-born American writer Julien Green who lived in Paris and wrote in French. Green was the first non-French national to be elected. It was not until 1980 that a woman, novelist Marguerite Yourcenar, was elected.

HISTORY OF FRENCH

The first written example of early French—not the version we know today—dates as far back as 862. French is actually one of the Romance languages, along with Italian, Spanish, Portuguese and Romanian. In fact, some scholars prefer the term Romanic languages, for what binds these languages is their common origin in the spoken language of the ancient Roman Empire. These languages evolved according to the ethnicity of the peoples of the conquered territories, as well as the legacy of the conquerors who forced the Romans out.

In Gaul (present-day France), the native Celts spoke Gaulish when the Romans arrived in about 100 BC, but not for long, as Latin became the language of the upper classes—the rulers, teachers and even merchants who traversed the Empire. Fortunately for the beautiful (and some say, extremely romantic) French language as we know it today, the Romans were supplanted by Germanic Franks, such that by the 5th century, the Latin language spoken in France had incorporated some Germanic words, in addition to Celtic ones. The lasting presence of the Franks and their great rulers (including Charlemagne, King of the Franks and the Lombards, and first Holy Roman Emperor) was instrumental in allowing the language to develop admidst wars and migration. This distinguished French from the other emerging Romanic languages.

This 'Old French' lasted for about 400 years, during which the dialect spoken in Paris became pre-eminent, as the power—cultural, as well as political—of the city grew. 'Middle French' lasted only a few hundred years, but it was important, for it was when separate French languages began to be fused into one, and when the Francien dialect of the Paris region supplanted the others, allowing the French language—and ultimately France—to become unified.

By the 16th century, François I was using French instead of Latin for official documents throughout the entire realm, taking it beyond a spoken language. By the time of the French Revolution, the language was pretty well-standardised across the realm. And it is this French, which has not stopped evolving, that is the basis of the French we speak (or try to) today.

LANGUAGE SCHOOLS

Learning French should be among your first priorities upon taking up residence in Paris; there are many language schools for foreigners. Depending on the course and the school, students at some of these schools qualify to apply for a student visa. Some also have programmes for *au pairs*, who must be registered in a recognised language course. The programmes of the schools below are officially accredited, but there are many others—check with the consulate in your home country, which may have brochures of language schools in Paris; the Paris Tourist Office website; *FUSAC*, which generally has detailed ads for such schools; and Europa Pages (http://www.europa-pages.com/france/). Pick a school that suits your needs and budget, and one that is convenient enough for you to attend and not slack off.

You will learn enough at any of these schools to get around and to read directions, instructions, advertisements and listings for cultural events, but improving is up to you.

- 5e: Cours de Civilisation et Langue Française de la Sorbonne; 47 rue des Ecoles; tel: 01.44.10.77.00; fax: 01.43.22.37.56; website: http://www.ccfs-sorbonne.fr/index.php. Serious language and culture courses at the Sorbonne; high school diploma required.
- 6e: Alliance Française; 101 boulevard Raspail; tel: 01.42.84.90.00; fax: 01.42.84.91.01; website: http://www.alliancefr.org. Worldwide network of language schools. General, business and customised language programmes, as well as courses in French culture, literature, etc.

- 6ᵉ: Institut Catholique de Paris; 21 rue d'Assas;
  tel: 01.44.39.52.00; website: http://www.icp.fr.
  Two semesters each year of courses in the language and
  culture of France for all levels. Summer course in July
  consists of 20 hours of lessons weekly, with excursions.
- 8ᵉ: Institut de Langue Française; 3 avenue Bertie Albrecht;
  tel: 01.49.53.96.45; website: http://www.inst-langue-fr.
  com. Short- and long-term courses in French language
  and civilisation, literature and cooking, as well as courses
  for test preparation. Evening classes available.

GETTING STARTED...
SOME PRONUNCIATION HINTS

Even before you enroll in a school, you'll be hearing French
and trying out those words you already know. (See the
Glossary in Chapter 10.) Listen carefully and see what you
can decipher when other people speak to you, although it
won't always be easy, for accents and intonations vary. It's
also hard sometimes for a newcomer to know the rules of
pronunciation, and when you ask three French speakers to
clarify something in grammar or pronunciation, they might
all have different answers! But that's what happens with
languages, for they are almost living entities that change
with the times and under external influences, especially
with younger generations imposing their own cultural
norms. Thus it's best just to know the current rules and
to obey them as well as you can—and to laugh at yourself
when you make a terrible mistake and vow not to make
the same mistake again.

First, it's important to understand that each syllable in
a French word is stressed fairly equally, with perhaps just
a slight emphasis on the last syllable (by lengthening the
duration of the syllable a tiny bit). For example, whereas
the word 'lí-brary' in English stresses the first syllable, the
French word '*li-brai-rie*' stresses each syllable equally. There
is little variation in this, even with words imported from
other languages. The city of Montevideo, which in Spanish
has the emphasis on the penultimate syllable, is pronounced
Mon-te-vi-de-o in French.

It's hard to discern the differences in pronunciation with some words, although there are nuances that you will learn eventually. For instance, *hôtel* and *autel* (altar) are pronounced almost identically, as are *faim* (hunger) and *fin* (end). There's no embarrassment in asking someone (politely) to repeat something — the French are pleased when a foreigner makes an effort to learn their language.

It Just Takes Practice

- É/é (*accent aigu*): the letter 'e' is pronounced as in the English word 'say'.
- È/è (*accent grave*): the letter 'e' is pronounced as in 'desk'.
- Ç/ç (*cédille*): the letter 'c' is pronounced with a 's' sound, as in 'see', and not a 'k' sound as in 'key'.
- ¨ (*le tréma*) over a vowel: the vowel is pronounced separately from the one directly before. Thus, the word '*laïc*' is pronounced 'lah-eek'.
- The letter 'r' is not at all produced from the front of the mouth as we do when speaking English, but from the back of the throat, near the uvula. If you try to pronounce the 'r' by lowering your tongue in front and raising it in back, you might feel like you are beginning to gargle, but the French will better understand what you are saying.
- The letter 'n'. If the letter 'n' comes after a vowel, it is not pronounced in itself. Instead, the preceding vowel is nasalised. Also, if there is an 'n' after a 'g', as in the word '*agneau* (lamb)', the combination is pronounced 'nya'.
- EU/Œ: This two-vowel combination has little reference in English. Words such as *peu*, *jeux* and *Sacré-Coeur* are pronounced like the English interjection 'er', but without the 'r' at the end. Form your mouth as though you were going to blow a bubble, then say 'er' by slightly puckering your lips.

French, of course, uses the Roman alphabet, and many letters are pronounced in the same way as in English. But letters are often pronounced according to their position in a word, and some are silent, such as the 's' or the 'x' when they appear at the end of words. The letter 'e' at the end of a word is not pronounced, unless it is accented. In fact, if a verb (for example, in the third person plural form) ends in 'ent', none of those letters are pronounced. So, *'ils doivent'* (they must) is pronounced 'eel doive'.

Also, the French do not usually pronounce the last consonant of any word, but this too can vary. If a word following one ending in a consonant begins with a vowel, that final consonant is pronounced, elided into the next word. So, if someone tells you that they slept *dix heures* (10 hours), what you will hear is 'deeser'. It can be complicated, for when someone tells you they have used *huit oeufs* (eight eggs) in their omelette, you will hear 'weeter', for not only has the last consonant of the word *'huit'* been elided into the following vowel, the final 's' in the word *'oeufs'* is unpronounced, as is the final consonant that precedes it. Do not give up hope, soon you'll get the hang of it too!

In terms of names, for the most part they follow the same rules. So although people—especially foreigners—might have their own ways of pronouncing their names, the French generally pronounce them in a French way. Thus, the name of the Italian poet Dante is pronounced 'Dahnt' and the ladies' dress shop Weill is pronounced 'Vey'. Sometimes the pronunciation of names is unclear even to Parisians: for example, the street name rue Desaix is pronounced by some as 'desay' and others as 'desex'.

Don't give up. Do your best and listen to how the French pronounce words and your pronunciation will improve. If French kids can learn all this, so can you.

MINDING YOUR BUSINESS

CHAPTER 9

'... Paris advances alone towards its destiny;
where the people lead no government can follow.'
—Maguerite Duras

THE EUROPEAN UNION

In the late 1950s, France became one of the six founding members of the European Economic Community (along with Belgium, Germany, Italy, Luxembourg and the Netherlands). Since then another 21 countries have joined—most recently some countries from the sphere of the former Soviet Union—bringing to 27 the total number of members of what is now known as the European Union (EU). These communities have pooled their economic resources to create a forceful single market throughout which services, goods and capital can move freely. The headquarters of the EU is in Brussels, Belgium (http://www.europa.eu).

There are no longer any trade barriers among member countries, and their citizens may live in any EU country they wish. The goal is to balance the national interests of each country with those of the overall community, allowing diversity while creating a community-wide identity. Thus, in addition to economic benefits, a unity is developing among countries that had heretofore been impossible. (This also means that war between member states is no longer likely.)

At the official level, governments are working towards this intricate balance. In general, the populace of France understands and accepts the benefits of the union; nonetheless people are increasingly concerned about the diminution of their national identity and about the number of foreigners allowed to live in their country. They also worry about changes to the culture and traditions of which they are so proud. There are no easy answers to these concerns. So, if you are going to settle in France and perhaps open a business, it is important to understand the ethos of your community and remember that France—along with all the other 26 countries—adheres to all regulations of the EU. In addition to the EU website (http://www.europa.eu) mentioned above, there are several others that might be helpful:

- European Commission; website: http://eceuropa.eu
- Price Waterhouse; website: http://www.pwcglobal.com
- US Commercial Service; website: http://buyusa.gov/europeanunion/doing_business.html

THE FRENCH ECONOMY

France is currently the world's fifth-largest economy. The government has partially or fully privatised many large companies, but retains controlling stakes in some, such as Air France and France Télécom. It is also dominant in the power, public transport and defence sectors. A major manufacturing economy, France is noted for its automobile, aircraft, machinery, chemicals and electronics industries.

PARIS BUSINESS SCENE

Although the official governmental policy is to decentralise the French economy, the Greater Paris area remains dominant in the economic scene. With a population hovering around the 12 million mark, Île-de-France (Paris and its surrounds) accounts for 70 per cent of all company headquarters in France, 30 per cent of research and development and 25 per cent of the labour force. Not only is Paris the country's political and administrative centre, it is also the centre of attraction for the more than 70 million tourists who visit France each year, making it the most visited country in the world. Paris is a centre for trade throughout Europe. About 8,000

It is said that some 26 million visitors come to Paris each year and that tourism accounts for some 140,000 jobs in Paris—about 12 per cent of the workforce.

foreign companies of all financial levels currently operate in the Paris area. The ultramodern business skyscrapers of La Défense, built to ensure that central Paris' age-old charm remains untouched, houses the headquarters of major French corporations and many multinational giants. (For a current listing, access http://www.parisladefense.com.)

In addition, embassies are headquartered in the French capital, as are other international organisations such as UNESCO (United Nations Educational, Social and Cultural Organisation; http://www.unesco.org) and OECD (Organisation for Economic Cooperation and Development; http://www.oecd.org). These create hundreds of diplomatic and supporting staff positions, with periodic rotation of personnel. Hundreds of non-governmental organisations (NGOs) accredited to UNESCO also bring professionals from all over the world to the Paris area. Thus, a significant expatriate community has settled in Paris and its suburbs, filling various professional positions. As a result too, many shops and services have sprung up to meet the needs of this community.

FRENCH BUSINESS INFORMATION

Fortunately, there is a wealth of government-generated information concerning the starting up of businesses in France. The most efficient way to begin is to access the many relevant websites and links—some are governmental, designed for the French, but the information is accessible to all. An English version is often available, indicated by an icon of a British flag. See also the section below for assistance specific to Anglophones. If you do a search on the Internet on 'doing business in France', you will find a long list of resource links to aid you in your research. Be aware of when the information was posted, for regulations change from time to time.

- APCE (Agence pour la Création d'Enterprises); tel: 01.42.18.58.58; website: http://www.apce.com. Offers official information on setting up a company in France, including information on options for company structure, taxation laws, etc.

- OSEO; tel: 01.41.79.80.00; website: http://www.oseo.fr. Provides assistance and financial support to innovative companies with strong marketing prospects during the start up and development processes.
- CCIP (Chambre du Commerce et de l'Industrie de Paris); 2 place de la Bourse, 75001 (Paris Delegation); tel: 08.20.01.21.12; website: http://www.ccip75.fr. Public agency that regulates and facilitates business and controls ports and railroads in France, the Paris Tourist Office and exhibition centres. CCIP represents 300,000 companies, which accounts for 25 per cent of all French economic activity. It also provides helpful information on setting up businesses in France.
- Invest in France, the official site for investing in France, has branches worldwide and provides extremely helpful information. To find the office nearest you, access its websites: http://www.investinfrance.org;
  Office in UK: 28-29 Haymarket, London SW1Y4RX tel: (44-020) 7024-3670.
  Office in USA: 810 7th Avenue Suite 3800, New York, NY 10019; tel: (1-212) 757-9340.
  Office in Canada: 20 Queen Street West, Suite 2004, Toronto M5H 3R3; tel: (1-416) 977 1257
- Business-in-Europe.com; website: http://www.business-in-Europe.com. A useful website detailing business opportunities and procedures to set up a business in France. Helpful brochures to download.
- INSEE (Institut National de la Statistique et des Études Économiques); tel: 08.25.88.94.25; website: http://www.insee.fr. The official French bureau for national statistics on all aspects of French society and economy.
- UBI (L'Agence Française pour le développement des entreprises); tel: 08.10.65.96.59; website: http://www.ubifrance.fr. French non-profit agency that fosters international development of French businesses. Brings together French business people and their foreign counterparts. Offers programmes and conferences.

La Grande Arche—the ultra-modern sculpture and symbol of La Defense on the western outskirts of Paris, where about 100,000 people work in the French headquarters of some 800 of the world's most important corporations.

ASSISTANCE FOR ANGLOPHONES
United Kingdom
Below are a few examples how individual countries assist their enterprises to expand internationally. The chambers of commerce in Paris can be particularly helpful. France is the United Kingdom's third largest export market after the United States and Germany. More than 1,800 UK companies have subsidiaries in France, and the prevailing opinion is that anything sold in the UK is likely to sell here. The British governmental department, UK Trade & Investment, offers information on doing business worldwide (http://www.uktradeinvest.gov.uk).

- Commercial Section of the British Embassy at 35 rue du Faubourg Saint-Honoré, 75008; tel: 01.44.51.33.44; fax: 01.44.51.34.01. website: http://ukinfrance.fco,.gov.uk/en/doing-business. Information about dealing with France.
- Contact Business Link; tel: (44-0845) 6009-006; website: http://www.businesslink.gov.uk. Offers information on imports and exports, as well as basic information on international trading.
- Chambre de Commerce Française de Grande-Bretagne; 21 Dartmouth Street, Westminster, London SW1H 9BP; tel: (44-207) 304-4040; fax: (44-207) 304-7034; website: http://www.uccife.org. Provides assistance for British investment in France.

United States
The United States and Foreign Commercial Service (US &FCS) is located at the American Embassy at 2 avenue Gabriel, 75008; tel: 01.43.12.23.70; fax: 01.43.12.21.72; websites: http://www.buyusa.gov and http://www.export.gov. The US&FCS helps American companies to enter the French market: sales, licensing agreements, joint and direct investment, etc. The service also works with French firms that want to represent American manufacturers, use American products or set up joint ventures. The Commercial Service can brief Americans on French economic conditions and specific markets.

Australia

ABIE (Australian Business in Europe), the government entity that promotes Australian international trade, is located at the Australian Embassy: 4 rue Jean-Rey 75723 Cedex 15; website: http://www.austrade.gov.au; ABIE tel: 01.40.59.33.85;

Canada

The Canadian Embassy at 35 avenue Montaigne, Paris 75008, has a Trade and Investment Department; tel: 01.44.43.29.00; website: http://www.dfait-maeci.gc.ca/canada-europa/france/menu-fr.asp

CHAMBERS OF COMMERCE

Chambers of commerce facilitate bilateral business by publishing current information, setting up meetings and seminars, and issuing directories of companies present in France.

- 7ᵉ: Chambre de Commerce France-Canada; 5 rue Constantine; tel: 01.43.59.32.38; website: http://www.ccfc-france-canada.com.
- 8ᵉ: American Chamber of Commerce; 156 boulevard Haussmann; tel: 01.56.43.45.67; fax: 01.56.43.45.60; website: http://www.amchamfrance.org.
- 8ᵉ: Chambre de Commerce et d'Industrie Franco-Irlandaise; 33 rue de Miromesnil; tel: 01.70.70.23.71; website: http://franceireland.com.
- 8ᵉ: Chambre de Commerce et d'Industrie Franco-Britannique; 31 rue Boissy d'Anglas; tel: 01.53.30.81.30; fax: 01.53.30.81.35; website: http://www.francobritishchambers.com

LEGAL FORMS OF ENTERPRISE

Business options for the would-be entrepreneur include setting up a new and independent business; purchasing and taking over an existing business; and leasing a business in which the owner retains the title but the lessee operates the business, assuming all risk. Before creating any enterprise, it is important to understand how much of your own assets will be at risk in each structure. A knowledgeable attorney should suggest the simplest structure possible and take care of all bureaucratic requirements. CCIP issues

Documentation Pratique with detailed information on each form of enterprise.

- *Entreprises Individuelles*: the simplest form whereby one person, whose assets are at risk, receives the profit or loss. No minimum capital investment required. Sole proprietorships, independent business people and sole traders.
- *Société en Nom Collectif (SNC)*: rarely found, it is a private corporation of at least two partners, jointly and severally liable without limitation for losses.
- *Société à Responsabilité Limitée (SARL)*: private limited company with a minimum capital of just € 1 and liability limited to investment. For medium-sized businesses requiring little financing, this is the simplest type of limited-liability company, with a minimum of two shareholders and a maximum of 50. Headquarters may be in a private home for a maximum of five years.
- *Societé Unipersonnelle à Responsabilité Limitée (EURL)*: like a SARL, but with sole proprietor as a limited-liability company. Liability is limited to investment in company.
- *Societé Anonyme (SA)*: corporate structure for large companies traded on the stock exchange involving at least seven shareholders and a minimum capital of € 37,000. Strict auditing standards are required.

A *succursale* is a branch office of any company that is registered in France: it must keep its own accounting books (except for the balance sheet), issue its own invoices and receipts, and pay taxes. A *filiale* (subsidiary) is a separate entity of a company operating under French statutes, with new partners and new capital stock. Both must be registered at the Tribunal de Commerce. A *bureau de représentation* is a small office that represents a company headquartered elsewhere.

For alternative strategies for starting businesses and marketing ideas in France, you might consult David Applefield, the publisher of *Paris Anglophone*, at 32 rue Edouard-Vallant, 93100 Montreuil (tel: 01.48.59.66.58; fax: 01.48.59.66.68; email: david@paris-anglo.com; website: http://www.paris-anglo.com).

ATTORNEYS AND EXPERT HELP

Many bilingual law firms in Paris specialise in *droit des affaires* (business law). All attorneys must pass the French bar exam to practise law under their own name. Because fees can be high, be clear as to your financial limits; on the other hand, be wary of any cut-rate offers. Some attorneys will sign a *convention d'honoraires* with their clients to set out the fee structure.

Make sure the lawyer you are considering is an expert in precisely the area you need—many are knowledgeable about employment legislation, which is important if your business requires hiring personnel. The American and British embassies publish lists of Anglophone attorneys in the Paris district but make no recommendations. Consulting agencies can also recommend bilingual attorneys.

A *notaire* may be helpful in rights concerning patents, copyrights and royalties, while an *expert-comptable* should help set up the financial reporting system to reflect the official French (and EU) method of accounting. The filling out of employee payslips, complicated in its legal intricacies, is often contracted to an *expert-comptable* rather than done in-house. A *comptable* (accountant) generally works in a company and does the financial record keeping on a daily basis. International consulting firms, although probably somewhat more expensive than local French firms, are expert in new business transactions and also serve as *experts-comptables*.

For professional help in understanding all the legal intricacies of business in Paris in English and administrative requirements, you might contact Jean Taquet, who specialises in civil and commercial law for expatriates (tel: 01.40.38.16.11; mobile: 06.16.81.48.07; fax: 01.40.62.94.27; email: qa@jeantaquet.com; website: http://www.insiderparisguides.com).

THE LABOUR POOL

Foreign-controlled firms currently account for 22 per cent of the French workforce; yet it would be wise to take into account the rigid labour laws and the costs of hiring employees when considering a business start-up.

Social benefits such as health insurance, unemployment insurance and retirement benefits, are costly for both the employer and the employee. Note also that French employees are entitled to five weeks of holiday per annum, or two-and-a-half days per month worked. Currently, the standard work week is 35 hours. As French businesses are cutting down on labour-intensive procedures to rely more on labour-saving technology, thus adding to the high unemployment rate, labour-intensive investments are especially encouraged.

Women make up just under half of the working population—subsidised childcare and tax breaks for home childcare workers help to boost this figure. Since the mid-1980s, men and women are by law equal in the workplace, yet women are still paid about one-third less than their male counterparts, and few women hold top positions.

Union membership has declined over the past decade and now accounts for about 12 per cent of the workforce.

Although strikes seem frequent, they too have declined by more than half in the past two decades.

The high level of unemployment has in recent years led to anger and civil unrest. Yet, official efforts to reform the current system in which it is difficult to fire employees from their protected positions and to hire new people, has also led to protests, sometimes violent. Everyone knows that the system must change, but nobody wants it to affect them.

BUSINESS ATMOSPHERE
French management remains traditional in its approach to business, which means that new ideas are slow to take hold. Hierarchical structures persist, and usually it is the top manager or director who ultimately makes the business decision, no matter with whom the initial meetings were held. Decisions are arrived at slowly, as all ramifications are considered and the French reluctance toward change has to be overcome, if at all. Yet, younger people on their way up the corporate structure—especially those who hold advanced degrees—have a more international outlook, and it is they who will change the face of French business procedures. Some are already expressing frustration with today's 'top-down' decision-making, although they understand that changes will come only as generations of leaders change or when France begins to slip in international markets. But make no mistake: while they may be more casual and open in their approach, and more willing to take on wider challenges, they are no less determined in achieving their business goals. And the general rules—the 'Do's and Don'ts' listed below, will still apply.

NETWORKING
Given the rigid structures and formal approach of the French business environment, it is important to cultivate all opportunities for personal contact. The Anglophone community in Paris is active in networking for people of similar interests. See Resource Guide in Chapter 10 for a list of helpful networking possibilities.

OFFFICE SPACE

Offices may be rented or purchased as a leasehold. If you purchase office space, be sure to select an appropriate *notaire*. Whether buying or renting, use a commercial, rather than

Do's and Don'ts in Business Situations

- Do make an effort to understand how the French culture and way of life differ from your own. Read as much as you can before you make your business contacts.
- Do make an effort to speak French, at whatever level you can. Without fluency in French, you will be at a disadvantage next to your EU colleagues and competitors.
- Do learn how the French do business, for it may be very different from the business customs of your home country. Hierarchical structures persist, and the French are formal, legalistic and extremely courteous in their business dealings.
- Do your homework. Find out all particulars about the companies you wish to deal with and write or call the appropriate contacts before arriving in Paris to set up meetings; confirm these meetings one day ahead.
- Do write all initial letters in French. If that is not possible, have someone translate them for you. Also, acknowledge all letters promptly and follow up a meeting with a letter, whether mailed, faxed or emailed, as appropriate.
- Do ensure that presentation materials are in French. If your French is not adequate, bring an interpreter to initial meetings or presentations.
- Do arrive on time for a business meeting. Remember that France uses the 24-hour clock. Thus, your business meeting set for 15h is at 3:00 pm.
- Do be formal in initial greetings (by letter, telephone or a face-to-face meeting), use the appropriate titles when addressing business partners.

residential, estate agent. Standard business leases are for nine years unless prior agreement is reached for another time frame. The lease will be renewed automatically for the same duration unless the tenant informs the landlord (or vice versa)

- Do shake hands at the beginning of a meeting and just before leaving.
- Do make sure that you have a business card ready to exchange at meetings and social events. It should contain your name and title, business affiliation, fixed telephone line and mobile numbers, fax number, email address and website of your company. Self-service machines for printing namecards can be found in some train stations and supermarkets. *Papeteries* (stationery stores) make stylish cards, but may take some time to be ready.
- Don't mistake a seemingly cold formality for lack of interest. Similarly, heated discussions and even negative comments about ideas and proposals may indicate a high interest in the project.
- Don't automatically assume that the French still like long business lunches. Long business lunches are less popular than in the past, owing to time constraints and the tendency to eat and drink less during business hours. Nonetheless, lunch is still seen as a pleasant method to cement a business relationship, but not to close a deal.
- Do not expect to have finalised orders or agreements after a first meeting, which is generally seen as an opportunity to size up the company or product.
- Lastly, take into account that in August nothing will get done, for there is no one around to do it. (This also means that if your business depends on a year-round cash flow, you should understand that Parisians disappear in August and sometime around Christmas and Easter.)

six months before the lease expires. EU nationals, Canadians and Americans are afforded the same lease protections as French citizens.

The British firm Jones Lang Lasalle at 58–60 avenue de la Grande Armée, 75017. Specializes in real estate and corporate services. (tel: 01.40.55.15.15; fax: 01.40.22.28.28; website: http://www.joneslanglasalle.fr).

Agents may also be found through the Chambre des Experts Immobiliers de France (FNAIM) at 129 rue du Faubourg Saint-Honoré, 75008 (tel: 01.53.76.03.52; website: http://www.experts-fnaim.org).

Temporary Offices

Fully equipped offices may be rented by the day, week or month. Most offer secretarial and translation services, message-taking, mail delivery, copiers and other office services; some are accessible six days a week. See *Location de bureaux équipés* in the *Yellow Pages*.

- Multiburo: http://www.multiburo.com
- NCI: http://www.groupenci.com
- Boss Buro Express: http://www.bbe.fr

THE JOB HUNT

Foreigners hoping to work in Paris should take into consideration that salaried jobs are hard to find. The persistently high unemployment rate of over 10 per cent has resulted in the tightening of regulations for hiring non-EU citizens. In addition, the government policy of the decentralisation of French industries over the past few decades has reduced jobs in the Paris area by about 200,000 positions. Fluent French is almost always a requirement; without it, job possibilities are minimal. For non-EU citizens, with the exception of certain cases as noted below, the appropriate working papers must be obtained before a position may be offered. Non-French companies may send personnel abroad for overseas assignments, but generally, overseas operations hire locally. Libraries in your home country should have resource materials on international companies and recruitment fairs for overseas positions. It

is not a good idea to come to France as a tourist, hoping to find employment and obtain residence status. On the other hand, a 2006 law is making it easier to get certain jobs in specific regions of France. Before making any choices, inquire at the appropriate organisations, and see whether you fit any of the criteria.

In addition, as the violent events of 2005-2006 exploded, partly owing to the high rate of unemployment—up to 25 per cent among the youth in the Paris suburbs—the entire populace became alarmed. But even as of this writing, government efforts in reform have not met with success in that same uneasy population. Thus, employment issues will no doubt remain in the forefront of governmental attention, but it is hard to know what reforms and changes will be forthcoming and what the populace—accustomed to protectionist policies for their own jobs—will accept.

WORK FOR EU NATIONALS

If jobs are available, most EU nationals with a valid identity card or passport may work in France without obtaining a permit. This includes citizens from the 15 member states that joined the EU before 2004, plus Cyprus and Malta. Citizens from the EU countries that joined after May 2004 must still apply for permits.

EU citizens may apply for most jobs, except those in the civil service or some high security positions in the private sector that require French nationality. Generally, employment rights and conditions, including benefits, salary, training, working conditions and Sécurité Sociale, are the same for EU nationals as for French citizens. EU citizens may stay in France to look for a job and even take one on without a *carte de séjour*. Once you have an employment contract and have worked for three months, you will be issued the *carte de séjour* and a French Social Security number, and health coverage will be activated.

In their job search, EU nationals should acquaint themselves with the services of EURES (European Employment Services), a joint programme of the European Commission and the public employment agencies of the EU countries and Switzerland (http://ec.europa.eu/eures/home. jsp?lang = en). EURES offers information, advice and job placement opportunities for EU citizens who wish to work in any EU country.

EU nationals and anyone who has a resident permit in France may also register with and directly use the services of Agence Nationale pour l'Emploi (ANPE), the French public employment services, whose website has a special section for young job seekers between the ages of 18–26. See http://www.anpe.fr.

British citizens should consult the job centre website (http://www.jobcentreplus.gov.uk) and click on Partners. Also contact the Franco-British Chamber of Commerce in Paris, which maintains a job file (see page 307).

Fully fledged British citizens may work without restriction in France, but this may not apply to Commonwealth citizens with UK residency rights. France deals with foreigners purely on the basis of their citizenship and not their residency, so such citizens may need to fulfil the requirements of their home country.

WORK PERMITS FOR NON-EU CITIZENS

Non-EU citizens will find it almost impossible to obtain a permanent work permit or to find a position just by looking. Nonetheless, you may inquire about procedures and requirements for temporary permits at the Agence Nationale de l'Accueil des Etrangers et des Migrations (ANAEM) at 48 rue de la Roquette, 75001 (tel: 01.55.28.19.40), or at the Main d'Oeuvre Etrangère (MOE), a division of the Direction Départmentale du Travail et de l'Emploi at 127 boulevard de la Villette, 75010 (tel: 01.44.84.42.86).

If you are transferred to France by a non-French company, you must have the *autorisation provisoire de travail* (temporary work permit), which is valid for the duration of the mission (no more than one year) and should have the same length of validity as the *carte de séjour*. This permit is renewable. Your company should fulfil most of the bureaucratic requirements and provide information and advice for settling in.

Sometimes a French corporation will hire a foreign executive or highly qualified technician. It must apply to the MOE as mentioned above, which issues the right to work. Once this is issued, the request goes to the ANAEM, which then sends it to the French consulate near the home of the potential employee. Only then does the visa process start. The consulate will request the submission of a dossier to apply for a *carte de long séjour*, which includes a medical exam. This should all be done as far in advance as possible, for it can take several months for the dossier to be completed.

France has, for some years, discouraged the hiring of non-EU nationals, as the level of unemployment for its own citizens is too high. Thus, it has the right to veto the request for a foreign employee if the monthly gross salary offered is less than € 4,000, and if there are unemployed French in the specific field. And since there is unemployment in just about any sector and for any position, the request may well be automatically denied, unless the employer can demonstrate the unique qualifications of the candidate. On the other hand, there are some positions—such as teaching at universities—that are not covered by this regulation.

PERMITS AND CONTRACTS

Some long-stay documents will indicate *salarié*, meaning that the holder is a salaried employee. A *carte de séjour temporaire salarié* is generally valid for one year, although there may be variations. Most cards show the type of professional work allowed and the French departments in which the holder is permitted to work, although one type of *carte de séjour temporaire salarié* gives the holder the right to work for any employer and anywhere in France. The permit may be renewed two months (or more) before its expiration upon presentation of an existing labour contract. Once a 10-year *carte de résident* has been obtained, the holder may work at any profession and in all capacities, including being self-employed, running a business, or even managing a corporation.

An *employé salarié* receives a monthly salary, from which Sécurité Sociale costs are deducted. Salaries are either stated as *salaire brut* (gross salary, before deductions) or *salaire net* (net salary, after deductions). The pay is often automatically deposited into the employee's bank account, which is efficient because all cheques are *chèques barrés* or crossed cheques (indicated by a bar across the check) and they must be deposited by the payee, not cashed. The employee receives a *fiche de paie* (pay slip) recording income and deductions. A *contrat de travail* (work contract) is required, following a *lettre d'engagement* (engagement letter).

Contracts are of the two types described below, but receiving three pay checks is also seen as binding. Make sure that all pertinent items are specified in the contract, including job description, salary, vacation and retirement benefits. Most contracts also mention the *convention collective*, which details employee rights. *Périodes d'essai* (trial periods) vary from one month for lower-level jobs, to three months for managers (*cadres*); they may be renewed once. The maximum *période d'essai* possible is a year, for executive positions. This system, benefits employers, of course, but it is standard.

- *Contrat à durée indéterminée* (CDI): a contract without a term limit, although there is generally a *période d'essai* before the contract binds either party. This protects the employee.
- *Contrat à durée determinée* (CDD): a contract for a fixed term, generally from three to six months, with a maximum duration of one year. These contracts may only be renewed once and for a total duration of 18 months.
- *Travailleurs indépendants* are self-employed professionals such as lawyers, CPAs or architects, who have obtained a licence to practise. Those engaged in project-oriented professions such as consultants, editors or translators also fall within this category. The *carte de séjour* required for *travailleurs indépendants* is easier to obtain, since neither URSSAF (the body overseeing the Social Security system), nor the Préfecture has the right to veto a request. Indeed, URSSAF simply verifies the legality of the request based on the activity proposed, although there are strict guidelines defining which jobs can be taken on by the self-employed and how they must be performed in order to qualify; the applicant must prove the soundness of the project to the Préfecture.

An independent worker must register for Sécurité Sociale and make contributions that are extremely steep—sometimes up to 40 per cent of gross earnings; inquire at URSSAF. Some companies prefer to use a *travailleur indépendant* rather than hiring a full-time employee, thus avoiding payment of high benefits. People considering working independently should therefore determine the amount they will be required to pay out from their gross earnings before setting their fees.

Holders of a *carte de séjour* who intend to engage in a commercial business, such as opening a shop, must also have the *carte de commerçant étranger* in addition to the *carte de séjour mention commerçant*. This is not necessary for someone with the *carte de résident*.

LOOKING FOR A JOB

When applying for a position, do so only in the field of your education and experience: French employers do not often hire people with the intention of training them.

Make sure your resumé is translated into French and attach a passport-size photograph. The cover letter should be no more than one page and preferably handwritten, not typed. Graphology is taken seriously and French employers rely on handwriting to determine a person's character. Large corporations are sometimes flexible on this, understanding that foreigners may not have been subjected to the same stringent handwriting standards as those of French schools and that foreign handwriting may not be analysed in the same way as French handwriting. Some companies also test for aptitude and personality, as well as a foreigner's fluency in French. An advertisement may ask for an applicant's *prétentions*, meaning the salary desired. It is best to find out the salaries being paid for comparable positions before responding.

Actually, open positions may not be publicly advertised. *Cooptation* (networking) is increasingly important for the more skilled positions, and *piston* (personal influence) plays a part when it can. Cultivating contacts, networking and knocking on doors may be as effective as any other means of finding a job. Sometimes a favoured person may be *parachuté* (dropped into) into a particular job without going through the application process.

Know Your Rights

The current standard work week is 35 hours, and no one may be required to work on Sunday. Five weeks is the minimum vacation allowance, and there are 11 national holidays. Vacation accrued is calculated as of 1 May.

THE JOB SEARCH IN PARIS

As mentioned, EU nationals and those with a work permit may use the ANPE, the public employment service. To register with the ANPE, contact ASSEDIC (Association pour l'emploi dans l'industrie et le commerce) at 08.11.01.01.75. You will be sent a form to fill out and to bring personally to its office at 4 rue Traversière, 75012. Registering with ASSEDIC automatically registers you at ANPE, and you have four weeks to meet with a counsellor who will help you in your job search.

There are more than 30 ANPE offices in Paris. Some branches specialise in particular professions, including *cadre* positions (see below). Inquire at any of the ANPE offices or at the central office at 123 rue Oberkampf, Paris 75011 (tel: 01.49.23.33.50; http://www.pole-emploi.fr). See *Administrations du Travail et de l'Emploi* in the *Yellow Pages* and *ANPE* in the *White Pages*.

Job seekers should access the city's cyber network (http:www.cyber-emploi-center.com). There are access points throughout Paris, and there are separate addresses for people under the age of 25. Reserve your computer time in advance.

FUSAC, the free advertising supplement for Anglophones, is an important medium for private employment agencies advertising bilingual positions. *Le Figaro* publishes the most important jobs supplement every Monday. *Carrières et Emplois*, issued on Wednesdays, repeats already published ads, and *Les Annonces* and *Le Marché du Travail* are also job ad publications.

Cadres are people with higher education degrees or with managerial experience. They may use the resources of APEC (l'Association pour l'Emploi des Cadres) at 51 boulevard

Brune, 75014 (tel: 08.10.80.58.05; http://www.apec.fr). For *cadre* positions, look in *Le Monde*, *Télérama*, *l'Express* and *Les Echos*.

Americans may deposit their resumés with the American Chamber of Commerce, which keeps them for two months as a resource for its corporate members.

TEACHING

French public universities may hire foreigners as visiting professors or lecturers, but only French citizens may teach in French public schools; exceptions are made for teaching assistants. There are also a variety of English-speaking private universities in Paris to explore (see Chapter Five).

Teaching in an international elementary or secondary school is a possibility. Applications must arrive no later than January for the following September. You should have a college degree, teaching certificate and proof of experience. Organisations such as International Schools Services (ISS) hold recruiting fairs (US tel: (1-609) 452-0990; fax: (1-609) 452-2690; website: http://www.iss.edu).

Teaching English privately is a possibility, but non-EU citizens will have a hard time finding a position in a language school. This is a popular occupation for young expatriates from the EU, who arrive in droves with official credentials for teaching English as a Second Language (ESL). People with RSA/TEFL certificates should see *Enseignement: langues* in the *Yellow Pages*. WICE, a non-profit anglophone organisation offers a TEFL certificate course.

STUDENT WORK PERMITS

Students from the EU do not need work permits. In certain cases, registered students from outside the EU may obtain an *autorisation provisoire de travail* (temporary work permit) and be allowed to work part-time during the school year and full-time between semesters. To apply, you'll need a valid student *carte de séjour*, student identification cards from the previous and current year, a statement from the school confirming student status and a written promise of employment from the company. (This does not apply to first-year students, who must prove that they have sufficient funds for the first year of studies.) Students at institutions that do not provide Sécurité Sociale medical care coverage are not eligible to work.

Students may work for a maximum of 20 hours per week during the school year and up to 35 hours during the three-month summer vacation (between June and October). By law, French employers must pay all employees at least the legal minimum wage, but many try to bypass this with foreign students. Sometimes it is possible to work in France for a year after studies are completed; inquire at your consulate. All earnings are taxable under the French tax system. French consulates may have copies of *Employment in France for Students*, which explains the details.

Students should apply to MOE/DDTE, the organisation mentioned above, which will then determine the appropriate course. Bring all residence and student documents, as well as a letter from the prospective employer showing your name and address; the position and wages offered; the number of hours of work; and the length of the employment. Students under 18 years of age must have authorisation from their parents.

Full-time students from American and some non-EU countries may work in France during vacations through a Work Abroad Programme approved by the French government. In the United States, contact Council on International Educational Exchange (CIEE) at 300 Fore Street, Portland ME 04101 (US tel: (1-207) 553-4000; fax (1-207) 553-4229;; website: http://www.ciee.org).

AU PAIR WORK
EU nationals only need a valid passport and not a pre-arranged position in order to come to France to work as an *au pair*. Non-EU nationals, however, must have applied for a *visa de long séjour* and obtained a *declaration d'engagement* with a French family. The contract must detail the hours, tasks and remuneration, and the family must declare the *au pair* a *stagiare aide familiale*, which permits health coverage.

All *au pairs* must register and take French lessons during their contract.

Au pairs generally take care of children in exchange for room and board, sometimes with a slight stipend. Other options exist, such as receiving room and board in exchange for light housework. *Au pairs* must be unmarried and between the ages of 18-30. The contract cannot exceed 18 months. *Au pair* positions are monitored by the Ministry of Labour. For agencies that handle *au pair* positions, see *FUSAC* and access the following website:http://www.europa-pages.com/au_pair/index.html.

Is It Really For You?

Think carefully before accepting an *au pair* position. The work, which consists of taking care of children full-time, usually includes some housework as well, and days off are few. Although it is an economical way to live in Paris, such a position may not correspond to the experience of living in Paris you had in mind before coming.

FAST FACTS

CHAPTER 10

'Paris France is exciting and peaceful.'
—Getrude Stein

Official Name
Paris

Flag
The flag of municipal Paris consists of a vertical band of blue (on the left) and one in red (on the right), the traditional colours of the city. In the centre is the city's coat of arms.

Time
Greenwich Mean Time plus 1 hour (GMT + 0100) in standard time and plus 2 hours (GMT + 0200) during summer.

Telephone Country Code
Country Code for France: 33
Area Code for Paris: 01

Land Area
105 sq km (40.5 sq miles)

Highest Point
Top of Montmartre hill (130 m/426.5 ft)

Climate
Mainly temperate, with the warmest temperatures during July and August. The coldest period is during December and January.

Population
2.3 million in Paris, with another 10.5 million in the surrounding suburban towns.

Ethnic Groups
Eighty per cent of the Greater Paris populace is born in Paris or from other French provinces. Foreign immigrants (primarily from North African countries) make up about 20 per cent. It is forbidden by law for the official census to ask questions about ethnicity or religion.

Religion
Some 80 per cent of the populace is nominally Catholic, although less than 20 per cent is religiously observant. With five million Muslims in France (about 8 per cent of the population), Islam is the second most important religion.

Official Languages
French

Government Structure
The city of Paris is the only city in France that is a single Department (75). It operates as a municipal entity, with an elected mayor and council. Each of the city's 20 districts has its own council with representatives on the Paris city council. The suburban communes in the Paris region each have their own municipal governments.

Currency
Euro (€)

Gross Domestic Product (GDP)
France: US$ 2.075 trillion (2007 estimate)
Paris: US$ 731.3 billion (2007 estimate)

Industries
Manufacturing, service and tourism

Airports
The two principal Paris airports are Charles de Gaulle International (northeast), which serves most intercontinental flights, and Orly (south), which handles most domestic and some international flights.

Conversion Tables
1 kilogramme = 2.2 pounds
100 grammes = 3.5 ounces
One litre = 1 quart, 2 ounces; about 4 cups
One litre = 0.26 gallons (US liquid); 0.22 gallons (Imperial)
One teaspoon dry measure = about 7 grams
One tablespoon = 14 grams
One Stone = 6.35 kilos

1 centimetre = 0.39 inches
1 metre = 3.3 feet
1 kilometre = 0.62 miles
1 mile = 1.6 km

0° Centigrade = 32° Fahrenheit
37° Centigrade = 98.6° Fahrenheit
100° Centigrade = 212° Fahrenheit

Women's Dress Sizes
American	8	10	12	14
French	38	40	42	44
British	10	12	14	16

Men's Suit Sizes
American	38	40	42
French	48	50	52
British	36	38	40

FAMOUS PEOPLE
Charlemagne (742–814)
King of the Franks and Holy Roman Emperor. Seen as the father of France, Germany and Belgium, and of modern Europe.

Joan of Arc (1412–1431)

Devout girl who followed 'voices' to lead the French in defeating the English at Orléans during the Hundred Years' War. Captured and delivered to the English, she was convicted of heresy and was burnt at the stake at age 19. Made a saint by the Church.

René Descartes (1596–1650)

Known as the founder of modern philosophy, whose most famous saying was "*Cogito ergo sum*" ("I think, therefore I am").

Louis XIV (1638–1715)

The 'Sun King' who fought wars to extend the power of France. Reigned for 72 years and built the opulent Chateau of Versailles. His last words were, "I am going away, but the State will always remain."

Voltaire (1694–1778)

Influential poet, playwright and satirist. He spoke out for social reform and defended civil liberties and religious freedom. His play *Candide* is still widely read.

Louis XVI (1754–1793)

An ordinary man, depressed and indecisive, he roused the ire of a nation in debt and a people mired in poverty, leading to the French Revolution. His Austrian wife Marie Antoinette (1755-1793) was also hated by the people. Put on trial during the French Revolution, both died by the guillotine.

Gilbert du Motier, Marquis de La Fayette (1757–1834)

A 'hero of two worlds', La Fayette fought on the side of the colonists against the British in the American Revolution. A reformer at home, he also took part in the French Revolution a decade later.

Napoléon Bonaparte (1769–1821)

Corsican soldier and military strategist, his successes in

broadening the lands of France led him to become Emperor. He instituted social, legal and administrative reforms, but disastrous military campaigns forced him into exile. After a triumphant return of 100 days, he was defeated by Wellington at Waterloo, and died eventually on the remote island of Saint-Helena.

Alexandre Dumas (1802–1870)
A writer popular worldwide, Dumas' most famous novels are *The Count of Monte Cristo* and *The Three Musketeers*.

Louis Pasteur (1822–1895)
Father of modern medicine whose discoveries are credited with lengthening the human lifespan. Developed a method to eliminate contaminated milk (pasteurisation) and immunisations to combat disease.

Georges Auguste Escoffier (1846–1935)
Elevated French cooking to an art, creating what is known as haute cuisine.

Jean Moulin (1889–1943)
Leader of the French Resistance against the Nazi invaders during World War II. Betrayed, Moulin was arrested and tortured, but gave no information to the Nazis. He died on the way to a concentration camp and has become for the French an enduring symbol of the Resistance.

Maréchal Henri Philippe Pétain (1856–1951)
French hero of World War I, Pétain headed the collaborationist puppet government of Vichy during World War II. He was tried as a traitor and sentenced to life imprisonment.

Général Charles de Gaulle (1890–1970)
Leader of Free France during World War II, he inspired resistance to the Nazi occupiers and collaborationist government in Vichy. He returned to Paris in triumph in 1945 and became President of Fifth Republic from 1958–1969.

Jean-Paul Sartre (1905–1980)

Proponent of 'existentialism', which argues that people are basically alone in a universe with no moral order, and that individuals themselves determine what is right and wrong and are accountable for their decisions and actions. A prominent figure among the Left Bank intellectuals.

Edith Piaf (1915–1963)

'The Little Sparrow' was one of France's greatest and most beloved singers. It is said that her funeral was the only time that traffic in all of Paris came to a complete stop.

François Mitterrand (1916–1996).

President of France from 1981–1995. A Socialist who brought a greater internationalism to France and improved French relations within the EU. He also oversaw domestic decentralisation and a series of *Grands Projets* (Great Works) that revitalised Paris.

Johnny Hallyday (1943–)

France's most famous rock'n'roll star, influenced by Elvis Presley.

Bertrand Delanoë (1950–)

The current mayor of Paris. Socialist and forward-looking, Delanoë is striving to improve the city and its quality of life. The first openly gay person to be elected mayor, he was stabbed in 2002 by a homophobic attacker; fortunately, his wounds were not severe.

Zinédine Zidane (1972–)

Football player of strength and elegance. A sports hero to the French.

THE USE OF ABBREVIATIONS

The French are enthusiastic users of initials, acronyms and abbreviations both in speaking and writing. When looking in the telephone book for a number, if you can't find a listing under its full name, try its initials (RATP, SNCF, FUAJ, etc.).

Below are a few commonly used abbreviations.

BHV   Bazar de l'Hôtel de Ville: major department store
BNP   Banque Nationale de Paris: major national bank
EDF   Electricité de France: biggest electric company
FUAJ   Fédération Unie des Auberges de Jeunesse: a youth hostel organisation
FUSAC   France-USA Contacts: a helpful publication for Anglophones in Paris
GDF   Gaz de France: gas company
HT   Hors tax: before sales tax
RC   Rez-de-Chaussée: ground floor
RATP   Régie Autonome des Transports Parisiens: the public transport system.
RDV   Rendezvous: meeting or date
RER   Réseau Express Régional: commuter train
RF   République Française: The French Republic
RIB   Relevé d'Identité Bancaire: official identification of a bank account
SIDA   Acronym for AIDS
SNCF   Société Nationale des Chemins de Fer: the national railroad
TGV   Train à Grande Vitesse: the express train
TTC   Toutes Taxes Comprises: all taxes included
TVA   Taxe sur Valeur Ajoutée: the sales tax (VAT)
VF   Version Française: a foreign film dubbed in French
VO   Version Originale: film in its original language
WC   Water Closet: the toilet

CULTURE QUIZ

SITUATION 1

You bought five handles for your kitchen cabinets in a Parisian hardware store. When you get home, however, you see that one is damaged, and besides, it turns out you needed only four. You go back to the store with the receipt to return the unwanted item, politely explaining the situation to the salesman. He is not at all accommodating, saying you should have noticed the problem before you left the store and that there's nothing he can do. He points to a sign on the wall that says 'no returns'. You:

Ⓐ Agree, saying, "oui, monsieur", you understand that, in general, nothing should be returned, but this item was defective. You add that you do not wish to be difficult but hope to continue patronising his shop in future.

Ⓑ Realise that the salesman's arrogant attitude is just a show, which can easily be overturned once he realises that he may lose your business. Thus, you tell the salesman that you will never again patronise his shop and, what's more, you will advise your foreign friends to do likewise, if he doesn't comply to your reasonable request.

Ⓒ Ask to speak to his manager or supervisor, as Parisian salespeople have obviously no power to make any decisions.

Ⓓ Politely tell the salesman that where you come from, all respectable shops abide by the motto 'the customer is always right', and firmly request that he reimburse you for the defective item.

Comments

Although it may take a longer and probably more stressful exchange with the salesperson than you would have expected, Ⓐ is the way to go about it in Paris. Standing your own ground, while reassuring the salesperson that you wish to maintain friendly relations with the store, is the best way to get French salespeople to acquiesce, albeit grudgingly, to your requests. Answers **B** and **D** will be of no use as the French do no react well to patronising or threatening talk. Asking to see his superior, as in **C**, will only leave you with the chore of having to do another round of lengthy negotiations, as the French attitude towards customer service is basically the same from the top to the bottom of the hierarchy. While in France, and especially Paris, never assume that the customer is always right. It pays to be meticulous in what you buy, checking everything before you leave the store. Get used to the French notion of customer service, which will hopefully change. In any case, quiet persistence usually works.

SITUATION 2

You have entered a boutique, said "Bonjour, madame" and indicated that you are just looking, at least for the moment. You browse and find a dress that you like, so you take it off the rack to hold it up in front of the mirror. The salesperson rushes to you, whisks the item away and asks politely whether you would like to try it on. You are annoyed (although you say nothing), for you had not finished browsing yet. So you:

A Indicate that you would like to look around some more. Thus you continue to browse and take a few other dresses off the rack, handing them to the salesperson to bring to the fitting room for you.

B Feel intimidated by the salesperson's controlling attitude and walk away from the boutique, heading for the more impersonal shopping centres.

C Whisk the item back from the salesperson and firmly tell her to please leave you alone, as you have not finished browsing yet.

D Follow the salesperson to the fitting room and try on the dress. If it doesn't fit, ask the salesperson to show you other similar outfits.

Comments

Both answers **A** and **D** are correct, if you intend to get any shopping done at the boutique, although **D** is the better option. In a small shop, customers generally do not remove items from the rack themselves. This is the domain of the shopkeeper, whose job is to help you. (This holds true of fruit markets as well—let the *marchand* or shopkeeper pick the fruit for you. Unless a sign says *libre service (*self-service), do not help yourself or paw through the fruit.) If you want to be left alone while you are browsing, go to a department store, as in answer **B**, where there are fewer salespeople per customer and where the personnel have a less personal attitude. Answer **C** will work against you if you eventually need the salesperson's help in finding or trying on an outfit, or if you plan on coming back to this store again.

SITUATION 3

There is a group of people standing haphazardly at one of the vegetable stalls at the *marché* (market). Someone approaches the stand, pushes to an empty spot closer to the front and winds up being served before you. What do you do?

A Make a fuss about it. As no one seems to be doing anything about it, the salesperson will probably allow others to jump queue as well, so you better speak up and point out the injustice.

B Do nothing. The person who has jumped the queue has disrupted the order of service for the others as well; if there's anything to say, let someone else do it.

C Gently say to the *marchand* as he finishes his transaction and before he serves the client who has not queued, "*Je pense que c'est à moi, monsieur*", reminding him that it is now your turn.

D Look out for any empty spots near the front and quickly position yourself behind the person being served. In Paris, unless you assert yourself, you will never get served.

Comments

This is a good opportunity to learn how to be patient. Making a fuss will get you nowhere nearer to being served, so answer **A** is of no use. First try **B**, letting others in the line complain for you. But if that doesn't work and it looks as though you are being totally ignored for some reason, try ❻. ❼will just compound the problem and make you no friends, so don't even consider it.

SITUATION 4

You are at a *traiteur* in your new neighbourhood, and the spread of dishes looks so delicious, you think you might like to patronise the shop regularly. After ordering, you realise that the slice of meat you have been given has too much gristle and fat for your taste. When you politely say so to the *vendeuse* (saleslady) and ask her for another slice, you notice that her lips are pursed and her demeanour has turned frigid. What might you have done differently?

❶ You could have taken a look at the slices of meat and, after noticing that they were fatty, leave the shop and go look for another *traiteur*, where the meats sold are leaner.

❷ Nothing. It is your right as a customer to choose the items you wish to buy, and it is the *vendeuse*'s job to give you what you choose. If she is not happy about this, that is her problem, not yours.

❸ Instead of saying that you didn't like her original selection, you might have said, "Oh, I'm so sorry to bother you, but might I have that slice to the left instead? Thank you so much, that's very kind."

❹ In your best French, you could have explained to the woman that fatty foods are harmful to one's health, which is why you stopped eating oily food years ago. She would have surely understood then—after all, who isn't concerned about health issues these days?

Comments

By asking the *vendeuse* to exchange the piece she had given you for another one, you probably made her feel that her initial choice was not good enough—this is not acceptable to the French. If you want to have any of the items exchanged, you needn't explain or put the woman in the wrong. Thus,

D would not work. The best way to go about it is to, firstly, apologise for any inconvenience caused, then ask politely if you might have a different piece, as in **C**. **A** and **B** are possible, but they will not help you in adapting to Parisian life. This situation should remind you to be vigilant: you could have pointed out in advance the slice you wanted, thus avoiding disappointment on your part and offending the *vendeuse*.

SITUATION 5

You have been invited by a French couple you have recently become friends with, to dine in a restaurant they have chosen. From the way your friends live and knowing that one of them is not working, you realise that their current financial situation may not be all it should be. Thus, you:

A Tactfully suggest a different, less expensive restaurant that you know they like.

B Accept their invitation, and after the lovely meal, offer to contribute to the bill.

C Find a good excuse to decline their invitation, suggesting that you wish to make up for it by asking them to a nice meal some time soon.

D Accept their invitation graciously but remind yourself to reciprocate at the earliest appropriate opportunity.

Comments

Except for **D**, all of the above choices would either annoy or offend your friends. In **A** and **B**, you would have indirectly brought up their personal financial situation by suggesting a less expensive restaurant or by offering to pay the bill, and referring to money is not done. Your friends had chosen a restaurant they thought you would like, and it is not up to you to change the plan. In addition, they would not have suggested an evening that would put them in the workhouse. Lastly, since your friends are taking the trouble to invite you to a restaurant, you should be gracious enough to accept their hospitality, and not decline their invitation or suggest that you treat them instead, as in **C**.

SITUATION 6

A colleague has invited you to his home for dinner. You want to make a good impression, so you dress carefully and bring along a nice box of chocolates. You arrive 20 minutes late, as is the standard, only to find that you are the first one there. It is clear that your host and his wife are busy in the kitchen. Your colleague shows you into the living room, which is large and beautifully decorated, with several other intriguing rooms opening off to the sides. Your host gestures to the couch and says to make yourself comfortable. You:

A Sit down and stay there until either other guests arrive or your host indicates otherwise.

B Take a quick peek into the other rooms, which look so beckoning, then sit down.

C Roll up your sleeves and offer to help in the kitchen.

D Browse around the living room, helping yourself to the aperitifs and snacks that are sitting on a table nearby.

Comments

First of all, please be assured that you have done nothing wrong by arriving 20 minutes late. You made an effort to conform to the cultural norms of your French hosts; unfortunately, even though you arrived late, it wasn't late enough for these people. This is one of those situations where you just have to make do. Once you have arrived at your colleague's home, however, you should sit down where indicated and stay put. You may look at books on the coffee table (if any), the view or the pictures on the wall (and comment about them nicely afterwards), but you should not help yourself to any food or drink unless you have been asked to do so. Thus **A** is the best answer. The important thing to remember, no matter what you do, is to respect the privacy of your hosts. Answers **B**, **C** and **D** would, as a result, make you seem intrusive and ill-mannered.

SITUATION 7

At the home of an acquaintance, you accidentally brush up against a case holding some beautiful china figurines. One of them falls and breaks. Naturally, you apologise...

When completed, the modern tramway system will circle all of Paris. The city's public transport network, which also includes the métro, bus, and RER, is one of the most efficient in the world.

Al fresco dining at a Parisian bistro. While Parisians might seem to lead a hectic life, they still enjoy a leisurely meal, along with the fine wine and conversation that accompanies it.

The Bastille Day parade passes by the Arc de Triomphe, while commemorating the storming of the Bastille prison in 1789. Taking of the Bastille symbolizes the beginning of the French Revolution, which paved the way to the fall of the monarchy independence and the rise of modern France. The world may call the holiday Bastille Day; the French, however, just say *le quatorze juillet*—July 14th.

Sunbathing along the banks of the River Seine. Paris may be a long way from the Mediterranean, but Parisians still enjoy a healthy dose of sun in summer, especially after their cold winters.

Paris is one of the most dog-friendly cities you can imagine. Well-behaved dogs are allowed at many restaurants, and smaller ones may even ride on public transport if they are held by their owner in baskets or sacks. Service dogs are allowed on all public transport.

Ⓐ ... profusely throughout the entire evening, in order to convey to your hostess how truly sorry you feel.

Ⓑ ... sincerely once and then drop the subject immediately. Who wants to ruin an otherwise lovely evening?

Ⓒ ... once in private, and then help pick up the pieces. You mention nothing about paying for the figurine, as the French are sensitive about issues relating to money. Instead, you send a bouquet of flowers to the hostess the next day.

Ⓓ ... once sincerely and publicly, help pick up the pieces and tell your hostess you are going to look for a replacement or to pay for one. You add that you will call your insurance company to alert them that there might be a claim. Nevertheless, you still send a bouquet of flowers to your hostess the next day.

Comments

Only **Ⓓ** is acceptable in this difficult situation. Your apologies should be sincere and profound, but you don't have to bring it up all evening, spoiling everyone's enjoyment of the event. Apologise, help repair the damage, offer to pay for the replacement, then drop the subject, but do send flowers the next day. Remember that in France, everyone has *multi-risque* (multi-risk) household insurance, so offering to pay for the repair or replacement of the item is both courteous and responsible.

SITUATION 8

You and some American friends from home have eaten quite well in a crowded restaurant, but now it's time to pay the bill and go home. Since the waiter is obviously occupied, one of your friends takes out his credit card and puts it on the corner of the table, assuming that the waiter will see it, take it, then bring it back to the table with the bill. Nothing happens and the waiter doesn't come. After about 10 minutes, your friend starts to get annoyed. Finally you catch the waiter's eye, and when he comes over, your friend points to his credit card but says nothing. Both your friend and the waiter are clearly annoyed. He brings the bill with the little credit card machine, the bill is paid, and everyone leaves, slightly uncomfortable that a pleasant evening has ended on an awkward note. Your friend grumbles about the French being anti-American, as surely the waiter should have seen the card on the table. So why didn't the waiter just proceed from there?

Ⓐ Your friend is right: some French waiters just have a natural aversion towards Americans in general.

Ⓑ Your friend should have called the waiter's attention by either politely calling out or signalling.

Ⓒ Your friend should have called over the restaurant host and asked him for the bill.

Ⓒ French waiters are proud. Your friend should have walked over to the waiter and handed him his credit card directly.

Comments

This is clearly a case of cultural assumptions colliding. Americans, especially, are used to the bill appearing automatically—usually just after dessert and coffee have been served—but French waiters are used to verbal cues or hand signals, or even a smile and a nod. Just putting a card on the table and expecting the waiter to jump to it, so to speak, is rude and does not show respect for the waiter. In France, being a waiter is a lifelong trade like any other; it is not a stopgap position for someone who is training for another career. As to anti-Americanism, there's much less of this than purported. People who make an effort to conform to the French sensibilities of *politesse* and respect will be treated in the same manner. Only **Ⓑ** is correct.

DO'S AND DON'TS

So here you are in Paris. Your belongings have arrived, your children are in school, you've most likely started to work at a job with new colleagues—even your dog has made friends in the park! What comes next? That's clear: building your life in Paris so you can enjoy what the city has to offer, with a minimum of 'culture shocks' that will make you feel like an alien from an unknown planet. Some cultural pitfalls can be sidestepped, so here are some tips to give you some confidence in starting your new life in Paris.

DO'S

- Do be polite to people. The most important thing to understand about the French is their reliance on manners and formality (although harried people anywhere can sometimes be rude). French codes of behaviour and mannerly rituals are strictly adhered to, and they are actually quite pleasant, once you get used to them.
- Do greet people whenever you can. When you board a bus, say *"bonjour, monsieur/madame"* to the driver, and to a chauffeur in a taxi before you say where you want to go. Say *"au revoir et merci"* when you get out of the cab. (You can't do this on the bus, because you must exit from the rear doors.) Greet, too, your local merchants and *restaurateurs*. Upon entering a small shop, say *"bonjour, madame"* to the salesperson, even if you just want to look around and aren't ready to buy. If in a larger office or store you need to get someone's attention—a person who, for whatever reason, has not looked up from behind the desk or counter as you approached—manners will do the trick. Say *"Excusez-moi de vous déranger, monsieur, mais..."* ("Excuse me for bothering you, sir, but..."), and when the person looks up, ask for what you need.
- Do observe good manners with both strangers and friends. If you are on a crowded bus or *métro* and an older person boards, offer to give up your seat. (This also holds true for pregnant women or those carrying small children.)

- Do excuse yourself if you happen to bump into someone while walking. "*Pardon*," you might say, or "*Pardon, monsieur/madame*."

- Do address women as "*madame*". Women should note that being called *madame*, even if you're young or unmarried, is not an insult. If you look to be over 30 years of age, you're called *madame* out of respect, so you should do the same when speaking. If a woman is clearly quite young, you may say *mademoiselle*.

- Do shake hands. The French shake hands a lot—the physical contact reinforces their feelings of amity and respect. Shake the hands of acquaintances or colleagues you meet on the street. At a restaurant you patronise frequently, the owner may shake your hand to signal that he knows you are a 'regular'. (For the staff, however, a smile and "*bonjour, monsieur*" will do. French waiters are not chummy and do not introduce themselves by their first name. Treat them with respect.)

- Do greet your friends with a kiss—the French are great kissers. Once you have made a French friend, you will no doubt move from shaking hands to kissing. Generally this involves a slight kiss on each cheek upon greeting and later, upon saying goodbye.

- Do respect people's sense of domain. At the market, do not pick out the fruit or vegetables yourself, unless there is a sign that says *libre service*; wait instead for the merchant to help you. In a shop, don't let your kids run wild and touch everything. At the office, always knock before entering other people's offices.

- Do remember who you are. Even after living in Paris for years and speaking what you think is fluent French, never try to pass for a native. Don't assume that just because you speak French, the merchants are friendly to you and you have close French friends, that you will be considered French. This will never happen.

DON'TS

- Don't use people's first names from the start. Using first names is not automatic; if your colleagues want you to call them by their first names, they will let you know. If invited to dinner with friends, you will most likely be on a first name basis with your hosts and the other guests, but this does not apply to dinner at the home of your boss or the more senior professional acquaintances.

- Don't move from using the *vous* form of address to the familiar *tu* unless given the green light; even when you are on a first name basis with your friends, it still is not an automatic move. Wait until your friend indicates a desire to *tutoyer* (use the *tu* form) or listen carefully to hear whether there hasn't been a subtle move toward this intimate term of address.

- Don't ask personal questions. The French guard their privacy and do not volunteer much personal information. With acquaintances, don't ask what they do for a living, how they voted, or where they've bought the clothes they're wearing—even if you'd like to visit that shop sometime. Let them make the first move.

- Do dress appropriately for the occasion. Appearance counts when you're out and about. If you're in a casual situation, you should still dress neatly, and if you're in a situation that calls for you to dress up, do so. Although young people wear jeans around town, older people don't. And if you look at those young people, they still look put together, jeans or otherwise.

- Don't speak loudly. Be alert to how loudly you're talking on your mobile phone while on the bus, in a crowded restaurant or in a museum. Don't give a belly laugh or guffaw (except while watching a funny film). Keep a low profile.

- Don't show impatience, ever. Not everything always goes your way, but it is ill-mannered to show impatience, whether to strangers or friends. Even if there is no orderly queue at a shop or stall at the market, generally the merchant knows who's next. If not, just wait until you are called upon to give your order.

- Don't start any encounter with an 'attitude'. Just because French people—especially the older generation—don't smile, don't assume they're rude or even unfriendly. If a salesperson in a store is busy with another customer, do not interrupt, even just to ask directions to the department you're looking for; wait patiently until it is your turn.

- Don't insist on getting apologies from the French. The French have developed a need to be right—or at least not to be wrong—and if you can get by without upsetting this 'rule', everyone will be better off.

- Don't always be on time! Be punctual for professional meetings and for dates with friends or colleagues in restaurants. If for some unforeseen reason you are delayed, call the person's mobile phone, apologise and say when you will arrive. But don't ever (ever!) be early or punctual for dinner at a French person's home. If public transportation has been particularly efficient and you arrive early, find a café nearby, order a drink and wait until 20–30 minutes after the time agreed upon.

- Don't talk about money. Money is one of those subjects that is pretty much taboo with the French, at least on a personal level. You can mention where you've seen items on sale and you can complain about how expensive life is in general, but don't translate this into talking about your personal situation with money, or anyone else's.

- Don't get too graphic. Avoid details such as your own health or that of your family, problems with your in-laws, or even specific problems with the bank or tax bureau. And don't go into long personal anecdotes.

DINING ETIQUETTE
Do's

- Do order a cup of coffee at the bar (or something else) first, if you're going into a café just to use their restrooms.
- Do place the napkin on your lap immediately upon sitting down.
- Do rest the hand that does not hold your fork on the table, not in your lap. Don't rest your elbow on the table.
- Do spread your butter bite by bite. Don't take a huge pat and put it on your plate.
- Do eat everything you can with cutlery, not with your fingers. This includes fruit, cheese, even French fries.

- Do place your knife and fork neatly and diagonally, across the top of your plate when you have finished eating.
- Do inform a waiter of your dietary needs (no butter, etc.) by asking how a dish has been prepared. But if a waiter says that a dish would be ruined without a particular ingredient, don't argue. Order something else.
- Do close your menu and put it on the table, when you are ready to order. If you keep looking at it (even just out of curiosity), the waiter will assume you are still deciding and will not approach the table to take your order.
- Do ask for the bill (*l'addition*) when you are ready to leave. The waiter waits for your cue.
- Do leave a small tip—about five per cent of the bill—in cash on the table, if the service has been acceptable. A basic gratuity of 12–15 per cent is included in the bill.

Don'ts

- Don't cut your lettuce leaves. If the salad has large pieces of lettuce, fold them with your fork and knife.
- Don't mop up gravy with bread in your fingers, use a knife and fork. Don't mop at all, unless you're with friends.
- Don't ask for coffee before the end of a meal. Coffee is served after the dessert, not with it.
- Don't smoke before asking for permission from diners at your table and those nearby. Come February 2008, a ban on smoking will come into effect.
- Don't talk business immediately at a business lunch or dinner. Catch up on the news before you zoom in; follow your colleagues' cues.
- Don't pour the wine yourself– the waiter, host, or sommelier will do it. But you pour your own water.
- Don't expect to take leftovers with you. There are no doggy bags in France. Don't even ask.

DINING ETIQUETTE AT SOMEONE'S HOME
Do's

- Do follow all the above general guidelines meticulously.
- Do bring something nice, but don't bring anything that

requires the hostess to divert her attention from the dinner. For instance, don't bring flowers for which she might first have to find a vase and then have to arrange.

- Do take only as much as you will eat if platters are passed and you are to serve yourself. It is a terrible gaffe to take or ask for more than you can eat.
- Do take some more if you are offered seconds and you are still hungry, but not of the soup or cheese courses. Don't ask for more, in general.
- Do follow the shape of each cheese, when helping yourself to the cheese course. Don't cut off the point of a triangular cheese, but slice a thin slice off the side, so everyone will get a good part.
- Do close the door behind you, after you have used *les toilettes*.
- Don't bring wine, which heretofore has been taken as a suggestion that the host's wine selection might not be up to your standards. However, this is slowly changing, so if your own country excels in producing a particular wine, you might bring a bottle as a novelty.
- Don't help yourself, unless it is a buffet. The host or hostess will notice when your plate or glass is empty.
- Don't leave when others are still lingering with coffee, but don't stay when it is clearly time to move on.

GLOSSARY

Even if you don't speak a word of French, you should have no trouble finding your way in Paris if you stay on the tourist track. Nonetheless, it's still a good idea to have a basic vocabulary, for the French appreciate visitors who try to speak their language—it is their country, after all.

All this said, if you don't have any French in your repertoire, the one most efficient sentence you might consider learning is *"Pardonnez-moi monsieur (madame), parlez-vous anglais?"* which means "Excuse me sir (ma'am), do you speak English?" And if you do speak some French, but have difficulty understanding someone, you can always say, with an apologetic little smile, *"Parlez lentement, s'il-vous-plaît"*, and most people will oblige by speaking slowly.

If you are here to stay for while, however, you should learn at least enough French to get by. It will be helpful in daily life, no matter how short your stay. It's also fun to be able to converse with others, even if you see them wince from time to time at your mistakes. Take some lessons to get you started. Most schools offer short-term courses, which can be fun as well as instructive. See Chapter Eight for language schools and for some hints on French pronunciation.

NUMBERS

Zero	*Zéro*
One	*Un*
Two	*Deux*
Three	*Trois*
Four	*Quatre*
Five	*Cinq*
Six	*Six*
Seven	*Sept*
Eight	*Huit*
Nine	*Neuf*

Ten	*Dix*
Eleven	*Onze*
Twelve	*Douze*
Thirteen	*Treize*
Fourteen	*Quatorze*
Fifteen	*Quinze*
Sixteen	*Seize*
Seventeen	*Dix-sept*
Eighteen	*Dix-huit*
Nineteen	*Dix-neuf*
Twenty	*Vingt*
Thirty	*Trente*
Forty	*Quarante*
Fifty	*Cinquante*
Sixty	*Soixante*
Seventy	*Soixante-dix*
Eighty	*Quatre-vingt*
Ninety	*Quatre-vingt dix*
Hundred	*Cent*
Thousand	*Mille*

DAYS OF THE WEEK

English-speakers should recognise the names of months , for they all bear some relation to the names of the months in English.

Monday	*Lundi*
Tuesday	*Mardi*
Wednesday	*Mercredi*
Thursday	*Jeudi*
Friday	*Vendredi*
Saturday	*Samedi*
Sunday	*Dimanche*
The week/ The month	*La semaine/ Le mois*

TIME

In writing, for timetables, television programmes, films and making reservations in a restaurant, etc., the French express time using the 24-hour clock. In speaking, however, many people say 8:00 pm rather than 20 *heures*.

1:00 pm	13h
2:00 pm	14h
3:00 pm	15h
4:00 pm	16h
5:00 pm	17h
6:00 pm	18h
7:00 pm	19h
8:00 pm	20h
9:00 pm	21h
10:00 pm	22h
11:00 pm	23h
midnight	*minuit*

COMMON EXPRESSIONS

Good day/ hello, sir (ma'am)	*Bonjour, monsieur (madame)*
Good evening	*Bonsoir*
How are you?	*Comment allez-vous?*
Very well, thank you.	*Très bien, merci.*
Yes, no, maybe	*Oui, non, peut-être*
Please	*S'il-vous-plaît*
Thank you; you're welcome.	*Merci; je vous en prie*
Good luck!	*Bonne chance!*

BEING POLITE

The French pay great heed to *la politesse*. Here are some standard phrases which the French use in daily life.

Goodbye and thank you	*Au revoir et merci*
Yes, please	*Oui, s'il-vous-plaît*
No, thank you	*Non, merci*
Thank you very much	*Merci beaucoup*
You're welcome	*Je vous en prie*
Pardon me (if you bump into someone)	*Pardon*
OK or I agree	*D'accord*
Excuse me (if you are apologising)	*Excusez-moi*
I'm sorry, but I don't understand	*Excusez-moi, mais je ne comprends pas*
Yes, I understand, thank you	*Oui, je comprends, merci*
Sorry to bother you, but...	*Pardonnez-moi de vous déranger, mais...*
Have a nice day	*Bonne journée*
Have a nice evening	*Bonne soirée*
You, too	*A vous aussi*

EMERGENCIES

Emergency!	*C'est urgent!*
Help me, please!	*Aidez-moi, s'il-vous-plaît!*
Call the fire department/ the police!	*Appelez les pompiers/ la police!*
Where is the pharmacy?	*Où se trouve la pharmacie?*

OUT AND ABOUT

The street	*La rue*
The pavement	*Le trottoir*
The metro	*Le métro*
The metro station	*La station de métro*
Where is the closest metro?	*Où se trouve le métro le plus près?*

Entrance	L'entrée
Exit	La sortie
Metro/ train transfers	La correspondance
Platform	Le quai
Bus	Le bus
Bus stop	L'arrêt de bus
Map	Le plan
Transport ticket	Le ticket
Ten bus/ metro tickets	Un carnet

MONEY TERMS

I don't have any cash	Je n'ai pas d'argent
Automatic cash dispenser	Distributeur
Is there a bank nearby?	Y-a-t-il une banque près d'ici?
Do you accept credit cards?	Acceptez-vous les cartes de crédit?
How much is this, please?	C'est combien, s'il-vous-plaît?
It's (not) expensive	C'est (pas) cher
It's a little too expensive for me	C'est un peu trop cher pour moi
I'm going to pay in cash	Je vais payer en espèces

LE SHOPPING

A department store	Un grand magasin
The pharmacy	La pharmacie
A book shop (a book)	Une librairie (un livre)
Dress, blouse, skirt	Robe, chemisier, jupe
Jacket, raincoat, hat	Veste, impermeable, chapeau
Gloves, scarf	Gants, écharpe
Shoes, socks, pantyhose	Chausseurs, chaussettes, collants

Shirt, tie, suit	*Chemise, cravate, tailleur (for women)/costume (for men)*
I'm just looking for the moment, thank you	*Merci, je regarde pour le moment*
Thanks, anyway	*Merci, quand même*
May I look around?	*Puis-je jeter un coup d'œil?*
I take size 10	*Je fais un quarante*
May I try it on?	*Puis-je l'essayer?*
It's too large/small.	*C'est trop grand/petit*
I'll take it	*Je le prends*
On sale	*Soldé*

DINING OUT

Waiters in most centrally located and well-known restaurants generally know enough English to interpret what you are saying. If you are adventurous in your restaurant searches, however, it's best to have at least a little knowledge of 'restaurantese'.

I'd like to book a table	*Je voudrais réserver une table*
For two/three people	*Pour deux/trois couverts*
At eight o'clock	*A vingt heures*
The menu	*La carte*
The fixed-price meal	*Le menu*
The napkin	*La serviette*
The cloakroom	*Le vestiaire*
The waiter/waitress	*Le serveur/la serveuse*
The tip	*Le pourboire*
The bill, please	*L'addition, s'il-vous-plaît*
Breakfast	*Le petit déjeuner*
Lunch	*Le déjeuner*
Dinner	*Le dîner*

The snack	*Le casse-croûte, le snack*
The first course	*L'entrée*
The main course	*Le plat/plat principal*
Dessert	*Le déssert*
A pitcher of tap water	*Une carafe d'eau*
Mineral Water	*Eau minerale*
Still/fizzy	*Plate/Gazeuse*
It's very good, thank you	*C'est très bon, merci*
What is the special of the day?	*Quel est le plat du jour?*
A little more, please	*Encore un peu, merci*
To your health	*A votre santé*

RESOURCE GUIDE

This section first lists telephone numbers that are important to have handy in case of emergencies. Two-digit numbers may be dialled without charge, while those starting with 01 are charged as local calls. Numbers that start with 08.00 are also free. Others that start with 08 (08.92, for instance) or those that have only four- or six-digit numbers (such as for SNCF or France Télécom) incur a number of centimes per minute—the cost per minute is announced at the beginning of the connection.

For information on activities in Paris, go to the Paris Tourist Office or access its website, which has extensive information on all facets of Paris life. The *mairie* (town hall) of your *arrondissement*, or the Hôtel de Ville (City Hall), should have brochures for residents that describe the services, programmes and even sports facilities sponsored by the city. See below for detailed information.

At the end of this chapter are some well-known networking resources in Paris, for both professional and social contacts.

EMERGENCIES & HEALTH
Emergency Numbers
- Police   17
- Pompiers (Fire Department)   18
- Gas Emergencies   08.00.47.33.33
- Emergencies anywhere in Europe 112

Dire Health Emergencies
- Fire Department Paramedics   18
- SAMU (Medical services and Ambulance)   15
  for suburbs of Paris   01.45.67.50.50

24-hour Medical Help
- Urgences Médicales de Paris   01.53.94.94.94;
  (house calls)
- S.O.S. Médecins (house calls)   01.47.07.77.77
- S.O.S. Pédiatries (house calls)   01.47.27.47.47
- Anti-poison Hotline   01.40.05.48.48

- Serious burns Hotline   01.58.41.27.22
- Serious burns—Adults   01.58.41.26.49
- Serious burns—Children   01.44.73.74.75
- Urgences Funéraires (Deaths)   08.00.88.00.88

Emergency Dental Health
- S.O.S. Dentaires   01.43.36.36.00
- Hôpital de la Pitie-Salpêtrière   01.42.16.00.00
- American Hospital (English-speaking)   01.46.41.25.25

24-hr Hospitals
- American Hospital
  63 boulevard Victor Hugo, Neuilly-sur-Seine
  Tel: 01.46.41.25.25
- Hôtel Dieu
  Place du Parvis Notre Dame (Ile-de-la-Cité)
  Tel: 01.42.34.82.34
- Hôpital Necker (Sick Children)
  149 rue de Sèvres, 75007
  Tel: 01.44.49.40.00

24-hr Pharmacies
For English-speaking pharmacies and those that carry British or American products, see page 130.
- Pharmacies Dhery (8e)
  84 avenue des Champs-Elysées
  Tel: 01.45.62.02.41
- Pharmarcie Européenne (9e)
  6 place de Clichy
  Tel: 01.42.82.91.04
- Grande Pharmarcie Daumesnil (12e)
  6 place Félix Eboué
  Tel: 01.43.43.19.03

Support Services
- S.O.S. HELP   01.46.21.46.46
  (Telephone crisis line in English)   (3–11pm daily)
- SIDA (AIDS) Support (24-hr daily)   08.00.84.08.00
- Alcoholics Anonymous   01.46.34.59.65

PRACTICAL INFORMATION ONLINE

- U.S. State Department information about France:
  Website: http://www.state.gov/r/pa/ei/bgn/3842.htm
- Brittish Expat Guide:
  Website: http://www.britishexpat.com/Moving-to-France.994.0.html
- American Embassy Information for Expats in Paris ("Blue Book")
  http://france.usembassy.gov/root/pdfs/bluebook.pdf
- Préfecture de la Police
  Website: http://www.prefecture-police-paris.interieur.gouv.fr
- Public sector links
  Website: http://www.service-public.fr/etranger/english.html
- Tourist Office Information in English
  http://en.parisinfo.com
- City of Paris Information in English
  http://www.paris.fr/portail/english/Portal.lut?page_id=8118
- Paris Ile-de-France Tourism website
  http://pidf.com
- 24-hour Post Office
  www.laposte.fr
- Weather Report
  http://france.meteofrance.com/

Hôtel de Ville (City Hall)

Place de l'Hôtel de Ville, 75004
Tel: 01.42 76.40.40; Helpline: 3975
Website: http://www.paris.fr
Open Mon–Sat, 10:00 am–7:00 pm; Sun, 2:00 pm–7:00 pm

- For the *mairie* of your *arrondissement*
  Website for the 1e: http://www.mairie1.paris.fr; for the 2e: http://www.mairic2.paris.fr, etc.
- For the young
  Website: http://www.portailj.paris.fr
- For students
  Website: http://www.etudiantdeparis.fr

France Télécom
- Customer Service   1014
- Helpline in English   08.00.36.47.75
- Repair hotline   1013
- Les Pages Blanches (residential listings) 118 012
- Les Pages Jaunes (business listings)   118 008
- Telephone numbers online: http://www.pagesjaunes.fr

Transportation
- RATP (Buses, Métro, RER)
  Tel: 08.92.68.77.14
  Website: http://www.ratp.fr
- SNCF (Trains)
  Tel: 3635
  Website: http://www.sncf.com
- Eurostar (to London and Lille)
  Tel: 08.92.35.35.39
  Website: http://www.eurostar.com
- Thalys (to Amsterdam, Brussels, Cologne)
  Tel: 3635 (say 'Thalys')
  Website: http://www.thalys.com

Lost & Found
- Bureau des Objets Trouvés
  36 rue Morillons, 75015
  Tel: 08.21.00.25.25
- Objects lost on public transportation
  Within 24 hours, go to station nearest loss or to the terminus
  of that line.
- Objects lost on trains
  Go to the train station having to do with that line.

Lost Credit Cards
- American Express   01.47.77.72.00
- Diners Club   08.20.82.05.36
- MasterCard, Maestro   08.00.90.13.87
  Cirrus, Eurocard
- Cartes Bleus, Visa   08.92.70.57.05

MAKING FRIENDS
General Networking

The large English-speaking community in Paris offers a variety of support and welcome groups, both formal and informal, as do other international interest groups. Most embassies have community liaison offices for their citizens in Paris, which may be able to supply specific contacts in Paris. SOS Help can also answer questions and make referrals on a wealth of issues of concern to the newcomer. The groups below can be helpful. Note that some are run by volunteers and hours may vary.

For detailed lists of country-specific associations and clubs, you might access these websites: British in France (http://www.britishinfrance.com); US Embassy Office of American Services (www. http://www.amb-usa.fr); Association Irlandaise (www. europeanirish.com/France).

- The American Church in Paris
  65 quai d'Orsay, 75007
  Tel: 01.40.62.05.00
  Website: http://www.acparis.org
  Christian religious and social gathering venue for the entire Anglophone community. Each October, the Women of the American Church sponsor the excellent 'Bloom Where You Are Planted' acclimatisation programme for English-speaking newcomers, providing a helpful booklet on living in Paris.

- Association of Americans Resident Overseas (AARO)
  Mona Bismarck Foundation
  34 avenue de New York, 75116
  Tel: 01.47.20.24.15
  Website: http://www.aaro.org
  Represents the interests of Americans overseas on issues such as taxes, Social Security, etc. Good for making friends with people of like concerns.

- Association of American Wives of Europeans
  34 avenue de New York, 75016
  Tel: 01.40.70.11.80
  Website: http://www.aaweparis.org
  Addresses current issues faced by American wives and promotes contacts and friendship.

- Association Irlandaise Paris
  22 rue Delambre, 75014
  Tel: 01.47.64.39.31
  Website: http://www.association-irlandaise.org
  Open to all who are interested in Ireland and its culture.
- The Green Room
  http://www.thegreenroom.fr
  A voluntary network designed to create a sense of community among the young Irish in France.
- American Women's Group
  32 rue du Général Bertrand, 75007
  Tel: 01.42.73.36.74
  Website: http://www.awgparis.org
  Social and cultural activities promoting Franco-American friendship, such as luncheon meetings, courses, tours.
- British Commonwealth Women's Association
  151 rue du Faubourg-St. Honoré 75008
  Tel: 01.47.20.50.91
  Website: http://www.bcwa.org
  Facilities such as clubrooms and a library; organises social and cultural activities, 'at-homes' and publishes a monthly newsletter.
- Canadian Meeting groups:
  http://canadian.meetup.com/6/
- France-Canada Association
  5 rue Constantinc, 75007
  Tel: 01.45.55.83.65
  Friendship association promoting contacts, conferences and cultural events.
- France-Amerique
  9-11 avenue Franklin-Roosevelt, 75008
  Tel: 01.43.59.51.00
  Discussions, lunches, etc. to improve cultural and economic relations between France and the Americas.
- Lions Club International
  295 rue Saint-Jacques, 75007
  Tel: 01.46.34.14.10
  Website: http://www.lionsclubs.org
  International service organisation.

- Rotary Club of Paris
  40 boulevard Emile Augier, 75116
  Tel: 01.45.04.14.44
  Website: http://www.rotaryparis.org
  International service organisation.
- Royal Society of Saint George
  Website: www.royalsocietyofstgeorge.com
  Activities for English people. Fosters contacts in Paris for English people and promotes English culture.
- The Standard Athletic Club
  Au Clos Obeuf, Route Forestière du Pavé de Meudon, 92360 Meudon-la-Foret
  Tel: 01.46.26.16.09
  Website: http://www.saclub.org
  Prestigious British club, which also includes members from various international communities.
- Toastmasters
  Website: www.toastmasters.org
  Meet friendly people and improve your self-confidence and public speaking skills. Check website for dates and venues around Paris.
- WICE (WICE Institute of Continuing Education)
  7 Cité Falguière 75015
  Tel: 01.45.66.75.50
  Website: www.wice-paris.org
  A wide-ranging organisation, offering a variety of English-language courses on living in France, French culture and politics. Special events.

Gay and Lesbian Networking

The gay and lesbian communities in Paris are among the most accepted in Europe. The French government has passed the Pacte Civil de Solidarité, commonly known as PACS, a 'contract of social union' that gives unmarried cohabiting couples—straight or gay—the same financial rights as married couples. There are also scores of gay-friendly hotels, restaurants bars, discotheques and shops. Every year, Paris hosts the largest Gay, Lesbian, Bi, Trans March on the continent. For some gay venues, see pages 247–248.

- Les Mots à la Bouche
  6 rue Ste-Croix de la Bretonnerie, 75004
  Tel: 01.42.78.88.30
  Website: http://www.motsbouche.com
  English-language books, gay guides, films, magazines and information of all sorts. Open daily (Sundays from 1:00–9:00 pm).
- Centre Gai et Lesbien
  63 rue Beaubourg
  Tel: 01.43.57.21.47
  Website: http://cglparis.org
  Extensive resource centre for gays and lesbians: information about the community and ongoing events, plus a library and meeting place for activities of various groups.
- Inter-LGBT.org.
  Voicemail: 01.72.70.39.22
  Website: http://www.inter-lgbt.org
  Email: contact@interlgbt.org
  An umbrella group for dozens of lgbt organizations, sponsoring activities of its own, including the popular Paris Printemps. Access the website for news, current activities, and links to other lgbt sites
- Maison des Femmes
  163 rue de Charenton, 75012
  Tel: 01.43.43.41.13
  Website: http://maisondesfemmes.free.fr
  Locale that offers information on a variety of feminist and lesbian groups. Also houses Les Archives, Recherches, Cultures Lesbiennes (ARCL), an important documentation centre open on Tuesday evenings (http://www.arcl.free.fr)
- Melo' Men: The International Gay Choir of Paris
  c/o Centre Gay et Lesbien, 75524 Paris Cedex 11 Website: http://www.melomen.com
  Well-known gay choir with performances in Paris and elsewhere.
- SNEG (Syndicat National des Entreprises Gaies)
  12 rue des Filles des Calvaires
  Tel: 01.44.59.81.01

Website: http://www.sneg.org
Gay and lesbian business group.

In addition, you might also access the following websites for information, events, chats and encounters.
- http://www.paris-gay.com
  An overall look at gay and lesbian Paris
- http://www.parismarais.com
  Information about the Marais and gay/lesbian resources in Paris.
- http://www.tetu.com
  Website of the popular magazine *Têtu*
- http://www.dykeplanet.com
  Extensive site for lesbians, including a 'Dykeguide'
- http://www.ladixiememuse.com
  Website for bimonthly lesbian magazine *La Dixième Muse*, also has a forum and chat room.

WORSHIP IN PARIS

Since the 6th century, the history of Paris has been intertwined with Christianity (see Chapter Two). However, for the last 100 years, there has been an official separation of church and state in France. Although some 90 per cent of the population claims Catholicism as its religion, it is said that only about 12 per cent are active worshippers. In addition to the 200 Catholic churches found in Paris, there are opportunities for worship in just about whichever denomination and religion you choose—and in the major languages of the world. See *Eglises* or *Cultes* in the *Yellow Pages*. For more English-language churches, check the Saturday edition of the *International Herald Tribune* under 'Religious Services'.
- **Anglican/Episcopal**
  American Cathedral in Paris
  http://www.americancathedral.org
  23 avenue George-V, 75008; tel: 01.53.23.84.00;
  Saint Michael's
  5 rue d'Aguesseau 75008; tel: 01.47.42.70.88
  http://www.stmichaelsparis.free.fr

- **Catholic**
  Neighbourhood churches open about 8:00 am and generally hold three masses daily. For masses and music at the Cathedral of Notre Dame, access its website: http://www.notredamedeparis.fr. Services in English can be heard at St. Joseph's Church at 50 avenue Hoche, 75008; tel: 01.42.27.28.56; website: http://www.stjoeparis.org

- **Christian Science**
  First Church of Christ, Scientist
  36 boulevard Saint-Jacques 75014; tel: 01.47.07.26.60
  http:www.tfccs.com

- **Interdenominational Protestant**
  The American Church in Paris
  65 quai d'Orsay 75007; tel: 01.40.62.05.00
  http://www.acparis.org
  'For all people of all nations', one of the focal points of the Protestant community in Paris.

- **Islam**
  La Grande Mosquée
  Place du Puits-de-l'Ermite 75005; tel: 01.45.35.97.33
  website: http://www.mosquee-de-paris.net/
  Call for worship times and information on other mosques. Inquire also at the Institut du Monde Arabe at 1 rue des Fossés Saint-Bernard, 75005; tel: 01.40.46.84.62.

- **Judaism**
  Divided into *Non-Consistoire* (ultra-Orthodox), *Consistoire* (Orthodox), *Massorti* (traditionally Conservative) and *Libérale*.
  Consistoire: Rothschild (Great) Synagogue; 44 rue de la Victoire, 75009; tel: 01.40.82.26.261
  Libérale: Kehilat Gesher (with services in English); 7 rue Léon Cogniet, 75017 and 10 rue de Pologne, 78100 Saint-Germain-en-Laye; tel: 01.39.21.97.19; http://www.kehilatgesher.org

- **Presbyterian**
  The Scots Kirk
  17 rue Bayard, 75008; tel: 01.48.78.47.94

FURTHER READING

HISTORY

France. Documentation Française. Free from The Ministry of Foreign Affairs.
- A comprehensive look at France—its history, politics, culture, economy, etc. Available in English from the Documentation bookshop on Quai Voltaire.

A Traveller's History of Paris. Robert Cole. Brooklyn, New York: Interlink Publishing Group, 1994.
- Excellent, compact history of Paris.

And God Created the French. Louis-Bernard Robitaille. Westmount, Canada: Robert Davies Publishing, 1996.
- A Frenchman's look at Parisians.

The Jews of France: A History from Antiquity to the Present. Esther Benbassa. Princeton, New Jersey: Princeton University Press, 1999.
- The turbulent history of the Jews in France, including during World War II.

Paris After the Liberation: 1944-1949. Antony Beevor and Artemis Cooper. London: Penguin Books, 2004.
- How Paris was shaped by the war and how it recovered.

Paris Noir: African Americans in the City of Light. Tyler Stovall. New York: Houghton Mifflin Company, 1996.
- Interesting and detailed history of blacks in Paris.

FAMOUS ACCOUNTS OF PARIS

Walks in Hemingway's Paris. Noel Riley Fitch. New York: St. Martin's Press, 1990.
- Quotes and anecdotes about the writers and artists who lived in Paris during the 1920s and 1930s, and suggested walks to show their haunts.

Autobiography of Alice B. Toklas. Gertrude Stein. Modern Library, 1993.
- Stein's classic book of expatriate life in Paris.

A Moveable Feast. Ernest Hemingway. New York: Touchstone Books, 1992.
- Hemingway's ever-popular book about life in Paris.

A Place in the World Called Paris. Steven Barclay. San Francisco: Chronicle Books, 2002.
- Quotes from people who have loved Paris.

Guide to Impressionist Paris. Patty Lurie. Cincinnati: Robson Press, 1997.
- Parisian sites painted by the Impressionists and how they look today.

WALKS IN PARIS
Time Out Book of Paris Walks. Andrew White. UK: Penguin Books, 1996
- Thirty-two walks around Paris, accompanied by informative and chatty descriptions.

Around and About Paris: Volumes 1-3. Thirza Vallois. London: Iliad Books, 1995.
- Important reference to keep on your shelf. Sprinkled with anecdotes, relates the history of Paris through recommended walks in every district, street by street.

Permanent Parisians. Judi Culberton and Tom Randall. Chelsea, Vermont: Robson Books, 2000.
- Places where famous people are buried in Paris.

ESSAYS
The Flâneur: A Stroll through the Paradoxes of Paris. Edmund White. London: Bloomsbury Publishing, 2001.
- Thoughtful essays about Paris.

Our Paris: Sketches from Memory. Edmund White and Hubert Sorin. New York: Alfred A. Knopf, 1995.
■ Essays and drawings of Paris.

FOOD

French Cheeses: A visual guide to more than 350 cheeses from every region of France. London, Dorling Kindersley, 1996.
■ A visual guide to more than 350 cheeses from every region of France.

French Wines: The Essential Guide to the Wines and Wine Growing Regions of France. Robert Joseph. London: Dorling Kindersley, 1999.
■ Everything you want to know about French wines.

PRACTICAL READING

French Toast. Harriet Welty Rochefort. Montreuil, France: Anglphone s.a, 1997.
■ Helpful, chatty look at living in France, with much insight and wit.

French or Foe? Getting the Most out of Visiting, Living and Working in France. Polly Platt. London: Culture Crossings, 1995.
■ Witty and informative book about living in Paris.

ABOUT THE AUTHOR

Frances Gendlin has held leadership positions in both magazine and book publishing. She was Editor and Publisher of the magazine *Sierra*, and was the Sierra Club's Director of Public Affairs. As Executive Director of the Association of American University Presses, she helped foster the interests of scholarly publishing worldwide. Through her own business, The Right Word, she helps writers with their projects and has taught English and business writing to foreign professionals. In 1997, she wrote *Living & Working Abroad: Rome*, and in 2001, *Living & Working Abroad: San Francisco*, two widely read guides to understanding and living in those cities.

While she was growing up, her family moved several times to different areas of the United States, each with its own characteristics and culture, climate and cuisine. This has led her to appreciate new cultures, to wonder about their differences and similarities, and to seek to understand them. All her life she has enjoyed travel and new adventures, meeting people she might otherwise not have met, and making new friends.

Frances Gendlin has lived in Paris for a decade, and life there is just as agreeable as she has conveyed in his book. Her fictional memoir, *Paris, Moi, and the Gang: A Memoir... of Sorts* can be ordered at bookshops, on amazon.com, and on other online sites.

INDEX

Titles in the CultureShock! series:

Argentina	France	Portugal
Australia	Germany	Russia
Austria	Great Britain	San Francisco
Bahrain	Hawaii	Saudi Arabia
Beijing	Hong Kong	Scotland
Belgium	India	Shanghai
Berlin	Ireland	Singapore
Bolivia	Italy	South Africa
Borneo	Jakarta	Spain
Brazil	Japan	Sri Lanka
Bulgaria	Korea	Sweden
Cambodia	Laos	Switzerland
Canada	London	Syria
Chicago	Malaysia	Taiwan
Chile	Mauritius	Thailand
China	Morocco	Tokyo
Costa Rica	Munich	Travel Safe
Cuba	Myanmar	Turkey
Czech Republic	Netherlands	United Arab
Denmark	New Zealand	Emirates
Ecuador	Pakistan	USA
Egypt	Paris	Vancouver
Finland	Philippines	Venezuela

For more information about any of these titles, please contact any of our Marshall Cavendish offices around the world (listed on page ii) or visit our website at:

www.marshallcavendish.com/genref